BEYOND THE CHAMPION

BEYOND THE CHAMPION

Institutionalizing Innovation Through People

Gina Colarelli O'Connor,
Andrew C. Corbett,
Lois S. Peters

STANFORD BUSINESS BOOKS
An Imprint of Stanford University Press
Stanford, California

Stanford, California

Special discounts for bulk quantities of Stanford Business Books are available to corporations, professional associations, and other organizations. For details and discount information, contact the special sales department of Stanford University Press. Tel: (650) 725-0820, Fax: (650) 725-3457

Printed in the United States of America on acid-free, archival-quality paper

Library of Congress Cataloging-in-Publication Data

Names: O'Connor, Gina Colarelli, author. | Corbett, Andrew C., author. | Peters, Lois S., author.
Title: Beyond the champion : institutionalizing innovation through people / Gina Colarelli O'Connor, Andrew C. Corbett, Lois S. Peters.
Description: Stanford, California : Stanford Business Books, an imprint of Stanford University Press, 2018. | Includes bibliographical references and index.
Identifiers: LCCN 2017018407 (print) | LCCN 2017022303 (ebook) | ISBN 9781503604506 (e-book) | ISBN 9780804798273 (cloth : alk. paper) | ISBN 9781503604506 (ebook)
Subjects: LCSH: Technological innovations—Management. | Organizational change.
Classification: LCC HD45 (ebook) | LCC HD45 .O258 2018 (print) | DDC 658.4/063—dc23
LC record available athttps://lccn.loc.gov/2017018407

Typeset by Newgen in Sabon 10 point.

As a research team, we dedicate this book to Bruce Kirk, director of innovation effectiveness at Corning, Inc., and Tracy Laverty, our PhD student. Both of these cherished people passed away during the time of our study, and both were influential contributors to it, in vastly different ways. We miss them terribly.

To my husband, Patrick, with love and gratitude.—Gina O'Connor

To my wife, Brenda: I'm better at everything I do because of you. Your support, counsel, and love are foundational to who I am and everything I accomplish. I'd also like to thank our two sons, Sean and Chase, two innovative minds. Keep following your entrepreneurial paths!—Andrew Corbett

I dedicate this book and body of work to my husband and grandchildren. Garrett McCarey, my husband, is my friend and supporter, but most of all he keeps me laughing. My grandchildren, Erin, Olivia, Stephen, and Ryan, are innovators in their own right. I hope this book is an inspiration for them to keep developing their innovation talents to make an impact.—Lois Peters

CONTENTS

ACKNOWLEDGMENTS

One day in 2010 Ted Farrington, research director at PepsiCo, called from out of the blue to ask when we were going to start the next phase of our research program on managing for breakthrough innovation in large, mature companies. We knew Ted because he had participated in the second phase of our research. This would be the third. Like the first two studies, it would be a significant undertaking. We gulped. We discussed it. Ted kept calling. The problems companies were facing in commercializing breakthroughs had certainly not been abated. Ultimately, we knew he was right.

Ted paved the way for us to return to the IRI, a wonderful, passionate organization of R&D leaders in large companies, who've sponsored our research since its inception in 1995. We already knew what the next research question of interest was, based on the most pressing challenges that surfaced in our second phase. We co-opted Bruce Kirk, our longtime supporter from Corning, to cochair with Ted the IRI subcommittee that would work with us throughout the project. It wasn't a difficult sell. Together we decided that our typical approach of ten to twelve companies was too much to handle, so we'd try for six. Within three months we had eleven. And so it goes.

This research program, the entire three phases, would not be possible without the enduring support of the IRI. Its members confirm the importance of our research and let us know that it resonates with them. When our results don't make sense to them, they talk it through with us, and we come to new levels of understanding. When they don't like what we tell them, they stick with us and come away with new understandings themselves.

Some members of the IRI have been steady presences for a long time, and it's the vibrancy of the organization that really helps us. Its structure includes a "Research-on-Research" committee, which oversees a portfolio of research projects on topics of interest to the R&D community, run by members. Ours has been one of those projects. With two cochairs (Bruce and Ted), and a show of hands indicating interest, we were off and running. ROR project committees meet three times per year. So that's how often we showed up to report on the project's status, develop and test surveys, provide interim results, and collect their feedback. The interesting thing is attendance at those meetings was fluid. Members from Bose, Masco, Dow Chemical, Rohm and Haas, Boeing, and a variety of other companies filtered through our committee over the years. It wasn't a stable group per se, and that meant we had many opportunities to get feedback, and many points of view to consider. Ted and Bruce were the stabilizing factor.

We must acknowledge the IRI, and its staff, who made this all possible. Ed Bernstein, president, was new to the organization when we began Phase III, and he's been inclusive, welcoming, and has done a great job of growing the organization, understanding its members' needs, and working to augment the IRI's offerings. The industrial research community is in need of this vibrant professional organization, and in our view, he and his staff have stepped up. Lee Green, vice president of knowledge creation, oversees the Research-on-Research committee and provided unrelenting support. We know we can call her at any time. Martha Malone, vice president of education, and Jim Euchner, editor of *Research-Technology Magazine*, help us find ways to publicize and teach what we've learned as a result of this great partnership.

We must also acknowledge Ted Farrington, who has been such a strong supporter of our work, and is really a student of innovation leadership himself. He's been an R&D director in a number of companies since we first encountered him at the IRI meetings, and has lent his perspective and his companies' participation in several of our studies. Thank you, thank you, thank you, Ted.

We cannot acknowledge Ted without acknowledging Bruce Kirk, who, sadly, passed away suddenly just after completion of our data collection, and just after he retired. Bruce was a keen observer, an excellent meeting facilitator, and a great advocate. His passion for driving innovation excellence serves as a role model to many.

Finally, we express our gratitude to our participating companies for this particular study. Many provided financial support, and they all opened their doors and allowed us in. The topic of this book can become personal, and it's not easy to share some of these difficult stories. Our company contacts identified people to us who'd experienced difficult career options; and those people gave us the good, the bad, and the ugly. They did not try to present a sugarcoated story line. Others gave us real-world examples of solutions they were trying to implement, or success stories that had occurred in the company, and made introductions so that we could follow up. The degree of openness we experienced has allowed us to gain the insights described in this book and offer them up for corporate leaders and innovators to improve management practices associated with innovation talent.

To Ray Yourd and Mike Gallagher at Bayer MaterialScience (now Covestro); Bruce Kirk, Deb Mills, Daniel Riccoult, and Charlie Craig at Corning; Manon Pernot, Herman Wories, Lucienne van der Werff, and Rob van Leen at DSM; Steve Toton and David Glasscock at DuPont; Martha Gardener and Michael Idelchik at GE Global Research; Lars Enevoldsen, Marjanne Gronhoj, Ole Tangsgaard, and Thorbjørn Machholm at Grundfos; Carl Loweth and John Reid at John Deere; Tim O'Brien, Louise Quigley, and Mike Pickett at Moen; Matthew Paquette and Mike Orroth at Newell Rubbermaid; Ted Farrington, Michael Keaneth, Rocco Papalia, and Andrea Foote at PepsiCo; and Leslie Cook and George Wofford at Sealed Air Corporation: thank you. You provided your time and insights in interviews. You identified colleagues that we should follow up with to learn their stories and their roles. You helped gain permission to print your companies' experiences in this book. To all of you, we thank you. Many of you are no longer in the position or even in the company in which we originally met, but we want to publicly acknowledge the contribution you made to this research effort. We know of the hard work you do every day to help innovation succeed, and we hope that in some small way this book helps your own causes.

For four years, we had put twenty companies under a microscope when Mike Giersch, vice president, strategic planning at IBM, turned to us and said, "You are sitting in the catbird seat!" The companies that had participated in our research had sent several representatives to hear results, debate them, and provide feedback. Just like that, we were the ones being studied.

Mike's right. We've been privileged. We are academics who live and breathe breakthrough innovation. We've had the opportunity to be students of it for more than twenty years, in partnership with many companies that are committed to building a sustainable capability for breakthrough innovation but find themselves fighting an uphill battle. Everyone blames senior management for the starts and stops, the lack of persistence. But we have arrived at a somewhat different conclusion. Of course senior leaders want breakthrough innovations. The trouble is, companies don't know how to produce them.

We don't know enough about the day-to-day activities of those involved in breakthrough innovation to recognize its emergence. We don't know what to expect of project teams working on potential breakthroughs. We don't really know what innovation expertise is, or how to cultivate it in our companies. We don't know how to communicate our progress to external stakeholders, either. So companies waste time, money, and other resources in their attempts. Eventually senior leaders lose patience.

This book is about a constant, nagging, critically important problem for managers of large, mature companies: how to increase their companies' success at commercializing breakthrough, step-out, game-changing, radical innovation. It's also about evolutionary innovation . . . anything beyond new product development that results in incremental innovation. It's about creating blue oceans based on technological advantage. It's about creating whole new platforms of growth for the company. It's about securing the company's future health through innovation. It's about managing under conditions of high degrees of ambiguity toward an objective of creating innovations that truly change people's lives for the better. We view breakthrough innovation as a required organizational capability, additive to companies' current processes for producing incremental innovations. We are not suggesting those capabilities be traded off, replaced, or diminished. But to succeed over time, companies must renew themselves, rejuvenate their businesses, and create whole new platforms of businesses. They cannot rely only on *path-dependent* growth patterns that follow current trajectories into the future. They must invest in *path-creating*, disruptive innovations, and build capabilities to ensure they do so constantly and at low risk to the company. They must invest in *strategic innovation*. A great variety of talent and creativity is required to accomplish this, some of which is not traditionally recognized or rewarded by large established corporations.

During the course of our study, we arrived at some strongly held perspectives about what large, mature, industrial companies must do to institutionalize a capability for innovation. But before we delve into that, we want to tell you why and how we conducted this research, and how our thinking has evolved about breakthrough innovation itself so you'll understand what underlies our insights and conclusions.

FROM RADICAL TO BREAKTHROUGH TO STRATEGIC INNOVATION

When we started researching this challenging and important problem in 1995, large, established companies had learned to excel at new product development processes that result in incremental innovations, which sustain current lines of business. But they'd lost their way when it came to game changers that delivered new-to-the-world benefits with the potential to revolutionize an industry. We labeled those as radical innovations in order to communicate the degree of change in the market and in the company that was typically required to deliver such a magnitude of value. We and others often juxtaposed radical against incremental innovation to clarify the differences between the two. Over time we've used many terms to infer that high level of innovativeness, including game-changing innovation, transformational innovation, and breakthrough innovation. And there are degrees of innovativeness that fall between the two extremes. Figure P.1 shows the two as endpoints along a continuum of uncertainty and terminology for points in between.

What we know about any of those on the right end of the continuum is that they have to be managed differently than new product development, because of the high degree of uncertainty on so many dimensions that breakthrough innovations face over the course of their development. It requires a completely different management approach from the one that executes along an operational excellence mentality.

The term *radical* intimidated people, not just because of the unintended political interpretations of it, but because of the extreme level of change it inferred. In fact, it's a rare occurrence. However, managing for high levels of innovativeness with varying degrees of uncertainty is not so rare. It's necessary for companies to survive.

Over time and as we've continued to watch companies evolve a capability for innovations that require managing under uncertain and ambiguous conditions, we have come to focus on the term *strategic innovation*.

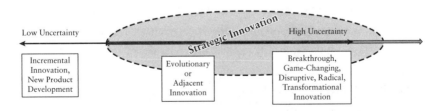

FIGURE P.1   Types of Innovation Along the Uncertainty Spectrum

By that we mean innovation undertaken by the organization that is intentional and can provide whole new platforms of growth through major market impact. Its objective is to create new businesses for the company, not just a new product within a current platform. That means that any strategic innovation initiative will likely create changes within the market, use novel technology or new combinations of technology, access resources and know how the company may not have, and will most likely upset the organizational applecart in one way or another. We see innovation on a continuum, and strategic innovation captures efforts that are beyond incremental up to and including new-to-the-world breakthroughs. Truly breakthrough innovation happens rarely, but innovation that becomes the force of corporate rejuvenation and alters the game in the marketplace needs to be continually fostered and developed. You will notice that we use the term *breakthrough innovation* when referring to projects or initiatives that could have had such an impact but were not handled with a strategic mind-set. Breakthroughs are great, but their likelihood of success is low if they're not also considered strategic.

THE TAKEAWAY

Can you imagine an organization today that would not have a marketing department or strongly developed marketing capability? Just a few decades ago, marketing as a function, profession, and department did not exist. It wasn't until the 1970s that marketing departments began to resemble anything like what we have today. We see the need for a similar evolution for innovation, and we will take you on our path of discovery in this book. Innovation is critical to the firms of today and will be the lifeblood of the firms of tomorrow. Firms can longer afford to have sporadic, half-hearted innovation efforts. With innovation at the heart of competitiveness, organizations need it to be institutionalized through its people, organization, and design. Strategic innovation is about generating the businesses of the future for the company, and it needs to be considered its own function.

A TRIO OF RESEARCH PROJECTS

This is the third book resulting from twenty-plus years of beating the innovation drum. Our thinking has evolved greatly, and our message has become clearer. Obviously, companies cannot expect to benefit from breakthrough discoveries and inventions unless they invest to commercialize them. To do that, companies need to build an infrastructure that can create new markets, business models, partnerships, strategies, and internal organizational arrangements. That infrastructure requires a certain set of skills and architecture, which are currently absent in most organizations.

Our research program began in 1995 with a generous grant from the Sloan Foundation and the sponsorship of the Industrial Research Institute,[1] a professional organization of R&D managers, directors, and chief technology officers of large established companies and governmental research labs. Together with the IRI we defined breakthrough innovations as those having the potential to offer one or more of the following: (a) new to the world performance features; (b) 5–10 times improvement in known features, or (c) 30–50 percent reduction in cost. The latter two criteria open up new application domains for the technology, enabling whole new platforms for growth.

The first book examines the processes that project teams applied as they undertook the challenge of commercializing a potential breakthrough innovation.[2] Our unit of analysis was the project itself. IRI members volunteered projects from within their companies that senior leadership identified as potential breakthroughs. None were commercialized yet. Some were just getting started in the development process.

We followed twelve projects in ten companies for five years. The companies included Air Products, Analog Devices, DuPont, GE, General Motors, IBM, Nortel Networks, Polaroid, Texas Instruments, and United Technologies. We interviewed project team leaders, members and their sponsors repeatedly . . . 186 interviews in all. During that time, some of the projects were killed off, as expected, and others met with varying degrees of success. Several changed the game in their industries. We investigated the challenges that teams faced and the ways they circumvented those challenges.

We identified four distinct dimensions of uncertainty that were pivotal to project management success: technical uncertainty, market uncertainty, resource uncertainty, and organizational uncertainty. From these a series of seven challenges for project leaders were described. The vast majority of projects we studied originated and progressed solely because of the strong will and persistence of a talented champion with ties to and protection from a senior management sponsor. Project teams and their leaders spent more time fighting against the norms of their companies, whose management systems, processes, and metrics were dedicated to responding to customer needs and operational excellence. These were not the norms and infrastructure needed for the high-uncertainty environment of breakthrough innovation. We concluded that companies could do a much better job of developing management systems and infrastructures that supported, rather than antagonized, innovation champions and their teams. We coined a term, *radical innovation hub*, to describe such a system. A hub is a central locus for breakthrough innovation activities: establishing, generating, and developing projects; providing coaching about dealing with ambiguity and uncertainty; accessing resources; networking; and gaining organizational legitimacy and receptivity for projects preparing to make the transition into business units or other receiving units.

In our view at the time, hub members would run interference between project teams and the mainstream organization and ensure that the connections with the mainstream organization occur as necessary so that the breakthrough was accepted into the company rather than rejected or ignored. The hub would develop the right kind of skills in people, oversee a portfolio of breakthrough projects, and set up appropriate governance mechanisms for each project and the portfolio. And it would play many other roles that we observed as gaps in companies' abilities to develop breakthroughs today. We noted the beginnings of a hub in three of the companies we studied, but that was all. And each of those was snuffed out by the end of the study period. Interesting and discouraging.

Our second book focuses on companies that were attempting to develop management systems to promote repeated success with breakthrough innovation.[3] We needed to know how companies that wanted a sustained breakthrough innovation capability were executing it. Was a hub the right approach? What alternatives were being tried? We went back to the IRI and proposed a second study. For this one, our unit of analysis was the company level, and the portfolio of breakthrough opportunities that was being managed through that system-level initiative.

We sought participation from companies that had a declared strategic intent to develop or evolve a sustainable breakthrough innovation capability. The majority of those that agreed to participate were just getting started. Twelve companies participated, including 3M, Albany International, Air Products, Corning, DuPont, GE, IBM, Johnson & Johnson Consumer Products, Kodak, MeadWestvaco, Sealed Air, and Shell Chemicals. Another set of companies joined soon after as a validation set. These included Bose, Dow Corning, Guidant, Hewlett-Packard, Intel, P&G, PPG, Rohm and Haas, and Xerox. Again we conducted regular interviews with all members of the innovation management system and those to whom they reported. We checked in with them regularly over a five-year period, and conducted 246 interviews over the course of that timeframe.

Grabbing Lightning is about building an innovation capability that will last. Company managers think of innovation as a process. In fact, new product development that results in incremental innovation can be treated as a process, since its approach fits into the normal systems and metrics of the mainstream company, whose objective is to convert its knowledge, customer loyalty, and experience into profits. But breakthrough innovation doesn't lend itself to processes that emphasize leveraging the company's current knowledge base, markets, and networks. New networks are required; new markets are to be created. Managers cannot project net present value or ROIs for early stage breakthroughs. There's too much uncertainty about the development path, market formation, disruption, competitors, value propositions, market applications, manufacturing challenges, business models, partnerships, strategic fit, and a host of other innovation challenges.

Managing under uncertainty, and creating new rather than leveraging the familiar, is not just a chance occurrence. It doesn't involve wandering blindly. Some people are very, very good at creating the new. They are excited by the prospect of charting courses in the unknown. So we arrived at the conclusion that, to be capable of breakthrough innovation, companies must develop an expertise in it, and to do that, it must be considered as and managed as a function, similar to marketing, R&D, purchasing, and legal. In fact, we observed that companies were, and are, beginning to do just that.

RESEARCHING ROLES AND RESPONSIBILITIES FOR AN INNOVATION FUNCTION

One of the key insights that came from the *Grabbing Lightning* work was that, of all the elements of the management system, the most challenging for organizations and innovators was talent management associated with people involved in developing and commercializing strategic innovation opportunities. Leaders repeatedly boast, "Our people are our most important asset!" Why, then, didn't those involved in innovation experience that sentiment? What was this new "chief innovation officer" job title all about? There were clues that companies wanted to institutionalize a strategic innovation function through people but, again, didn't yet have a framework for doing so.

We had just published a short article expressing some thoughts on ways this problem could be alleviated when we received an inquiry from the Thought Leadership Institute (TLI),[4] a professional organization of human resource management professionals.[5] The TLI leadership had seen the article and were interested in helping their member organizations develop the human capital for strategic innovation. Around the same time, we received an invitation from a member of the IRI, to take up another phase of the research. His call was timely, since we were bothered by the findings that people management was such a stumbling block.

To participate, companies had to have declared their strategic intent to evolve a breakthrough innovation capability, and had to have expressed concern about talent management issues. Nine IRI companies who volunteered met the criteria and joined. We also sought two companies in Europe that we were aware were pursuing talent development strategies and programs for breakthrough innovation. Participating companies include Bayer MaterialScience, Corning, DSM, DuPont, John Deere, GE, Grundfos, Newell Rubbermaid, Moen, PepsiCo, and Sealed Air Corporation.

In this study, we again focused on the person responsible for the breakthrough innovation management system, and requested that s/he identify all members associated with it, including at least one representative from the HR or organizational development function. Again, we visited each company and interviewed all those people our primary point of contact identified as participants in the innovation management system, and then asked each to identify others they knew of or accessed in the course of their work. We interviewed as many of those individuals as possible.

We asked people to describe their backgrounds, skills, career paths to date, current responsibilities, relationships with their supervisors, direct reports, and other points of interface. We asked about the frustrations with their current roles and their careers so far, their points of pride and success stories, and their professional aspirations. We asked about the expectations for the projects or initiatives they were working on, and for themselves. We inquired about succession planning and permanency of their role. A total of 181 interviews were conducted.

In the final months of the study, we contacted them all again to see what had happened to them. We tracked them on LinkedIn and via e-mail. When we couldn't reach them, we asked their colleagues to connect us. Ultimately we learned the outcomes for all 141 participants.

This book's focus is on the single biggest challenge that companies identified as they work to institutionalize a strategic innovation capability: that of developing and managing innovation-related talent. It's back to people. While project champions are both the bane of their managers' existence and the glory of their companies' folklore, they are extremely rare. A healthy organization cannot rely on these unique individuals for its future growth platforms. Therefore, we set out to understand the roles that are emerging in innovation. We saw that many of those roles are as temporary and lilting as the wind. They are not institutionalized in companies today. Once the specific person who has filled that job moves on, the role dissolves. We have come to realize that companies can make major improvement in this arena, which we trust will dramatically improve their innovation outcomes. Without some permanency in innovation roles, how can companies ever develop an expertise for strategic innovation?

Chapter 1 of this book presents the problem of managing for high-uncertainty innovation, through recent examples, and takes a look at the approaches companies have tried that have not yet provided an answer. Chapter 2 sets up the framework of a management system for strategic innovation and alerts you to the recent progress in our understanding of how to manage this previously overwhelming objective. In Chapter 3 we return to the people aspect in detail and give you a bird's-eye view of the issues that those in innovation trenches face regarding their careers. You may be surprised by some of those stories. In Chapter 4 we offer a framework of roles and responsibilities for an innovation function that follows from an understanding of what expertise is actually required to make it come to fruition. Chapters 5, 6, 7, and 8 delve deeply into each of those roles, and provide not only company leadership but also the organizational development and HR communities with rich information to help design those jobs and select the appropriate talent. In Chapter 9 we take up the difficult challenge of developing and rewarding innovation talent. We address the issue of career paths because we see over and over again that the rare talent that does exist in innovation functions may be stalled from a career progression perspective, but need not be. Finally in Chapter 10 we summarize these thoughts and go on to ask what other institutions can be doing to increase the speed with which an innovation profession and innovation function come to fruition.

You may find our prescriptions controversial. As we've presented our findings and suggestions for action in conferences, companies, and innovation summits, we have been challenged by audiences, even by our supporters at the IRI. But the more they heard, and worked with these ideas, the more they began to agree with our logic. We hope you will, too. And if you don't, please do let us know. We continue to learn. And, together, we innovate.

BEYOND THE CHAMPION

I   WHY AREN'T COMPANIES GETTING BETTER AT BREAKTHROUGH INNOVATION?

Together with a research chemist he had hired, George Eastman founded the Eastman Kodak Company in 1892 after a fifteen-year series of inventions and refinements that ultimately led to the ability to take a snapshot picture and develop film using a novel rolling technique. The inventions included dry plate photography; the equipment to produce such plates; "negative" paper; transparent, flexible roll film; and the camera that would enable its use.[1] Kodak became an icon among large industrial companies, providing the mass market access to the hobby of photography through its development and commercialization of the pocket camera. Subsequent business platforms were based on Kodak's later inventions of motion picture film, color film, and film that enabled "talkie" movies.

As late as 1976, Kodak commanded 90 percent of film sales and 85 percent of camera sales in the United States.[2] By 1988 Kodak employed more than 145,000 workers worldwide.[3] By its peak year, 1996, Kodak held more than two-thirds of global market share in film and cameras and was worth more than $31 billion. The Kodak brand was the fifth most valuable in the world.[4]

In January 2012, just fifteen years later, Kodak declared bankruptcy. Its global workforce had shrunk from its 1988 height to thirteen thousand.[5] Ironically Kodak is recognized as holding the patents that claim the invention of the digital camera. Yet not only did this great company fail to commercialize the digital camera first; it resisted embracing the business opportunity even as digital technology was licensed from it and came to market through others.

Kodak is not unique in its near-death experience associated with refusing to engage in the new technological order. Nortel Networks hid its head in the sand in June 2009 as its core business was shattered by the advent of Internet-based communications.[6] There are countless examples of companies that flourished on the basis of successful introductions along predicted technology trajectories but that simply could not arrange themselves to accommodate major technological or market changes, much less lead them. Even more frustrating, many of those same companies harbor advanced technologies that could bring immense value to the marketplace; however, they lack the expertise to innovate beyond their core products. Many potential breakthroughs are left sitting on the shelves in R&D labs, collecting dust.

It is not that Nortel didn't see it coming, and the same can be said for Kodak. In fact, both had established innovation hubs: groups or departments whose mandate was to develop breakthrough new businesses for their companies. At Kodak the group was the Systems Concept Center. At Nortel it was called the Business Ventures Group. Both were run by smart people who reported directly to their companies' chief technology officers. Why didn't it work? Indeed, why do we hear these failure stories over and over again?

WHAT IS THE REASON?
As obvious as the problem is, explanation as to why it endures is up for debate. Several reasons have been accepted as conventional wisdom, thereby allowing leaders of large companies to shrug their shoulders and indicate there's not much that can be done. These include the following.

Core Capabilities Become Core Rigidities.[7]   Most would agree that the culture of operational excellence necessary to keep customers and stockholders satisfied precludes the kind of exploration, learning, and redirecting that is natural for developing and commercializing breakthroughs. These potential new business platforms are fraught with high levels of ambiguity and risk, and so they require different processes, systems, metrics, and talent than mainstream management systems are designed to support. Mainstream cultures thrive on leveraging what they know rather than pioneering the unknown. The original breakthrough innovation that fueled so many companies' infancy and growth becomes the barrier to their next frontier. What starts as a core capability, a company's sustainable competitive advantage, becomes a ball and chain around its neck. Chemical film processing put the chokehold on Kodak. It was the telecommunications infrastructure at Nortel. IBM's near-death experience in the late 1980s was due to its worldwide success in mainframe computing. Ironic, right?

Over time companies stultify innovation. Processes become more influential than people. They take on a life of their own. New product development processes are well honed in companies today, but they are designed to produce incremental innovations that serve current markets and leverage what the company knows best. They don't produce new platforms of business born of novel technologies that require different business models. Metrics that measure progress and success are based on knowable, predictable market and financial returns. None of these exist in the world of breakthroughs, which oftentimes upend current markets completely. We have seen over and over that large established companies fail to leverage new opportunities even when they themselves create those possibilities.

Senior Leadership Incentive Structures.   A second reason offered for failure to successfully experiment with path-creating change is the financial incentive system for corporate leaders and boards, especially in US-based companies.[8] A recently published study of CEOs and CFOs reported that, to avoid missing their own quarterly earnings estimates, 80 percent were willing to forgo R&D spending.[9] Political pundits suggest that SEC rules in the early 1980s easing stock buybacks have enabled executives to manipulate share prices through the timed release of positive news so that their incentive compensation payouts are maximized.[10] Stock-based incentive compensation for executives encourages them to make decisions based on what traders and hedge funds want, which are short-term gains in stock price.[11]

Indeed, pressures to elevate short-term stock prices at the expense of long-term investments are so enormous that some US-based companies are moving their legal homes to other countries whose infrastructure and financial markets place greater value on long-term investments. The CEO of Mylan N.V., a drug manufacturer who moved from Pennsylvania to the Netherlands to avoid a hostile takeover, is quoted as saying, "This is a stakeholder company, not a shareholder company."[12] Recognizing an organization's multiplicity of constituents may cause leaders to take a longer-term view, and that sounds reasonable. Yet in both the United States and in Europe, private-equity companies are buying seats on company boards to eventually take over voting rights and flip the companies for large financial gains, after stripping them of corporate-level, long-term investment capabilities.[13]

While these explanations are surely important influences on behavior, we'd like to offer a third that we believe bears examining and could diminish the impact of the first two. Companies need to develop bench strength for innovation. What are we doing about selection, development, and retention of innovation talent? Could companies build a talent base and infrastructure system to create "newstreams" just as well as they reinforce "mainstreams?" What if we could identify expertise in this arena and institutionalize it? Would companies improve their capability for commercializing innovation? Would the financial markets recognize this investment?

We believe the answer is a clear yes. Management theory and practice has become increasingly sophisticated over recent history. We're expert in marketing, finance, and in information systems management. We have cracked the code on manufacturing systems management, on quality management, and we are attacking data analytics now. It's time to step up and become expert on innovation . . . the kind that brings new orders of magnitude of value to the marketplace and therefore to the company. We've been researching this phenomenon, which we've labeled "breakthrough innovation," for decades now and have learned a lot. It is time to put it to practice. To do so will require new thinking about innovation talent management.

Our research shows that, in large part, companies have shot themselves in the foot when it comes to building a sustained capability for breakthrough innovation. They've not taken as strategic an approach as is necessary to develop innovation capability. A large part of that problem has to do with how companies manage one of their most precious assets: human capital. In Kodak, Nortel, and many other companies, the roles and responsibilities required for a successful breakthrough innovation capability were not clarified, described, or institutionalized. People volunteered. There were no tools, frameworks, or attention given to recruiting, selecting, and developing innovation talent. People cycled in and out of innovation hubs that had cool names but no staying power. In a number of the companies we researched, innovation hubs existed but were populated with part-timers or people cycling through for short-term professional-development experiences. The "other part" of their jobs required attention to near-term, immediate issues focused on current customers, current operations, and the consequences of those issues on the next quarter's stock performance. In some cases the groups we studied were filled with inventive, creative types, but they lacked personnel to incubate, experiment, and grow the businesses that resulted from the creative genius of their "think tank" partners.

In all these cases, and for any one of these reasons, the innovation hubs did not have the opportunity to develop expertise they could leverage over and over again. They could not practice, improve, and become increasingly sophisticated at what they did. Of the companies we studied, talent management practices for people who filled innovation roles were lacking. Selection, development, and retention approaches for innovation personnel were overlooked, undervalued, and/or misunderstood.

The people who work on the breakthrough innovation efforts are considered off the beaten path. For any ambitious employee looking to become a person of influence in the company, time spent in an innovation role is considered a "time-out" in his or her career. In fact, participants were viewed as misfits in the organization. There was no career path for people who prefer to work on developing potential breakthrough new businesses other than a higher potential of being released during lean times or when the flavor of the day was something other than innovation.

The average life span of a new ventures group in large companies is just a little more than four years,[14] and the personnel affiliated with breakthrough innovation projects and hubs are not always treated well when the dissolutions occur.[15]

Conventional wisdom holds that breakthroughs occur when highly driven project champions, shielded from company rules and policies by a senior leader sponsor, are allowed the freedom to break conventional practices and do what needs to be done. Some companies call them mavericks. Some call them hero-scientists, and others call them intrapreneurs. Once in a while this approach works, but more often they are the outliers. In most cases, in the stories you never hear about, the champion model fails. The disgruntled intrapreneurs leave the organization or remain and burden themselves and their organizations with cynical attitudes or deflated spirits. Even in those instances when it works, intrapreneurs contribute to company folklore but may not be willing or able to help the company develop a sustained innovation competency.

Returning to the Kodak story, the employee who invented the digital camera, Steven Sasson, was clearly a brilliant R&D scientist and a phenomenal inventor. In fact, President Barack Obama awarded him the National Medal of Technology and Innovation in 2009. In conferring its Innovation Award on Sasson in 2009, the *Economist* called the digital camera a "seismic disruption" that rendered the existing technology virtually obsolete.[16] And his alma mater (Rensselaer Polytechnic Institute) inducted him into their hall of fame in 2011 . . . just before Kodak declared bankruptcy. Steve Sasson was a great inventor, but he was not an intrapreneur. He did not have the championing qualities companies seem to depend on to push, prod, cajole, and nag leadership to respond to opportunities or to impending threats. He invented the digital camera in 1975 and moved on to his next project. Did he do his job well? Yes! But there were multiple other tasks and activities that needed to occur, and no one was assigned to take them up.

This book is predicated on our belief that companies cannot improve their innovation outcomes unless there are people charged with managing a system devoted to that objective. While this sounds obvious, the fact is that there are few companies today with formal, consistent roles associated with new business creation that leverage R&D investments beyond the core business. There may be projects, task teams, and passionate people who make up interesting titles for their business cards (and we've seen a number of them!), but few companies have a clear, enduring organizational design for commercializing new business platforms based on breakthrough discoveries, inventions, or strategic objectives. Few have clear roles articulated, personnel selection criteria delineated, or career development opportunities embedded, as is the case for virtually every other function in the company.

Through our research we have identified a number of interesting roles and responsibilities that companies experiment with. No single company has the whole picture. Our results derive from assimilating best practices, observing challenges companies and individuals face in executing innovation, and filling in the gaps. Companies can get better at breakthrough innovation and develop a capability for what we call strategic innovation. Senior leaders say they want just that. We believe this book will help speed the process.

ORGANIZATIONAL EXPERIMENTS

Since the 1970s and 1980s when this problem was first articulated, companies have experimented with a number of approaches to get breakthroughs.[17] They've tried process-based, cultural, and structural approaches of many flavors, along with financial approaches. Some companies cycle through them all, again and again. So far none have endured or become the template for others to follow. Your company probably has remnants of each.

Process-Based Approaches.   When Robert Cooper recognized and described the weaknesses in large companies' new product development process, and prescribed a Stage-Gate® approach to improve it, he took the world by storm.[18] The insight was to work in a cross-functional team, and to consider marketing, engineering, manufacturing, and cost implications as needed in pursuing a new product concept through a prescribed series of development steps. Gate reviews imposed discipline and enabled the company to make explicit decisions at specific junctures as to whether or not to continue investing. Gate reviews resulted in "go" or "kill" decisions, thus allowing decision makers to prevent losses on projects that would never succeed commercially as soon as possible. The process brought efficiency to what had previously been considered a handoff, serial process that resulted in outdated, costly products. The Stage-Gate® and other similar processes are deeply institutionalized in most large, mature industrial companies today and have dramatically improved cycle time and effectiveness of the new product development process for familiar markets and technologies.

Many managers inform us that they apply a similar approach to breakthrough innovation, because it is familiar and works within the organization's operating norms. To allow for the higher uncertainty and risk associated with breakthrough innovation, they impose a "Loose Stage-Gate®" process. What that means is that gate criteria are allowed to slip or are relaxed: the project is allowed to proceed to the next stage even if it meets just part of the gate criteria, subject to its meeting the remaining criteria at a subsequent gate.[19]

Hmm . . . Well, we're not convinced, and we have not seen it work. A completely different approach is needed for innovation that will set the future for the firm—one that is exploratory and learning oriented, rather than confirmatory and responsive to market demands. We need an approach that incorporates organizational change as part of its core activities. A breakthrough project under development does not depend on current available resources, organizational arrangements, or business models; it is open to accessing new resources and creating new organizational arrangements and business models. It does not depend on market research but rather on market creation. Prescribed project management steps will not work, since learning in one stage determines the next steps to be taken. Gate criteria, therefore, cannot be preordained. Each learning loop sets its own objectives. Gate review committees become strategic coaches rather than evaluators.

Empirical research supports our observations and company managers' experiences. Results of a study of 120 projects that used the Stage-Gate® process showed that the application of strictly enforced and objective evaluation criteria for improved control makes projects more inflexible and leads to a failure to actually learn.[20] The more novel the project, and the more turbulent the technological environment, the worse its market performance under a Stage-Gate® approach. This same research also found that loosening the gate criteria does not help and, in fact, does not impact market performance at all. Unfortunately, this approach is the most commonly adopted for managing breakthrough innovation among all the companies we investigated.

Companies are also trying entrepreneurial process approaches, such as the Lean Startup Method,[21] as an alternative to the Stage-Gate® model. Developed for the software-based start-up environment, the approach prescribes the kind of field-based market learning orientation we encourage. But the Lean Startup Method is more suited to its title—start-ups—than to the corporate environment. Organizational strategy, structure, and politics are crucial issues when handling breakthrough innovation in large companies, and this method doesn't help project managers address those concerns. It is also a process that does not align with the management system of operational excellence, and so it needs to be situated in a management culture that allows those who use it to succeed. There has to be a better way.

Culture as a Driver.   Another approach to succeeding with breakthrough innovation is the culture approach. We heard several companies declare that breakthrough innovation occurs because "We have an innovative culture here." They're proud of it. They repeatedly state it. It's written on the walls and on the website. Internal networks are active, people share information readily, and company rules may even dictate that every employee can spend up to 15 percent of their time each week on a project of their choice that may result in something big.

Most companies that innovate successfully this way are run by their founders. Google, Amazon, and LinkedIn all come to mind when one thinks of innovative cultures. Others, such as Hewlett-Packard, Analog Devices, Polaroid, and Apple, were innovative when run by their founders, entrepreneurs who called the shots regarding which products would come forward and which would not. Fully half of the top ten most innovative companies on *Fortune*'s list of the top one hundred in 2014 are run by members of their founding team.[22] The founders set the culture.

That's great. But those companies are not the subject of this book. We're concerned with mature, established companies who must find a way to innovate after the founding team has long since handed over the reins.

Of those, 3M is among the most famous for this cultural approach. "Grow and divide," "Make a little, sell a little," and "15 percent time devoted to innovation" are cultural norms that 3M instituted long ago, and to which it credits its patience for developing and incubating a number of new opportunities, such as the Post-it note or the optical display technology that led to privacy screens for computers. 3M's innovation culture leads to a "let a thousand flowers bloom" outcome. It produces many innovations but not too many breakthroughs. 3M did not make the *Forbes*'s top one hundred most innovative companies list in 2014. Recently it has focused on adopting a lead user process,[23] formed a new medical materials and technologies group to drive breakthroughs in that market arena,[24] and changed CEOs four times since 2001. It's tough to maintain a culture of innovation under those conditions.

Maintaining an innovative culture that results in breakthrough new businesses is extremely difficult for large mature companies. Lou Gerstner, past CEO of IBM and author of *Who Says Elephants Can't Dance?*, notes that IBM's culture was his greatest challenge when he was struggling to save it from the brink of bankruptcy in the mid-1990s.[25] He was reflecting on Rosabeth Moss Kanter's original observation that professional management, that is, bureaucratic management, is inherently preservation seeking, compared with entrepreneurial management, which is inherently opportunity seeking. Managers in established companies succeed by administering known routines in a uniform manner. They use past experience to guide them in establishing and refining those routines. Deviations from these routines spell failure.

In contrast, the major concern of entrepreneurial organizations is to create and exploit opportunities—however that can be done—without regard to what the organization has done in the past and without regard to resources currently under its control.[26] So, while a cultural approach to sustaining capability for breakthrough innovation in large established companies is important, it cannot be depended on as the sole answer.

There must be more: a management system in which it operates and expertise in innovation itself.

Structural Approaches. Recognizing that cultural norms supporting breakthrough innovation are difficult to sustain in a mainstream organization devoted to operational excellence and keeping customers satisfied, companies sometimes set up special groups committed to carrying out an innovation mandate. Some of these organizational designs, such as Skunk Works, popularized by Lockheed Martin, and off-site incubators, most notably Xerox PARC, sequester innovation groups from the mainstream. The reasoning behind that choice is to allow as much independence from the mother ship as possible so that technical resources, manufacturing systems, and revenue models can be developed completely independent from corporate's current approaches.

Skunk Works projects tend to work when the objective is clear at the outset, senior leaders are committed to the presumed outcomes, and the organization is strategically prepared for the new business that will ultimately result. Anything short of these three criteria and Skunk Works turns into someone's favorite project that ends up going nowhere. Off-site incubators have resulted in wonderful innovations, such as the graphical user interface (GUI) system, the mouse, and many others. However, they oftentimes end up on the commercialization docket of other companies. The link to the company's core business or strategic intent is typically too tenuous to result in any of the benefits being transferred back and changing the mainstream organization.

New ventures groups, such as those developed and popularized by Nokia, Nortel, Lucent, and Procter & Gamble, gained favor in the late 1990s partially as a way to stem the flood of talent from these large companies to Silicon Valley. These groups are typically linked to corporate R&D and therefore have the potential to contribute to the strategic intent of the company. Most, however, have struggled with that link and have become a mechanism for diversification more so than organically grown breakthrough new business platforms, given the relatively low levels of involvement of senior leaders and the uncertain corporate commitment to the nature of the investments they are making. Nortel, for example, initiated the Business Ventures Group (BVG) in 1996, an in-house incubator whose purpose was to enable employees with creative ideas to develop them in a start-up environment within Nortel rather than defecting to Cupertino. The design included an entrepreneurial culture, a set of coaches, external and internal investors, and a governance structure that would run interference between the portfolio of small companies and the typical expectations and processes of the mainstream company. The BVG's director was a vice president who reported directly to the CTO of the company. However, when the company changed CEOs, so, too, was its growth strategy altered. The new CEO favored acquisition over internal development and substantially reduced R&D spending. The CTO retired, and the BVG was defunded.

Ironically, Nortel could not make the change from the telecom era to the Internet era, which was the original mandate of the BVG. In 2009 Nortel declared bankruptcy and ceased operations. In October 2008, one of the BVG's portfolio companies was acquired by EBay/PayPal for nearly one billion dollars, which was greater than the market capitalization of Nortel at the time.[27]

Similar stories exist with Lucent's, Xerox's, Motorola's, and Nokia's venture groups. Nokia, a tire manufacturer in Finland who had risen from the ashes to laudatory profits through its success in transforming itself to a diversified company with holdings in electronics, rubber, materials, and more, was widely regarded as one of the companies at the forefront of new venture creation capability because of the design and success of its new ventures organization,[28] which is credited with developing and commercializing Wireless Application Protocol (WAP) and ultimately forming Nokia Internet Communications, which supported the move into handsets. However, Nokia couldn't keep it going, and ultimately it sold its phone business to Microsoft, who has since laid off twenty-five thousand workers, nearly all that it had acquired from that business deal.[29]

Finally, organizations may initiate innovation programs, such as IBM's Emerging Business Opportunity (EBO) program.[30] Introduced in 2000 in response to a call from CEO Lou Gerstner, the EBO program was designed and managed from the Corporate Strategy Office. During the time it ran, it was a great success, initiating twenty-five new ventures and delivering close to $10 billion in new revenues within the first five years, with ongoing revenue streams for more years to come.[31]

As IBM defined it, an EBO focused on "white space" opportunities with the promise to become profitable, billion-dollar businesses within five to seven years. The program was based on the recognition that different growth horizons require different management systems.[32] The Horizon 3 management system was designed specifically for seeding new potential business options, with the recognition that those opportunities were operating under a high degree of uncertainty and needed to be managed accordingly.

EBOs were typically assigned an experienced IBM executive leader to manage the venture during its start-up phase. An experimental, learning-based approach to project management was applied. Pilot projects, almost always involving clients, validated and refined initial ideas for the EBO's products or services. Once an EBO grew to sufficient size, it was overseen by an existing IBM business unit. They were always incubated within one of IBM's many business units, but they were governed by the top corporate executives.

In 2006 IBM moved away from a focus on Horizon 3 businesses and applied the principles of managing EBOs to a broader set of growth opportunities, including business process changes and expansion into emerging economies.[33] At this point the EBO program is a fond memory. It is currently not referred to on the company's website. While many of those twenty-five EBO leaders have had rewarding careers and carry that experience with them, the VP of corporate strategic planning who oversaw the management system retired.

Programs come and go. Functions do not.

Financial Incentive Approaches.   We've seen two quite different financial incentive-based approaches that firms use to institute an innovation capability. The first, adopted by companies that plan to spin ventures out, is to issue phantom stock so that intrapreneurs share ownership in their ventures. By and large this model has evaporated, because it sets up an "us and them" mentality. If intrapreneurs can share in the equity of their businesses, why don't all hardworking employees share directly in the financial upside of their respective projects and functions? And if the company plans to retain the venture rather than sell it, how would one value the venture in order to issue phantom stock?

Every company that we've studied or spoken with eventually has backed away from this approach. While intrapreneurs claim they take more risk than other employees do, their risk levels do not approach those of entrepreneurs. They still receive their regular paychecks, and they rely on company resources and capabilities. As one executive pointed out, if the company wishes to make innovation an institutionalized part of it, employees who work on innovation projects should not be granted financial favors. Key to his point is that they also should not be punished, of course (which, as we see in coming chapters, is not always the case).

A second financially driven approach firms take is to build and exploit a corporate venture capital (CVC) fund. Investments in small start-ups outside the company's walls help the corporation understand technology trends in key areas of interest, and ultimately position the firm to acquire promising start-ups. Having made its first appearance in the mid-1960s, the CVC model has endured more than the others.[34] Today more than 750 companies list CVCs in the Global Corporate Venturing database,[35] and their investments cross many sectors. While this approach is a wonderful complement to internal, organic growth, it does not help the company if it functions in isolation. An innovation capability must complement the investment in externally sourced technologies.

DISTINCTIVE MANAGEMENT APPROACH NEEDED: AN INNOVATION FUNCTION

Champions, Skunk Works, venture groups, and programs may all have their place, but so far none has had the kind of impact our companies require or solved the dual problem of successfully commercializing breakthrough innovations for the market *and* creating new growth platforms for the company from which they originated.

Our research leads us to conclude that innovation must be managed as any other typical business function, accompanied by an appropriate management system charged with the mandate to find and nurture the company's businesses of the future. To develop the expertise needed, there must be formalized roles at multiple levels. Over time, people filling these roles will develop expertise. Companies need people with innovation skills in addition to passion. Companies will recruit for those roles, select carefully, and develop people. When a person moves on in her career, they will replace her with someone of equivalent acumen. In this manner, innovation capability will become institutionalized in companies. While new product development (that is, incremental innovation) can be managed as a process, breakthrough innovation cannot. Innovation is a function. It's not R&D, and it's not marketing. It is its own function.

It turns out that we're not the only ones beginning to see this option: Russ Conser, former director of the Shell GameChangers group, enthusiastically supports the notion. "We will be amateurs at Breakthrough Innovation until we get the talent management part right," he confirmed when we interviewed him. Others share the concern. The Thought Leadership Institute (TLI), a professional organization of HR and organizational development leaders, and the Industrial Research Institute (IRI) each surveyed its members about the issue of talent management for breakthrough innovation. Although the number of responses was small (twenty-nine IRI members and twenty-two for the TLI), their responses, shown in Table 1.1, aren't surprising and send a clear message.

The vast majority of both groups indicate they realize that the goals of operational excellence and breakthrough innovation are different enough to require distinctions in assessing talent for those roles. But on average, fewer than one-third do. And the percentage of respondents who believe they cultivate and develop innovation talent is also low . . . much lower for those from the R&D community than from the talent management community, but still low overall. Finally, the survey shows that, while it is viewed by both communities as fairly risky to one's career to undertake breakthrough innovation, the rewards for commercial success are high. So the message that comes through is, "Go for it, but at your own expense!" Or, put another way, "We want you to do it, but we won't give you any support; we make no promises, and you'd better not fail" (even though breakthrough innovation is fraught with false starts, stops, pivots, and all the things that look like failure in an operational excellence world). Not a great message for companies who pride themselves on competing via innovation.

TABLE 1.1   Talent Management for Breakthrough Innovation

	Percent of Industrial Research Institute Respondents Who Answered "True"	Percent of Thought Leadership Institute Respondents Who Answered "True"
WE KNOW WE SHOULD DISTINGUISH . . .		
It is important to distinguish between the goals of operational excellence and breakthrough innovation in assessing talent for my company.	80	77
BUT WE DON'T.		
My company distinguishes between the goals of operational excellence and breakthrough innovation in accessing talent pools for potential hires.	28	36
My company distinguishes between the goals of operational excellence and breakthrough innovation in its hiring processes.	21	36
DO WE CULTIVATE BREAKTHROUGH INNOVATION EXPERTISE?		
My company believes that any person in the "high-potential" category is capable of managing breakthrough innovation.	38	27
My company trains individuals in the art of breakthrough innovation.	10	23
My company helps with career planning/management for breakthrough innovation project leaders.	7	32
My company has specific criteria for selecting individuals to be responsible for breakthrough innovation programs.	24	32
My company helps with career planning/management for breakthrough innovation program leaders?	14	27
HOW ARE BREAKTHROUGH INNOVATION PARTICIPANTS REWARDED?		
Risk		
People hesitate to get involved in breakthrough innovation projects because of risks of project failures.	45	41
If a breakthrough innovation fails careers can be ruined here.	31	36
Reward		
Individuals who have successfully developed and commercialized breakthrough innovations are highly respected in our company.	69	73
It is expected in this company that, to move up in the ranks, individuals have to be involved in some risky projects.	14	23

Why do companies send this message? We believe it is because they don't know what to do. But in fact, much more is known today about management practices for breakthrough innovation than even five years ago. It's time to become as sophisticated about innovation as we are about marketing, finance, information systems management, quality management, operations, and R&D.

This is the next opportunity for a major step forward in management practice. We can get it right. By doing so, we help companies, the marketplace, and society benefit from those dusty inventions sitting on shelves that should be changing the game.

THE TALENT MANAGEMENT GAP AND ITS LINK TO STRATEGIC INNOVATION

Our premise is that the concept of breakthrough innovation is evolving. With a clearer understanding of how it actually occurs, we can now build management systems that support its unique characteristics of uncertainty and ambiguity, and we can become more proactive at addressing those uncertainties. It becomes more strategic and less opportunistic. We know now how to hunt for and recognize emerging disruptive technologies. We know more about open innovation strategies and partnership arrangements for accessing resources and competencies without full-force investment before we're more certain.

Talent management for innovation must be addressed for companies to develop expertise that survives a single successful champion. This is an overlooked aspect of a management system for breakthrough innovation. This is not rocket science, and you may believe your company handles it well. Following are true accounts from people who work in the well-known companies we studied. We call them our "pain stories": good, smart people who were penalized for their engagement with breakthrough innovation, or who were expected to succeed in aspects of the innovation process far different from the expertise they brought to the table.

The R&D champion who spotted an opportunity to apply a discovery in avionics to medical-imaging technology in one of our companies was responsible for bringing it to the attention of the vice president for research. It was a breakthrough concept if applied appropriately in the medical field. However, the president of the medical-imaging business unit at the time wanted no part of it, indicating that the business unit did not have the manufacturing capacity to handle this new technological approach, nor did they need the business given their growth rates with the current technology. Why fiddle with a successful product platform? The champion continued to press, and the business unit finally sought an external manufacturing partner, having perceived a threat when it heard that a competitor was experimenting with a similar technology. The manufacturing partnership failed, in part because there were so many process innovations required, and the business unit was unable to invest in developing that deep of a relationship with the external partner to help it devise the new production approach. Ultimately the champion built the business within R&D, using R&D's facilities traditionally used for fabricating prototypes to conduct the needed higher-volume manufacturing. Within a few years this medical-imaging business grew to become a major game changer in its field and for the company, but our champion's boss retired, and he retired too early. He told us, "The idea of having someone champion the project, have a vision for it, and push it and push it and push it and push it is what makes it successful." But pushing too hard can raise the hair on the backs of other important political players' necks. He didn't have a chance of succeeding politically once his senior sponsor could no longer provide cover.

In another of our participating companies, a business director for an emerging business told us that there was no upward mobility for him in his current role. His line of reporting was through the chief technology officer, who lacked business creation expertise. He therefore received little guidance regarding the business's development, and certainly would never assume his boss's role. He perceived that his only way to succeed was to make sure his business succeeded so that he could become its general manager. He'd been nurturing the opportunity for four years in the hopes that this would happen, but it was taking too long, and there were no guarantees. Even with all his hard work, uphill battles, and signs of success, he'd been promoted only once during the time he was incubating this business, which was viewed as strategically important for the company. The colleagues in the operating unit that he'd left to assume this role had been promoted multiple times. The business director claimed that he was not doing this gig for the money, but for the possibility of a big success story (the once-every-ten-years big hit). He appreciated the visibility he was getting from senior management, but, unfortunately, the one that mattered most to him retired during this time. Eventually he left this role and moved back to his previous business unit. Today he's the divisional vice president. That's great for him, and perhaps good for the division he's running, but not so great for the new business he left. This ambitious guy had to wait too long for the recognition and position of influence he sought. Incubation takes a very, very long time.

Finally, we encountered a vice president of science and technology in yet a different company who considered his most recent assignment as punishment for transgressions he'd committed in his attempts to grow a new business area. While his current title was certainly impressive, he was not happy with the associated responsibilities, which were to develop and lead innovation best practices across the company. "I am in the penalty box. I feel like an experienced quarterback with a broken leg . . . on the sidelines." Why had this talented person been sidelined? He'd had a big idea, built a venture, and then was passed over as CTO of the venture he built. He deduced that he'd not been politically sensitive enough when he spoke to others in the company about the venture. He'd burned a few bridges and had not had appropriate strategic guidance to help him understand the consequences of his venture's success on other aspects of the company's strategy. By the time we finished our study, he'd opted to take early retirement and is now consulting to companies on how to drive technology-based innovation.

These are but a few of the many pain stories we've collected. Talented innovators make political faux pas, lacking proper coaching and strategic guidance, or suffer the consequences of working on highly uncertain projects that cannot meet predicted timetables. They're not stupid. They're not lazy. This is the nature of breakthrough innovation. There are far too many examples of people in the wrong roles, or people working without a link to the right leadership, or companies' ineffective use of innovation talent. On several occasions we encountered research scientists put in the position of having to create market connections and build business platforms on the basis of their discoveries. At one of the companies we studied, a breakthrough opportunity occurred. A promising scientist volunteered to drive the business. He did, but it took him seventeen years to build a business that was recognized as part of the mainstream company. How often does the window of opportunity stay open for that long?

CONSEQUENCES

These stories may seem unlikely or dramatic. Yet many more exist in every one of the companies we've studied. At the end of our four-year study, we contacted each person we had interviewed to learn of any changes in his or her role over the study period. Here's what we found:

- Of 129 people classified as filling innovation roles, 66 people (51 percent) had left the position after three-plus years—a fairly typical turnover rate of roles in the corporate setting.

- Of those, 71 percent left the company's innovation function. They had either moved to a business unit or left the company, rather than being promoted within innovation . . . hmm, loss of expertise.

- Of those who left the company 87.5 percent are working in an innovation function for another company or have started their own company.

- More people exited the company than moved within innovation roles.

  - 17 percent of study participants left the company over the four-year period.

  - 14 percent moved into new innovation related roles within the company.

The implication? By their actions, companies are indicating that they favor losing their innovation talent to competitors over rewarding and retaining it. We know that innovation talent is rare, and we have also learned that many people who have those skills and expertise would rather move companies than take on operational roles. One innovation director told us:

If they put me in charge of a business where there are no opportunities to grow or innovate, they would waste my color . . . I'm not married to any company. I'm attached to who I am, and what I would like to do.

SO WHERE DO WE GO FROM HERE?

Over the past several years, there's been a trend to identify a new role of chief innovation officer, but identifying their mandate has been tougher. Executing on it is tougher still. A study by Capgemini Consulting reported that, in 2012, 43 percent of executives responding to their survey indicated that their companies have an innovation executive, compared with 33 percent the previous year. For many companies, the title of chief innovation officer is ambiguous. The *Wall Street Journal* commented on the study by suggesting that the CNO[36] role was industry's "new toy. Company boards feel that they ought to have one. They just aren't sure what to do with it."[37] While some companies report finding people who have the right skill, mind-set, clout within the organization, and bandwidth to be able to lead innovation activities, they do not necessarily know what is expected beyond "more innovative ideas."[38]

Allocating one expert to handle innovation for a company is unrealistic. What is becoming clear is that companies need deep expertise in innovation. And that means identifying what those roles are. If that doesn't happen soon, companies will retract their investments even in the CNO position (and, in fact, many have done just that since 2012), and we'll be back to square one. Companies who compete on the basis of breakthrough innovation must address the problem of talent management in order to build an innovation expertise.

In Chapter 2 we describe the evolution we see among companies to get professional about innovation . . . to move from a concept of breakthrough innovation to strategic innovation. Strategic innovation sets its scope on the far future and cultivates a portfolio of options that will become the company's next platforms of business. It's ambiguous. It's uncertain. It needn't be unmanageable or excessively risky. It needs to be strategic. We'll describe the management system for strategic innovation and the competencies that firms must develop to successfully commercialize breakthroughs and other innovative new platforms of business. These were identified in our earlier studies and have been validated by numerous companies in many settings.

But this book focuses on the talent development aspects of the management system, because at its core, instituting innovation roles is the weak link we find in most companies' innovation management system attempts. We offer a framework of roles that align with the necessary competencies of discovery, incubation, and acceleration that form the basic building blocks for strategic innovation. Later in the book we take up the issue of career paths for innovation personnel. As you have seen, people in innovation roles are more likely to leave their companies than those in other roles, and, perhaps more important, they are more likely to work in innovation roles for other companies than to move to non-innovation-related roles. This means that attention to career paths and job satisfaction for such personnel could greatly enhance a company's reservoir of expertise for strategic innovation and strengthen its competitive advantage rather than surrendering it to others.

2

WHAT WE NOW KNOW
ABOUT MANAGING
STRATEGIC INNOVATION

In Chapter 1 we asserted that innovation must claim its place as a function within companies, alongside marketing, engineering, production, purchasing, R&D, and others. Conceived in this way, strategic innovation is not a process, a program, or the result of a long-shot, once-in-a-while opportunity that occurs thanks to a strong-willed intrapreneur. Rather, it is an organizational mainstay with specific responsibilities. The innovation function has a clear purpose and a management system designed to reinforce its aims.

The elements of a management system are displayed in Figure 2.1.[1] Simply put, such system is the set of structures, processes, and norms that allows a unit to function efficiently and effectively.

All the elements of a management system must reinforce one another in support of the system's mandate. If any single element counteracts another, the system will not work optimally, sending confusing messages to those working within it and those expected to support it. "We don't walk the talk around here" is a phrase we hear frequently when employees are experiencing this sort of confusion.

Management systems are crucially important for enabling organizations to thrive beyond their original founders. Founding teams—like George Eastman and his trusty chemist at Kodak, Bill Hewlett and Dave Packard

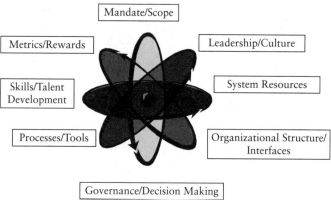

FIGURE 2.1   Management System Elements
Source: Reprinted with permission from John Wiley & Sons, from Gina Colarelli
O'Connor, Richard Leifer, Albert S. Paulson, and Lois S. Peters, *Grabbing Lightning:
Building a Capability for Breakthrough Innovation* (San Francisco: Jossey-Bass, 2008).
Copyright © 2008 by John Wiley & Sons, Inc.

at HP, or Larry Page and Sergey Brin at Google—instill a strong culture
and set of norms for how things get done. Once the torch is passed to a
second or third generation, these charismatic leaders are often replaced by
"professional management." It is at this point that management systems
operate as the mechanism that helps companies perpetuate their goals
and ensure that employees' behaviors are aligned with the organization's
objectives.

For most mature companies, the overarching mandate is to maintain
ongoing operations—to efficiently and effectively manage current markets,
technical know-how, and operations to turn a profit. Herein lies part of
the problem: companies tend to apply one management system across the
board. The operational excellence mandate often lies in sharp contrast to
that of an innovation function—which is to find and develop new business platforms for the company based on more risky, uncertain, and potentially game-changing opportunities. Thus, an innovation function is a
subsystem within the company that requires its own management system,
aligned with its unique objectives.

Such an extreme innovation mandate may scare business leaders. Many
do not want to commit to breakthrough innovation as a matter of every-

day business, claiming it is too rare, too difficult, and too risky. But anything beyond incremental innovation—those opportunities for which the target market, technological solution, underlying needs, business model, and organizational fit are not obvious—fits within an innovation management system. Similar to breakthroughs, these types of innovation leverage *some* of the company's organizational setup and current capabilities, but not many. There is still plenty of uncertainty on many fronts to address, and a robust, healthy management system for higher uncertainty innovation must exist to support these initiatives. In other words, the innovation function is not just for lightning in a bottle.

A number of interesting contrasts emerge when we compare management systems for operational excellence with those designed for strategic innovation. We'll consider each in turn.

As mentioned, the *mandate and scope* of mainstream management systems include efficient, effective management of current markets and operations, leveraging known and well-understood technology. Speed to market is crucial, and competition is fierce. Innovation management systems, in contrast, address new business opportunities in yet-to-be created markets or untapped spaces. Who needed a phone to also operate as a camera until they had one in their hands? Yet, in 2014, people reportedly uploaded an average of 1.8 billion digital images every single day.[2] The prediction is that 1.3 trillion photos will have been captured in 2017.[3] This is but one example. Stronger bridges, faster integrated circuits, drones, solar cells, clothing that rejects stains and collects data . . . the list goes on and on.

Next in the lineup of management system elements is *leadership and culture*. In an operational excellence setting, they are oriented to planning and delivery. Decisiveness is crucial. Closure is important. Building on what we do best trumps trying something new. Moving quickly to beat competitors is a must. Defensive moves outnumber offensive plays. A culture of innovation, on the other hand, encourages learning and redirecting as needed; it is oriented toward creating possibilities rather than managing probabilities. Leadership in an innovation culture operates with a "build and create" mentality while recognizing that the company's limits require strategic decisions about where to stake the company's investments in R&D and market creation. That said, innovation is not a free for all, and innovation leaders are well aware of the strategic responsibilities they face. Guiding an organization in a disciplined manner to hunt down all possible pathways within an opportunity space and connecting those opportunities to the intended future of the company are at the forefront of an innovation leader's concerns. So, while discipline and leadership are needed, the command and control culture, defensive moves, and quick decisions of mainstream management systems will stamp out strategic innovation in a heartbeat.

Organizations seem to change their structures all the time. In fact, many claim that flat organizations are the way to go, and some no longer maintain organization charts. That's not the majority, but this approach sure does make the news. By and large, these *organizational structures and interfaces* are clearly delineated, and changes to them create organizational disruption. If a company reorganizes its business units, it's a big deal. When people are promoted or take a lateral move, the position is posted and filled by another hire.

Decisions about the innovation group's organization structure, reporting relationships, and mechanisms for interfacing with the mainstream organization, however, have tended to be fluid and flexible. For some time we thought that was because innovation required such organizational fluidity. And it does at the company level. If a company needs to set up a new business unit to house its emerging new businesses, it should. However, we've seen that structural ambiguity within the innovation group creates confusion. To whom the group reports sends a clear message to the rest of the organization about its role. Clarifying the responsibilities of those within it is crucial. A management system for innovation must have the same clear lines of reporting and positions as any other function. The roles themselves and reporting structures have to fit with the jobs to be done—developing the new business options for the company's future.

System resources are the budget and people allocated to ensure the strategic innovation mandate can be addressed sufficiently. For mainstream functions, annual resource allocation decisions occur through the strategic planning and budgeting process. When innovation is treated as a function, it receives resources in this more typical manner. Otherwise, resources are granted on a project by project basis and are not predictable. If a project is viewed as highly promising, it becomes the "glamour project" of the year, and the company may throw too many resources its way. Assigning lots of people to a project fraught with uncertainty doesn't help. Instead, it attracts too much attention and raises expectations that the project will succeed.

The most important aspect about innovation system resources is that they be consistently allocated year after year and sized to match the desired size and current maturity of the portfolio of opportunities. The scope of the innovation portfolio needs to be aligned with a firm's capacity for growth through strategic innovation.

Once those decisions are made, those managing the portfolio should allocate seed funding to projects to learn more. Each project does not need high-level review for resources, so long as they are aligned with the company's stated strategic intent. After that, let the experiments begin. This situation is certainly contrasted to traditional project funding, for which an annual budget may be allocated, and the job of the project manager is to operate within it. For innovation, we need a lump-sum budget that is managed across the portfolio to aid learning experiments. It's a real options approach, based on a consistent, persistent annual budget that the chief innovation officer and his leadership team dole out as needed.

Governance is about identifying who makes decisions about the strategic innovation portfolio and the criteria they use to do so. In the mainstream management system, leadership for ongoing operations prioritizes the execution of current plans. There is typically a clearly defined set of criteria for deciding whether to continue or kill a project, or whether or not to make an investment of time and resources. Hierarchical decision making works. But decisions in an innovation world, which is full of ambiguity, are not so clear. In the world of innovation, decisions are made by a broader set of people, since gaining buy-in for these new businesses from a number of constituents is required for the level of resources needed to grow them and the directions in which they may take the company. Consensus isn't necessary but conversation is.

Processes and tools are used to guide organizational behavior in an operational excellence world. They bring discipline and help produce predictable, reliable outcomes, which is of crucial importance for large, complex organizations. The application of such processes works quite well when desired outcomes are known (e.g., deliver quantity X of product Y to customer Z by March 1, with zero defects in product quality), and when best practices exist and are well understood. That is certainly not the situation when it comes to the world of strategic innovation. Every undertaking requires experimenting and learning about new technical and market possibilities, as well as considering how a market might develop as the opportunity space grows. That does not mean that processes and tools aren't useful. But they have to be the right ones, developed for the purpose of helping guide decisions under ambiguous circumstances without closing options off too soon. Perhaps even more important, the people working in innovation cannot become subjugated to the processes nor can they use those processes as a crutch or excuse for failing to learn and deliver insights.

Are the *skills sets* that are needed for mainstream and innovation management systems different? In Chapter 1 we saw that R&D and HR professionals think so. When an organizational manager is hiring a new person into her group in one of the traditional functions of the mainstream system, she looks for deep expertise in the function. Interestingly, that has not been the case with many innovation-related functions that we've observed. Instead, hiring managers tend to look for people with skills in the particular technology or market domain of a specific project. Functional expertise versus innovation expertise seems like a rather sharp contrast, but it is not if one begins to consider innovation as a function, a profession of its own. We have all encountered people who innovate on behalf of the company time and time again, and can do so regardless of the nature of the technology or market application. More than anything, their skills are associated with learning how to learn. Put them in an operational role where they are responsible for delivering the same reports, products, or other kind of output on a regular basis, and they do not perform well. But innovation management systems require this type of person, their learning skills, and the room to develop their expertise.

Finally, the *metrics* used to determine how an innovation management system is performing cannot be the same as those we use to assess our mainstream organization's health. Stock price, profitability, and market share all focus on the present, or may incorporate the market's expectations about the near future. The very near future. Similarly, the *reward systems* in the operational excellence world are structured to reinforce meeting targets and ensuring no surprises happen. No deviations from the plan. That of course is not the reality of innovation.

How does one measure the impact that an innovation group has had over the past year? Surely the likelihood of any single project's success as a breakthrough is low. When we move to strategic innovation, it's higher, but not close to the success rate expected of incremental innovation. Is that failure? What happens to the people on that project? If they stuck to a plan and didn't pivot, is that appropriate behavior? Absolutely not. An innovation management system is best measured based on the richness and relevance of the portfolio of options it develops for the company's future, and the actions its people have taken to nurture them. These cannot be measured in terms of net present value or internal rate of return, since those are unknowable until the markets come to fruition. Over time the company can examine the source of its new businesses and analyze the influence, either directly or indirectly, of the innovation group. In the meantime, activity-based performance metrics are needed.

As we can see, the elements of a management system for the mainstream and innovation hubs within a business are the same, but the specifics differ dramatically. A management system for innovation helps a company persist at developing its future, rather than as a once-in-a-while focus.

WHAT CONSTITUTES A STRATEGIC INNOVATION CAPABILITY?

We tested the management system model in twenty-one companies.[4] Through our analysis, we came to see that strategic innovation capabilities are composed of three distinct competencies, their interfaces with one another, and their interface with the rest of the organization. These capabilities, supported by a high-performing management system for innovation, set the innovation function up for success. The competencies are discovery (D), incubation (I), and acceleration (A). The ways that they interface with the rest of the organization will change based on the pressures the organization faces and its ability to absorb new growth opportunities. We call that the organization's capacity for innovation.

The interface must be managed, typically by a single person holding a senior-level role such as a chief innovation officer (CNO), or a corporate vice president for innovation with a second in command, an orchestrator, who manages the innovation portfolio and works behind the scenes to help move the nascent businesses along from one phase to the next. In many cases, an innovation governance board will make major investment decisions. But someone has to be held responsible for innovation in established companies. As the saying goes, "If someone doesn't own it, nobody owns it." History shows that new business incubators, new ventures divisions, or other groups that are responsible for major innovation in companies don't last. Nortel Networks' didn't. Lucent's didn't. Xerox's didn't. Even 3M's didn't. Their average life span is about four years. The idea that a CNO powers the innovation function up and down, given the company's ability to absorb new businesses, is key to ensuring that innovation capability is not lost, and remains part and parcel of the company. Strategic innovation capability over time is pictured in Figure 2.2.

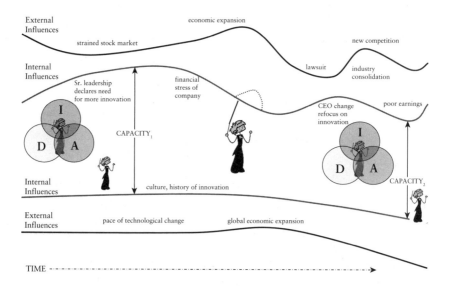

FIGURE 2.2   Model of Strategic Innovation Capability
Source: Reprinted with permission from John Wiley & Sons, from Gina Colarelli O'Connor, Richard Leifer, Albert S. Paulson, and Lois S. Peters, *Grabbing Lightning: Building a Capability for Breakthrough Innovation* (San Francisco: Jossey-Bass, 2008). Copyright © 2008 by John Wiley & Sons, Inc.

THE BUILDING BLOCKS: DISCOVERY, INCUBATION, AND ACCELERATION

Each of the competencies—D, I, and A—must be developed in their own right. The skills and metrics for discovery, for example, are different from those of incubation, and both differ from acceleration. Figure 2.3 summarizes the three competencies that organizations must master as a starting point for building an innovation expertise.

The first building block is the *discovery* competency. Discovery is about the creation, recognition, elaboration, and articulation of opportunities. The skills needed for discovery are exploration and conceptualization skills. Discovery activities can be the internally focused laboratory research that we are used to thinking of, but also include hunting inside and outside the company for great ideas, licensing technologies, or placing equity investments in small firms that hold promise. All these activities are associated with generating opportunities that could grow to become new business platforms, and many companies engage in all of them to increase the likelihood of getting a few great ones.

We have seen a number of interesting approaches companies are taking to discovering potential strategic innovations. One maintained a dedicated staff of creative geniuses, labeled the "alpha team" who was responsible

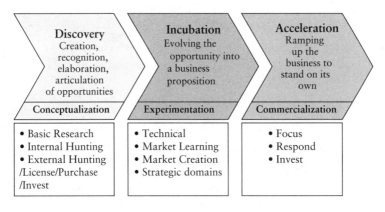

FIGURE 2.3   Three Competencies for Strategic Innovation
Source: Reprinted with permission from John Wiley & Sons, from Gina Colarelli O'Connor, Richard Leifer, Albert S. Paulson, and Lois S. Peters, *Grabbing Lightning: Building a Capability for Breakthrough Innovation* (San Francisco: Jossey-Bass, 2008). Copyright © 2008 by John Wiley & Sons, Inc.

for developing radically innovative ideas. Another firm employed idea "hunters" (the title listed on their business cards) responsible for identifying opportunities both inside and outside the company. A third company formed an "externalization" team devoted to the development of future trend analyses based on visits to universities, government agencies, and other external entities, and also built a "hunters' network" of creative individuals throughout the company. In yet another, a permanent team of technical and business development middle managers composed the "Technology Identification Process" team, who was charged with finding new opportunities to help fuel R&D projects with the potential to become new platforms of business.

Three companies we studied were experimenting with "exploratory marketing groups," which served as partners to the exploratory research groups in corporate R&D labs. All of them were situated in R&D, although they were rarely there . . . they were out scouting for opportunities to leverage the firm's technology prowess. Finally, one company relied on a network of external contractors to generate and develop wild ideas and inventions. This network was maintained and funded by a senior executive who elected not to hire them on as employees for fear that their creativity would be stifled by the company's culture.

So it's clear that discovery is about much more than bench science. It's about opportunity generation based on advances in science and technology, coupled with sheer imagination and a heavy dose of market analysis. But all we are doing in discovery is generating options for our company. No one knows which ones will become the company's future.

Incubation is the second competency companies need. Of the three competencies, incubation takes the most time and patience. Incubation is the competency associated with exploring opportunities and evolving them into business proposals. A business proposal is a working hypothesis about what the technology platform could enable in the market, how the market space will ultimately develop, and what form the business model will take. Incubation isn't complete until that business proposal (or, more likely, a number of proposals based on the initial discovery) has been tested and appears to have significant promise.

The skills required for incubation are experimentation skills. Experiments are conducted not only on the technical front but also for market learning, market creation, and for testing the match of the business proposition against the company's strategic intent. The technical, market, resource, and organizational uncertainties involved require that individuals be comfortable with ambiguity and lots of false starts.[5] Those participating in incubation must be creative in their search for new knowledge and in devising learning trials.

The companies whose management system evolution we studied did not systematically engage in incubation. Of the twelve, only one was doing much incubation when we first began observing. Over the next several years, however, nine others recognized the need for this activity and attempted to build it into their practices. Most added business development or strategic marketing personnel to their teams. Others evolved a new version of project manager. Some called them business leaders. The company that had an "alpha team" of creative geniuses developing business concepts added a "beta" group to begin experimenting with those concepts in the marketplace, in the company's labs, and with strategic partners.

Incubation appears to be the most fragile and least understood of the three competencies. Some of the companies de-resourced incubation as their innovation mandates evolved toward projects that were aligned with the company's current businesses. We call this "mandate creep" and identify it as a frequently encountered challenge faced by strategic innovation groups. Others incubated projects for a very short time, found one easy pathway to market, and transitioned the project to a business unit, completely underleveraging the innovation's potential as a platform from which a whole family of products could be launched.

Most of the companies used coaches to help teams who were incubating projects, though not formally, and the coaches weren't always expert at new business creation. Some of the most impressive coaching we saw involved helping the fledgling businesses gain "clarity of strategy" by talking with the project teams about markets, business models, technology development directions, financing, partnerships, staffing, and organizational alignment. Good coaches pressed teams to prove out the value proposition and guided them to elect courses of action as choice points arose that strengthened the link between the emerging business and the company's vision for its future.

Acceleration is the third competency. There are typically few emerging businesses in the acceleration portfolio at any one point in time, because it requires the most resources and organizational change. In acceleration we are ramping up the fledgling business to a point where it can stand on its own relative to other business platforms in the operating unit that will ultimately house it. Whereas incubation reduces market and technical uncertainty through experimentation and learning, acceleration focuses on finding ways to convert early customer leads to predictable sales forecasts. But alas, new types of uncertainties arise—those associated with configuring resources to scale the business and claim its space within the portfolio of the company's ongoing businesses.

The activities of acceleration include investing to build the business' infrastructure and operating routines, while focusing on and responding to market leads and opportunities. The metrics associated with acceleration capture growth rather than profitability.

Companies struggle with where acceleration should be located. Most company leaders try to accelerate their emerging innovations inside an operating unit, with the promise that they'll be patient while it grows. They rarely are. This model cannot work unless senior leaders provide persistent oversight. In most of the companies we studied, nascent businesses that are located in the business units are pressured to adhere to the revenue models, operating norms, and current customer base that the business unit serves. The degrees of freedom for matching the business model to the market's needs are highly constrained. Accelerating businesses require investments of money and attention, and the business unit's leadership is typically not in a position to provide those investments given the many pressures they face for delivering near-term profit. Under these circumstances, the elements of the management system are misaligned. Managers of accelerating businesses will be held to metrics they cannot meet.

Corporate-level accelerators, or a strategic business unit devoted to housing early stage growth businesses, are better organizational approaches unless an emerging business's operating model fits neatly with that of the business unit (BU) destined to become its new home. Only when the new business can show a predictable path to profitability, satisfied customers, and an operating model that has been accepted by corporate leadership can it adequately compete for attention and resources in a traditional business unit. Small businesses require investment, and the business unit is typically not in a position to do that.

Projects, Platforms, and Portfolios.   In watching the participating companies evolve their strategic innovation management systems over several years, we noticed another interesting pattern. Most of them kicked off their innovation initiative by issuing a call for ideas, any ideas that could be classified as potential breakthroughs. They were deluged with ideas in the beginning, most of which were smaller, or incomprehensible, or unrelated to the company's vision of the future. Within a short amount of time, most companies settled on a few domains they expected to be leading in the future. They articulated imagined possible futures and ways in which these technological innovations would be dominant and would define the company. "If we don't invest now, we won't get there, and we need to own that space," one CTO told us. We called these domains of strategic intent. They're not connected to the company's current strategy or to its current assets or expertise. Instead, they result from a view of multiple emerging technologies and social movements that could collide to form dramatic new opportunities.

In the mid-1990s, for example, Corning's just-retired CTO thought about the mapping of the human genome and its consequences for a glass company. After some convincing, Corning invested in hiring biologists into its R&D center and began developing equipment for diagnostic testing at the genetic level. Today Corning has a healthy medical products business. But to get there, they started and killed many R&D projects, all of which were directed at contributing to this commonly understood platform of genetic testing. Any single project might be labeled as failed, but together they developed into a platform of expertise and product lines that are the foundation of an entire business.

As companies define and articulate their domains of strategic intent, they find that cross-platform spillovers of learning and application arise.

Multiple domains of strategic intent are an important way to diversify their efforts and benefit from their investments. So each platform may be composed of a set of small experiments known as projects, and the platforms combine into a larger portfolio. All of this is to say that the strategic innovation (SI) capabilities of discovery, incubation, and acceleration tend to operate at three levels: project, platform, and portfolio. Individual projects within a platform serve as mechanisms for learning and building the platform. The portfolio of SI platforms constitute the entire set of projects overseen by the innovation function. At each level for each competency different types of expertise and talent are required.

DIA as a System.   Balancing activities across discovery, incubation, and acceleration is a strategic decision that depends on funding and strategic imperatives. In addition, the characteristics of the portfolio's diversity are strategic questions. Most portfolios are diversified along the risk spectrum. Traditional portfolio managers ensure they have some sure winners along with some long shots to make sure there'll be a return. But breakthrough innovations are all risky, so a portfolio like this will not be diversified along that dimension. How, then, should one think about diversification? Should one diversify along business domains? Along technology competency domains? Along time pacing across D, I, and A? How can a company evaluate the health of the strategic innovation portfolio? These are issues that companies are just beginning to face. Viewing the DIA system as one management system, and innovation as a function, can help managers think about these issues in a clear light.

One can imagine many ways for the set of DIA competencies to fail as a system. Here are a few that we've seen:

- *Can't Get Heard.* Lots of money is poured into discovery, but no one invests to explore the business opportunities through incubation. Many of the people we spoke with in the participating companies expressed this frustration. That's why we mention that incubation is the most absent of the three competencies.

- *No Courage to Continue.* At one company, we were told that as the company came to understand the market opportunity, it didn't have the courage to continue to invest and execute on their learning . . . what they learned was too foreign to them. So they did some incubation, but did not persist through acceleration, and did not benefit from the opportunity.

- *Big Ideas, Incrementally Executed.* This occurs when a company moves projects straight from Discovery to Acceleration. They devote lots of resources to discovery, but then commercialize only the most immediately apparent application and call it a day. Companies in this situation are not doing new business creation: they're doing new product development. There's a big difference.

- *Open Innovation at the Extreme.* Many companies believe they can build breakthrough innovations by in-sourcing the technology and incubating it. While that may be true, they cannot allow the discovery capability to atrophy and shrivel. It's key to understanding real opportunity, no matter where it originated.

- *Interface Management Problem.* In one company, the project leader had explored many potential applications for the technology, but when it came time to grow the business, the newly appointed program manager did not leverage that learning. In a territorial tour de force he began exploring new markets from scratch. This is a great example of why the DIA system requires an orchestrator, to monitor the system's linkage to the company's capacity but also to ensure that the system's interfaces are well greased.

Each competency (DIA) has to be considered in its own right, in terms of leadership, talent development, governance, organizational structure and location, tools and metrics. In addition, the three competencies must be melded as a system with feedforward and feedback loops, which is why they're shown as three interlinked circles in Figure 2.2.

Finally, the whole thing has to be orchestrated in line with the company's current capacity to deal with real innovation. That capacity is determined by internal and external forces, denoted in in Figure 2.2 as the dark and light lines surrounding the DIA activities. The dark lines symbolize external forces on the company, including the stock market's performance, pace of technological change, and the competitive landscape that the company is facing. The light lines indicate internal forces that alter the company's appetite for innovation, including its earnings picture, leadership's strategic priorities, and the company's historical approach to gaining competitive advantage. Notice that the lines on the top of Figure 2.2 are wavy, but those on the bottom are relatively smooth. This indicates that some of these forces change dramatically and others take a long time. As the orchestrator realizes, these forces combine to form the company's current capacity for innovation. At times the capacity will be munificent, and the company will want innovation immediately. At other times, it's constrained, and the company will want to defund innovation completely. Neither extreme is realistic or smart. The CNO and orchestrator monitor the company's capacity, work to counterbalance those swings, and maintain an innovation portfolio that fits the capacity of the company, while also ensuring the continued development of the innovation expertise and options for new business platforms. Without that match and the CNO's continued influence to remind the organization of its strategic intent, this effort will be another in the long line of defunct attempts.

THE BIG PICTURE AND SMALL STEPS FORWARD
Given this endgame, where should companies start or seek to improve their innovation capability? We noted in earlier research that of all the elements of a management system that we've observed in the companies we've studied and worked with since, talent development has surfaced as one of the most challenging for companies. It's not so much that it is challenging as that it has not received much attention, resulting in undesirable consequences for firms attempting to improve their SI capabilities. Without clear roles and responsibilities, these management systems cannot become institutionalized, and companies cannot improve their expertise. They start over and over with glamorous innovation initiatives with fancy names like moonshots, breakthroughs, transformational innovations, game changers, and on and on. Pretty soon, employees can't take them seriously.

So far we have made the point that the skills and expertise required for SI differ from those needed to run the ongoing operation and core business. Based on the model presented above, though, we can say more. What we now know is that, within the innovation function, there is greater complexity than we've previously acknowledged. Discovery, incubation, and acceleration must all be addressed, and each requires different types of talent. In addition, we know that a SI capability requires managing more than a random set of projects. They're organized into platforms aligned with the company's strategic intent, and a portfolio of platforms helps the innovation function cover some of the more important bases of the future and therefore hedge its risk.

The implication for the talent development challenge is to recognize that all innovators are not the same and neither are all innovation roles. Ignoring this reality causes frustration among innovation talent or those who desire to move into innovation. It also sets companies back in developing an innovation expertise. In addition, innovation leaders must understand how to evaluate innovation projects, platforms, and portfolios in light of the uncertainty involved, the organization's capacity for innovation and strategic intent for its future. Innovation leaders must orchestrate investment in breakthrough innovation capabilities and talent in line with this evaluation.

In Chapter 3 we bring to life the disaffection that innovation personnel experience in their careers, and the lackluster management practices associated with managing innovation talent that have come to light in our most recent study. We discuss presumed reward systems and why they are poorly conceived. Much of what you read will likely feel familiar. Once we understand the issues, we can start to design the innovation function required to address them.

3   INNOVATORS BEWARE
Talent Management Through Neglect, Misunderstanding, and Punishment

Our people are our greatest asset.

Innovate or die.

These two phrases are central tenets of corporate competitive strategy, and so it is not surprising that we are examining the intersection between them: the talent management side of innovation. Most prescribed approaches for developing an organizational capability for innovation acknowledge the crucial role of the individual.[1] CEOs proclaim the importance of getting the right people on the job.[2]

What is surprising is the current state of affairs that innovators face in most companies. By *innovators*, we are referring to people who undertake the responsibilities associated with creating opportunities out of ideas or inventions, and those who develop those opportunities into businesses. We are talking about the people who take inventions and turn them into commercial reality. How they are recognized, selected, developed, and rewarded for their seemingly crucial contributions is unsystematic at best and bewildering at worst. Here are a few perspectives from personnel in different companies that we've interviewed:

Normally if projects fail, the technical people get placed somewhere, but the commercial people get the pink slip. And I recognize . . . that makes people quite nervous.

The way I describe the universe at [our company], and I think it's true of a lot of large companies, is there are two safe places. One safe place is doing long-term research, and one safe place is running an existing business—when I say safe, I mean for your career.

I can't point to anybody in the company today who you could say, wow, they've had a very successful career, successful meaning they were able to incubate some businesses, and they were compensated accordingly. Some have been promoted, but not into the executive level.

If we're really honest, [our company] doesn't try to develop business development people. I wouldn't say that our senior management values this kind of stuff. I don't know what you're hearing from the people you talk to, but those of us who have been doing this our whole career, there's not a system or a process to advance people or recognize high potential people who do this kind of work.

In this chapter, we show the disaffection that innovation personnel experience in their careers, and look at some of the more counterproductive practices companies are using to manage their innovation talent.

We are not suggesting that corporate leaders intentionally treat innovators poorly. What we find is that managing innovators is not even on the radar screen of most companies. First we take a look at the risks innovators face in their careers, and then describe a set of talent management practices we have observed that could be—shall we say—improved. Once these weaknesses have been identified, we're well on the way to identifying solutions.

CHALLENGES TO INNOVATION EXPERTS' CAREERS

As we researched companies' efforts to develop innovation management systems, we noticed the frequency with which people changed jobs, expressed frustration about their careers, or shared war stories to remind one another about the low likelihood of positive outcomes. A closer look uncovered five types of career risks to individuals who work on higher-uncertainty innovation: project failure, unpredictability, scale, recognition discount, and career atrophy.

Project Failure.   The most widely recognized risk is that associated with a failed project. This risk is heightened if the firm's overall performance is not meeting expectations, and pressures from Wall Street or the private investment community are mounting. These pressures exacerbate uncertainty levels within the team by forcing members to project positive signals even if things are not progressing well. A new business development manager who was overseeing several projects in a company with severe financial challenges told us, "It's difficult for the teams to let us know that the project isn't making headway or gaining traction. If it gets killed, they may very well get the pink slip." In another company the portfolio manager told us, "If [the emerging business opportunity] is on a growth path, then they will get absorbed pretty quickly; if it is not, then the people will not be safe anywhere."

Even when companies are not financially distressed, failure is sometimes attributed to the team members rather than to the risk level associated with the project. One project coach argued that failure needs to be handled differently, in a manner that explicitly recognizes project risk levels:

We still treat things at a project level rather than a portfolio level. So if a project fails, this can mean "you're out." We need to focus more on individual portfolios. For example, an individual can have six out of ten successes.

Several of the companies we looked at did take a portfolio approach, and indeed we see this trend increasing. In one, somebody told us that "if the project fails, it's because of the risk, not the team. We have great people here." Another innovation manager works to protect her good people by ensuring that their next assignment will succeed: "If a project fails, I deploy those people on to more certain projects the next time so that their organizational credibility is restored."

It is important for people to feel safe if they are going to work on risky projects. Otherwise, management will never get the honest scoop from them. When people sense that it is risky to be associated with a project that might fail, there are negative effects for the individual, the project, and the company at large. The individual cannot be transparent with what he is learning as the project struggles to mature and will be perceived as a poor project leader, the project does not benefit from adequate coaching or a strong pivot, and the company ends up funding projects that in actuality show too little promise.

Perpetuating a culture that stigmatizes failure hampers the individual's actions and performance from the start. Of course this does not mean that there are no poor performers in the innovation business. Our point is that project failure is not necessarily an indication of the team members' capabilities. And this is just the first of many challenges they face.

Unpredictability.   Organizations thrive on predictability. Strategic innovations, on the other hand, are fraught with uncertainty, making sales forecasts, repeat purchases, costs, yields, and any other metric used in mainstream organizations nearly impossible.

An example of how this unpredictability can affect an individual's career path can be seen in a project that we encountered in our research, which showed early signs of success. In its earliest stages, an R&D "hero-scientist" brought on a sales and business development manager, Paul, to work with him to build a market for a game-changing new computer chip. The effort took years, but Paul persisted and found a number of application markets for the technology. When the nascent business was moved from R&D into a business unit, Paul expressed a desire to become the program manager for the business. His request for promotion was denied, though he was retained as the director of sales and moved with the fledgling business. When the newly appointed program manager requested sales forecasts in order to complete his plan and budget for the year, Paul provided low numbers because of the uncertainties still at play. Those numbers were increased twice, once by the program manager and again by the division vice president. When the program did not meet those sales objectives, Paul was "put in the penalty box," as he told us. He left the company shortly thereafter, extremely disgruntled. During our final interview with him, he explained: "I've put many years of my career into developing this opportunity. I've gone bald and gained forty pounds working on this business. And this is the company's response?"

Business units do not handle unpredictability well. As Paul's story shows us, rather than setting up better structural systems, we tend to blame the person. Obviously, this is not a great way to attract new business creation personnel. We need to design better innovation career systems and structures that can handle unpredictability.

Scale. A third risk is being associated with a venture whose size pales in comparison to that of established businesses in the company. When IBM instituted its Emerging Business Opportunity program in 2000, the company began selecting rising stars to lead these high-risk, yet promising, ventures. In response, confused new venture leaders questioned whether or not they were being demoted, since the budget and head count associated with the new opportunities were smaller than groups they had previously managed.[3]

A similar situation at another company involved an ambitious new hire with a technical background and an MBA from a prestigious business school, Mitch. He signaled that he wanted to lead an innovation team. An opportunity had arisen to take a successful technology and see how it could be applied to a slow-moving, capital-intensive industry. Mitch reasoned that the technology's potential breakthrough in the marketplace would be a boon for the company and an industry game changer. His peers (other recent MBA hires on a high-potential leadership track) knew that Mitch, like them, aspired to become a general manger in the company someday, and cautioned that sticking with the traditional career promotion path in the mainstream business was the smarter way to go.

Mitch was encouraged by his manager's offer that he'd have the opportunity to run the new business should he succeed with it, as an alternative pathway to a position in general management. He appreciated the development opportunity and the exposure he'd have to senior leadership, who viewed this venture as an important step for the company. After several years and impressive progress, the start-up opportunity failed for a number of reasons. Mitch realized that the brass ring of becoming a general manager was not going to happen on this path. Worse, while he was recognized as a talented person—given the way he handled the emerging venture—he had fallen behind his peers on the promotion schedule. He hadn't managed big enough projects. His only option at that point was to cycle out to a business unit in a role for those three to five years behind him so that he could catch up. Needless to say, he left the company not long after. Mitch had not demonstrated that he could manage a business of a size and scale that company leaders believed was necessary to demonstrate readiness for the next level of promotion. They were impressed by his talent, but somehow it didn't count toward promotion.

While able innovators are working away to sow the seeds of the company's future, they are being inadvertently punished. Leadership needs to realign its thinking and realize that, in today's world, managing scale is not the only prerequisite for the path to the C-suite or general management. The skills that Mitch demonstrated and developed—dealing with ambiguity, finding new partners, putting together disparate pieces to develop a new market or industry—are becoming increasingly critical to a company's long-term success. Aspiring leaders who demonstrate those abilities should be recognized.

Recognition Discount.   A fourth risk is associated with where and how credit is given for the early phases of innovation. To get to the point: starters don't get credit, finishers do. Innovation managers from several companies offered these thoughts:

In order to be in this (innovation) business, you have to be happy to see others take credit for your ideas.

Everyone remembers the failures, but no one remembers who came up with the successes.

If (project x) makes $10 billion ten years down the line, no one's going to say that our group started that business.

I could help launch $4, $5, $6 billion businesses over the next five years and I won't get promoted to VP.

The person who made the last remark offered the following explanation. Innovation projects are not always traced back to their origin. As an emerging business picks up steam, it tends to transfer locations in the company and add people from traditional functions. To ensure that others in the organization recognize the initiating group's role in creating a successful business, the innovation portfolio leader must remind the organization of the emerging business's origin. Promoting the original group's contribution to the company turns out to be a crucial part of the innovation leader's role, but we observed that very few such leaders invest the necessary effort.

All this adds up to an impossible scenario: to be a game-changing innovator, one must have a strong ego, patience, and a willingness to take a back seat to others when it comes to doling out credit. We're not sure how many innovators fit that profile!

Career Atrophy.   A final risk we'll highlight is that innovators can be perceived as taking a break in their careers. It's easier to point out the group's failed attempts than its successes, given the recognition discount risk we mentioned earlier. People in innovation can lose credibility as they are associated with a record of unsuccessful attempts, and time spent in the group can be perceived as time wasted. Even projects that receive enthusiastic market responses may be dismissed as a poor fit for the company, and therefore shut down after a significant investment of time and resources. This dynamic results in social isolation for innovation workers within the firm. Mark, one of the innovation group leaders that we interviewed, stated, "Our group was perceived as a 'timeout' in your career. Some internal networks were concerned that moving to (our group) was a dead end that would hurt your upward mobility."

The sense that these groups can be dead ends is evidenced in the way they are sometimes staffed. In one company, the New Business Creation Group was staffed from the redeployment pool, meaning people searching within the company for new jobs because theirs had been eliminated. This practice promotes the perception that innovation-related roles are training grounds at best, career placeholders at worst. In another company, people were assigned to the innovation group just prior to their retirement. That practice could send a strong message about the need for experienced, well-networked people in the innovation group, but it can also signal that the group is a playground for those who've earned their stripes rather than a place for intensive effort that merits high expectations.

Over time Mark concluded that the perception of his group is improving because individuals leaving it are now able to secure better assignments at exit:

With successes and increasing confidence among the upper-level managers, that situation is changing. We are becoming much more favorably viewed. We are increasingly seeing that some of the people we exited out are performing very well in the business units. So, this helps our equity.

The increased value associated with those exiting the innovation group is a testament to the fact that they have honed beneficial skills and gained important experiences while they were in it. Innovation shouldn't be perceived as a career dead end. More important, it shouldn't be perceived as a rotation on the way to a better place. Where are the vibrant, exciting career paths within an innovation function?

WEAKNESSES IN TALENT MANAGEMENT PRACTICES FOR INNOVATORS

We consider the topic of career paths in some detail in Chapter 9 when we discuss ways to retain innovation personnel, but first there is a more fundamental issue that we need to address: innovation roles, those beyond R&D, are not institutionalized as part of a company's regular HR system and organizational design. As a consequence, when an innovation champion retires or leaves, there is no guarantee that the role will be backfilled. And there is no way to develop succession planning for innovation leaders if their roles are associated with the people who hold them rather than with a clear set of expected responsibilities.

This fact breaks down into several pieces. If companies can address these five problem areas, they will open the door to professionalizing innovation and making it a sustained capability.

1. Role Legitimacy and Permanency

Innovation roles beyond R&D are not formally recognized in most companies. Most of the organizations we've studied assigned high-potential employees to breakthrough projects as one rotation on a path to becoming a general manager, but had almost no permanent, formalized positions in an innovation function.

The people we spoke to were stymied by this question: Who's developing expertise in innovation if there is no stable group of innovation personnel?

While innovation experts are perceived as valuable employees, it is as if the company does not know how to handle them from a talent management perspective. Those people who manage to remain in innovation roles tend to invent their own job titles. One such person articulated what so many we encountered actually practiced: "More or less illegally, I put '(Company Name) New Business' on my business card." Another listed "Idea Hunter" on his. Other fabricated job titles included Innovation Evangelist, Head of Innovation Hub, Director of Business Model Innovation, Innovation Engineer, and Manager- Innovation Opportunity Modeling. These are great labels, but since they are not recognized by the established human resources management system, they fade away when the person moves on to his next job. In other words, many of the people we encountered in our research are recognized for what they do, but their accomplishments are associated with them personally rather than a specific role in the company structure. This practice risks the loss of the company's ability to continuously improve its capability for strategic innovation.

Innovation roles beyond invention are so vaguely understood that company managers can't describe what characteristics they're looking for in potential candidates for such positions. They rely on volunteers, and that doesn't always work out. Company managers told us:

"Historically we have tended not to assign personnel but rather try to entice people."

"We have a big gap in terms of getting people to champion entrepreneurial teams. . . ."

Why? Because they're voluntary, temporary assignments that frequently end as Mitch's did.

In one consumer products company we studied, a task team was formed to develop a new offering that required a different revenue model and a different vendor relationship. The new business was to be incubated in one of the company's largest operating units, whose leadership balked at the prospect of introducing these changes. Senior corporate leaders intervened, assembled a team led by a rising star in the company, and off they went.

The first product in a promising new lineup was launched and met with moderate success, but wasn't the instant blockbuster the company had hoped for. (This is typical of breakthroughs, by the way. It takes a while for the market to understand the full value of its benefits.) The operating unit could not afford to support a thin margin business, and the project was disbanded. What happened to the team members?

- No one on the team was accepted back into the jobs they'd left to take up the new project.
- All team members were barred from any role in the operating unit in which the project was being incubated.
- The technical personnel found new jobs at higher levels in the organization.
- The commercial people left the company.

Practices like these make it very difficult to develop a stable of innovation experts, and that makes it impossible for the company to improve at Strategic Innovation over time. If the team had been recognized as part of an Innovation function working on a portfolio of opportunities, they'd have been recycled onto another project within that same product platform to re-engage the market from a different direction. Instead, this project was chalked up as a failure and the people associated with it suffered the consequences.

Several companies identified people who remained in their innovation roles for a long period of time as "pillars," or "tent poles." The Director of Strategic Marketing in one company, who was responsible for incubating new businesses in one of its business units, told us:

"You need pillars, and you need movers. If I've got a couple of pillars around me, maybe one pillar in my direct report, and then maybe a pillar in the report to them, then the other people can come in and move through. That is the kind of blend that I look for."

Another strategic innovation group manager finally balked at the rotational nature of her group and began requiring new members, and their functional supervisors, to agree to a three year stay. "It takes one year to train them, one year for them to at least try, and finally, by their third year, they're making a contribution to the team," she explained.

Legitimate roles that survive the people who occupy them, and are refilled when those who hold them move on, would help companies improve their strategic innovation capabilities.

2. Role Ambiguity and Responsibility Expansion

Companies are not yet clear on how to define innovation roles. The resulting vagueness makes it difficult to guide and coach people. Given this degree of role ambiguity managers tend to expect the persons filling those positions to expand their responsibilities as the projects mature and continue to nurture those projects into their next phase. Without a clear role description, responsibilities for various innovation activities fall on people who are not trained and do not view this as their jobs. This sets up both the innovation function and the people involved in it to fail. We have observed innovation personnel stay with projects from Discovery through Acceleration, though their strong suits resided in one or the other of the DIA capability arenas. As one senior leader told us, "We're putting them in monstrous roles."

One company, for example, solicited proposals from the highest levels for "rocket" projects, i.e. those with breakthrough potential in their industry. The call went out across the company's R&D community, and eventually a number of project proposals were funded. Interestingly, the only people assigned to the teams were R&D personnel. While technical progress was made on many of the projects, most also required new business models, new customers and plans for how they'd fit with the current divisions' operating schedules and marketing programs. All but one were eventually shuttered, since it was mistakenly assumed that the research scientists on the job could perform all of the tasks associated with Strategic innovation, most of which had never been defined, but ended up being marketing and strategy oriented. The company no longer funds a rockets program.

This is but one example among many of company's attempts to invent without the capability to commercialize. When opportunities offer the potential for a whole new platform of business, they rarely fit neatly into the known territory of the company's current business models, and so business units tend to reject them. Expecting those who generate the opportunities to also deliver them to the market is unrealistic. Similarly, expecting those who can experiment in the market to spot the value proposition to then scale up the new business is unrealistic. These skills are different enough to warrant using different types of people.

3. Selection Issues

Without clearly defined roles, it is difficult to establish selection criteria. We can tell you some of the issues companies are struggling with now.

Hire the Passionate Ones? Or the Competent Ones?   We found that most of those who volunteered for innovation jobs, especially as the innovation management systems were getting started, were from the R&D community, and had no new business creation experience whatsoever.

In one company, the strategic innovation initiative was led by an R&D Director who wanted to find a way to salvage the exploratory research budget that was under threat. He adopted a widely accepted company term for *breakthrough innovation*, and claimed he was starting a local version of it in his division. He was given the funding and the people. Alas, he had no idea how to move ideas from the lab to the market, and he lost the group.

In another company, a "commercial development group" had been formally instituted within central R&D. When the group's leader retired after many years, the company was looking for a replacement. An R&D director took the job. He had an entrepreneurial mind-set but had never worked in one of the company's divisions, nor had he any exposure to business principles or practice. He learned by contacting academics—not exactly a fast track to driving change in a large company. Within three years, he had left the company (to start his own), and the commercial development team was dramatically reduced in size. Because of the poor selection criteria applied to that role, company leadership doubted their investment in the group and cut the budget. Was it the role or was it the qualifications of the person hired to fill it that caused the problem? We'd vote the latter. Could that person have learned? Absolutely, and he did. Just not quickly enough.

Selecting inappropriate candidates for innovation jobs results in several consequences. First, corporate leaders begin to doubt their organizations can be successful at strategic innovation. Use of the term becomes taboo, and associated investments are cut when, in fact, the problem was the people selected to make it happen. Second, when innovation experts sense that other members of the innovation function lack the proper skills, they, too, lose faith. They may compensate for incompetent colleagues by refusing to pass projects along to them, which stalls progress in the innovation pipeline. Third, the passionate but poorly prepared grow frustrated as they look back on their investments of time and energy and see little progress. And finally, the company has spent resources with little to show.

Hire Based on Subject-Matter Expertise: But Which Subject?   Another interesting selection issue is that subject matter experts tend to be favored over innovation experts. We found that many companies hired people with specific domain expertise, either in a specific industry or technology arena. These people were hired from outside the company, which caused two problems. First, they did not know the company's norms and strategies, and they lacked the internal networks that are so heavily leveraged for strategic innovation. As one manager expressed, "You really need to have people who know that market, and that is difficult because they do not know our company and its strategy."

That kind of knowledge can be developed over time, but the second problem sometimes makes that impossible. That is, if the project fails, the company is left with a talent resource that it no longer needs. One company had hired an arsenal of top-caliber talent in a variety of life sciences that they ultimately could not justify as strategic to the company. The disgruntled scientists described how they were recruited with promises of committed investments for discovering new frontiers in their disciplines. But once they arrived and got to work, their projects were defunded, strategic direction changed, and they were assigned "small stuff" or laid off.

Eventually the company's management provided better job security for subject-matter experts by budgeting for them as part of the company's general and administrative expenses rather than their earlier approach of associating them with project-specific funding. Allocating them as a general and administrative expense makes sense only if the company has committed itself strategically to creating a new business in a particular domain. Then, even if one project fails, others will be taken up until the company has figured out its approach to creating a business in that arena. Until then most companies solved the problem by using external consultants for subject-matter expertise until they were certain that they were going to make a strategic investment.

While subject-matter expertise is necessary on the technical side, it appears to be less so on the business development side. Several managers that we encountered had accumulated experience across multiple projects that allowed them to develop this expertise. Business-creation skills such as the ability to understand opportunities across technology and market domains are fungible. These people are facile in their ability to understand the implications of inventions for market opportunity, even if they don't understand everything about how it works. In fact, we find that they don't love getting into the technical details too much.

Company strategic innovation managers are recognizing that these new business creation personnel are experts, but their subject matter is the field of innovation and new business creation rather than any specific market or technology area. One innovation manager told us: "We need to change the way we imprint people. If you could say, 'Hey, I am a new business developer' or 'I am an exploratory marketing expert . . . and by the way I can do that for any type of area,' we would be better off."

Young Turks or Seasoned Vets?   The passion model is predicated on the idea that youth brings energy, enthusiasm, creative drive, and an openness that someone who's been around the company for years lost long ago. Some of the companies we studied preferred youth, but the majority favored the experienced. The arguments are shown in Table 3.1.

In the few companies that hired junior talent, young people were assigned to opportunity-finding tasks as part of the discovery function.

TABLE 3.1   Opposing Views on Age and Experience Requirements for Innovation

Hire Junior-Level Talent	Seasoned Talent Needed
Begin building innovation capability through junior talent.	Innovation roles occur at the pinnacle of peoples' careers. Put them in various organizational roles and then, after those experiences, they'll be ready to lead a new business area.
New business creation is its own expertise and can be trained.	Innovation doesn't require specifically trained expertise. Apply general management skills. It's more important to have accumulated experience and networks in the company.
Networking is enabled through the person's acumen and his leaders.	Understanding "how things work" in the company is more important than any specialized expertise in order to get things done. Need credibility.

Incubating new businesses was left to those with internal networks and more experience. The problem with this arrangement was that the incubation personnel had not necessarily worked on innovation or new business creation. Most had technical backgrounds and some business unit experience, which is a great combination. But they had come up through the operational excellence culture, and either didn't fit there or didn't work well in the innovation spectrum.

There's clearly work to be done to identify worthy selection criteria for innovation personnel. One thing we do know is that it's not a one-size-fits-all approach.

4. Organizational Design

Organizations go through restructuring all the time. We get that. New divisions, new reporting relationships, and new initiatives come and go. Even so, we challenge companies to perform a design audit of their innovation function. You'd be amazed at the room for improvement. Pockets of potentially breakthrough innovation activities live and breathe in organizations but are not coordinated or viewed as a system. That creates terrific inefficiency.

R&D managers in one company complained vociferously about its poor processes for transitioning burgeoning strategic innovations into business units to be nurtured and grown. It's interesting that they blamed the process. Who was supposed to make it happen? There were no people identified to receive these nascent businesses and make the miracle of market dominance happen.

Several of our company representatives in R&D organizations identified people (by name, not by title) in business units whom they considered their partners. When we followed up with those people (directors of strategic marketing, advanced marketing, and new business development), we learned that they didn't see it that way. R&D did their thing. These new business groups in the divisions were generating their own ideas and opportunities, as opposed to carrying out R&D's! No one viewed the organization as a system, and surely not as an integrated one.

In one company we visited, we interviewed people every forty-five minutes, without much of a break. Our location was the corporate R&D center, and as can be imagined we spent most of the day talking with R&D directors, project leaders, and portfolio planners. Our very last interview was with a brilliant scientist. We were halfway through the conversation when we asked him who he called when he had a breakthrough. He replied: "Well, it depends on what it is. If it belongs in Division X, I call Y. If it belongs in Division B, I call C." "Who are Y and C?" we asked. His answer was they were directors of new business development in the business units. When we asked why we had not been told of these people's existence in preparatory interviews or earlier that day, he mentioned that while he knew these people personally, there was no real system or perception of a need for linking R&D's work to those groups. We could not believe it, but that is not the only place we encountered this story. We proceeded to call each one of those people and learn about their roles and responsibilities. Each reported to a division manager, of course. None considered it their responsibility to pick up where R&D had left off with breakthrough opportunities and try to cultivate them. If companies thought about an organizational design for their innovation function, we could dramatically improve our ability to leverage the investments in discovery, incubation, and acceleration that are happening in a piecemeal fashion today.

So one organizational design issue associated with innovation is that it is incomplete or disjointed. The other issue that arose in our research was inappropriate reporting relationships within an existing innovation function design. For example, one person we interviewed was leading the business development of an entirely new platform. He'd come up through the marketing and commercial part of the company and had an entrepreneurial bent. However, he reported to the director of research. This smart, ambitious intrapreneur indicated to us that his boss, not having experienced anything beyond R&D, was of little help:

> So one of the real challenges I have is the way we're structured. We have this new business development, or incubation group. It's structured under our science and technology organization. And so you have business people working for very experienced scientists who are managers. So my boss—he's been a CTO at (several) companies, but fundamentally he's a scientist, he's not a businessperson.

If companies designed reporting relationships for those within the innovation function in a thoughtful manner, we could dramatically improve our ability to leverage the talent pool that's working to grow the business platforms of tomorrow.

5. Performance (Mis)Measurement

How do you measure the performance of someone who works on projects whose potential is unknown, for which the market may not yet exist, and for which the technology is unproven? Not only is the task of evaluating their work difficult; it is compounded by the fact that roles for innovators are still unclear. Do we consider how many projects they take on? How far across the development cycle they carry those projects? Commercial outcomes? How many they've forwarded on to a business unit?

No. So much of what contributes to those outcomes is not under the person's control. Yet these are all used to measure innovation personnel performance. We heard it time and time again.

One experienced new business creation leader provided some great insight into how he evaluates his employees tasked with finding opportunities.

> We evaluate on the quality of their analysis, and keep in mind that it's going to be some time after that that we know the final outcome or success of that market initiative. They're so far removed from commercial success, it's hard to evaluate them on the outcomes. So I spend time with them, maybe a half day each week. I'm assessing them and listen to what they're doing, and if I think that they're

just generally missing things that they should know, I consider that in their performance evaluation.

In addition, he noted that market analysis and value proposition analysis, even in the realm of the uncertain, is not just gut instinct. "We often get the outcome right, but we don't often get the data exactly right." He explained that the market size numbers of first application areas that perceive value may be incorrect, but the act of conducting those explorations provides enough data to make a reasonable judgment. When evaluating his people, he's looking for those cleverly designed and well-executed explorations and experiments that drive solutions in the face of large uncertainties.

As one new business creation portfolio team member told us, "We need guidance, not process." We were struck by this description because it captured what many others said, and that is that strategic coaching is critical for breakthrough innovation. Another company had each emerging business leader come with team members of his choosing to a monthly meeting with the chief strategy officer, the chief technology officer, and company controller. Rather than the top leaders peppering the team with questions, the team members set the agenda, depending on the challenges they were facing at the time. It was a coaching session. The senior team members viewed their job as helping break down barriers and gaining a clearer picture of an emerging strategy for the business as new evidence was coming in from the lab and the marketplace.

The importance of coaching as a means not only of getting work done but also of evaluating people signals that expertise in managing for strategic innovation improves as one gains more experience with it. One vice president for business development told us:

I think I have dealt with a lot of different innovation situations long enough that, you know, I don't rely on intuition. I think intuition is maybe sometimes a tie breaker, but you still have to look at the market fundamentals and other things, and I think that just having been through a lot of iterations over time has given me a greater comfort level with how to spot those things.

A young woman in new business development in another company also mentioned the admiration she had for her boss, who protected her from being diverted onto near-term projects and "owned" the continued investment in long-term business development, even though they were situated in a business unit with severe profit pressures. Our young interviewee extolled her boss's virtues of supporting her and providing opportunities for her to gain exposure to senior leaders. "She believes in engaging others and giving recognition. She believes in putting them in the spotlight. I get my face time with them."

In terms of taking risks, we found people frequently suggesting the importance of a boss who can (a) position the experiment as an important investment rather than a wild risk, and (b) help design those experiments to provide maximum learning value. When asked about risk taking that did not yield a favorable outcome, a successful innovation leader, reflecting on his career, articulated it well:

Particularly over the last few years, I've probably been in situations where I took greater risks in doing some things and not all of them have worked out. I wouldn't say I've been rewarded for those necessarily, either monetarily or with a high five, but those experiments have been recognized as good decisions, and that we should have tried them. Maybe some of them didn't work out or give the answer we wanted, but they were well done.

Quality of the design and execution of meaningful experiments is a powerful evaluation criteria. The problem is, most of the people we interviewed were not subject to those metrics. In fact, most were not attended to very closely at all. Scientists are rewarded for excelling at research and hypothesis testing, not on the outcome of the test. Even when the company files for a patent based on one of its scientists' discoveries, they recognize that a patent affords an opportunity to its owner, but that is all. The patent versus real value is unknown until others begin to cite it, build on it in their own research, or license it for use, which occurs years later.

Why not evaluate strategic innovation experts the same way?

NEXT STEPS

There is no doubt that companies recognize the need to formalize new roles for innovation specialists. Of the twelve companies whose management systems for strategic innovation we researched in depth, eight initiated or added to those groups during the course of our study. Companies are announcing VPs of innovation or chief innovation officer roles, as well as necessary support groups for these senior leaders, signaling the importance of innovation. Yet companies are still struggling in their management of this talent because there is so little development of the roles beneath the leader, and no promotion paths have emerged. Given this challenge and others we describe in this chapter, why would anyone today choose a role in innovation, other than as a fun development opportunity? And how can companies stand a chance of developing a legitimate innovation capability?

It is time to recognize strategic innovation as a business function in its own right, just as the functions of marketing and operations have been so recognized, and to expect innovation to be a sustainable ongoing capability in companies, serving as a fount of corporate renewal and growth. Institutionalizing innovation via career paths and talent development is an important step in the right direction. Currently there is little in the way of succession planning for the leader of the innovation agenda. When one individual leaves, we observed, innovation agendas, processes, personnel, resources, and metrics are all up for reappraisal. Why should we start at zero base each time? Why manage innovation differently from other functions that we've learned to handle with sophistication? Firms have the opportunity to behave more systematically with respect to strategic innovation and can start by improving their approaches to talent development and management.

Our next step is to introduce a framework for innovation roles and justify it. We turn to that task in Chapter 4.

4

INNOVATION ROLES
A Framework for Designing the
Innovation Function

In the first few chapters we described a way to think about breakthrough innovation differently than you have likely seen elsewhere. Established organizations are not getting better at breakthrough innovation, and through our work we've seen that a major element of the root cause comes from how organizations select, develop, and manage people. We are claiming that companies need to move beyond the champion model to one of strategic innovation. They need to move beyond one or a few "glamour projects" to a portfolio approach that develops multiple options of new business platforms, and that requires a full complement of innovation roles. In this chapter we re-examine the organizational structure for strategic innovation and the array of roles needed in order to let breakthrough and evolutionary innovations flourish.

Currently we see a breach between what organizations want to do and what their structure allows them to do. Simply put, talent management practices for most firms are mismatched with organizational desires and needs for strategic innovation. Firms want innovation but often fall into traps that prevent them from putting the structures in place to get what they want. Structure for innovation? Yes. On the surface this might seem to be the exact wrong direction but our experiences tell a different story.

So far we have made the following observations and claims:

- Companies have tried many approaches to improving their capability for commercializing breakthrough innovation: instituting new processes, modifying the organization's culture, experimenting with new organizational structures, and instituting financial incentives. None has provided a silver-bullet solution to this pressing problem on its own.

- To build expertise, company leaders should no longer think of breakthrough innovation as an exception but as an added organizational capability. That means management should consider it as one of the multitude of business functions in the company, and apply a management system whose objective is to find and nurture the company's business platforms of the future. All the elements of that management system, including the function's structure, metrics, resources, processes, people, governance, leadership, and culture, should be aligned with that objective. Under these circumstances we can view it as strategic innovation. It's uncertain, it's ambiguous, and in some cases it's risky, but it's strategic. It's the future.

- An organizational capability for strategic innovation is composed of three distinct building blocks: discovery, incubation, and acceleration. Each requires a different type of skill.

- To mitigate risk and create options for their futures, companies should consider their innovation initiatives as a portfolio, where failure of the majority of projects is more than compensated for by the outsize performance of the few that succeed. Each project is a learning experiment, and together they can form the basis of a new competency area that is strategically important to the company.

- Innovation portfolios are composed of a number of potential new business platforms that will most likely—in one form or another—become the business areas of the future. Within each of these platforms, multiple projects are undertaken to experiment with the form that the emerging value proposition could and should take, and to build the competency necessary to win in the given new business domains.

- Thus, within discovery, incubation, and acceleration, activities are taking place at the project, platform, and the portfolio levels at any given time.

- Talent management practices associated with strategic innovation are lacking in most organizations. Companies are not yet sophisticated enough about effective approaches for identifying, selecting, developing, and retaining people with the aptitude for operating in the high-uncertainty spectrum required of strategic innovation. These gaps lead to negative consequences for individuals interested in and capable of developing and commercializing potential breakthroughs, and they send a mixed signal to those considering this line of work.

The implication of these observations is that we cannot apply a one-size-fits-all approach to talent management for an effective innovation function. In this chapter we introduce a framework of innovation roles that follows from these insights, and we address the questions that company leaders raise as they grapple with our counterintuitive prescriptions. But first let's address the one-size-fits-all model: the legend of the intrapreneur.

INTRAPRENEURSHIP IS A FALLACY

When Gifford Pinchot wrote his famous book introducing the concept of intrapreneurship to companies in 1985, the message was clear: intra-preneurs break the rules.[1] The "Intrapreneur's Ten Commandments,"[2] repeated in Table 4.1, somewhat irreverently direct those with a will to create new businesses to behave like rebels.

TABLE 4.1 The Intrapreneur's Ten Commandments

I. Come to work each day willing to be fired.
II. Circumvent any order aimed at stopping your dream.
III. Do any job needed to make your project work, regardless of your job description.
IV. Find people to help you.
V. Follow your intuition about the people you choose, and work only with the best.
VI. Work underground as long as you can—publicity triggers the corporate immune system.
VII. Never bet on a race unless you are running in it.
VIII. Remember, it is easier to ask for forgiveness than for permission.
IX. Be true to your goals, but be realistic about the ways to achieve them.
X. Honor your sponsors.

Rebels don't depend on too many others; they work with their tightly assembled teams to accomplish an entire task themselves. It's a great idea but not very realistic. Successful intrapreneurs are well known within their companies. They become legend, part of the folklore of the corporate culture. But how many people who love innovation try, fail, and give up? How many have some degree of the intrapreneur's ability and persistence, but not enough to finish the job? Plenty. Our research shows that, even those who would like to manage across the entire innovation spectrum of discovery, incubation, and acceleration, and at the project, platform, and portfolio levels, simply don't have the skills. More to the point, not many want to!

Organizations that compete on the basis of innovation beyond incremental new product development need to create specific roles for their people. Not roles that put them in some form of an organizational straight jacket, but clear roles that allow them to get the job done for the company. Strategic innovation is a "team sport": it's so big that no one person has the skill set to do it all. Individuals want defined roles that allow them to take advantage of their innovative strengths—roles that give them some autonomy while still providing guidance for where they should invest their energies. The passion model is great, but it's not enough in a large, established company.

This perspective is akin to the process that serial entrepreneurs go through in classic start-ups. Some people get things started: they invent a concept and build the initial business. These same folks may want little to do with scaling it up, though, and that is why serial entrepreneurs exit and allow professional managers to grow the businesses they started. Existing organizations face similar issues. However, they need structure beyond the individual project since strategic innovation requires that a portfolio of opportunities be nurtured. Given this, we advocate a similar talent management approach to that used by venture capitalists, who switch inventors out as the venture matures for those better suited to take it to the next stage of development. Consider the following statements from a number of the innovators we've interviewed:

I don't feel I have the right profile for running a standard business. I'm far more talented at setting up new stuff, or at least that's what I like. So I'd rather work on new areas to find ways to grow them than to continue with those that are already running. I guess my strength is that I can take an idea and concept to something that's real and tangible, and I've got good business acumen, but I would want to hand it off to more of a general manager now, to scale it. I'd have oversight to the vision of it, but then I'd probably want to start over again.

I think if [the company] would put me in a project at an early phase, even if it's a promotion in terms of whatever salary—I don't think I'm the right person on the job.

I don't want to run a business.

These statements and others like them show that innovators differ: some prefer the front end of new business creation, and others prefer the back end. Some like to conduct small field experiments, others like the more strategic aspects of creating a business platform. One size does not fit all, and there is plenty to do. Figure 4.1, reprised from Chapter 2, is augmented here and provides a reminder of the distinctive requirements of the discovery, incubation, and acceleration competency areas. Underneath each competency area is a set of roles that we observed from among the many people we interviewed.

Of course, we did not see each of these roles formalized in every company. There are many instances in which responsibilities are not assigned

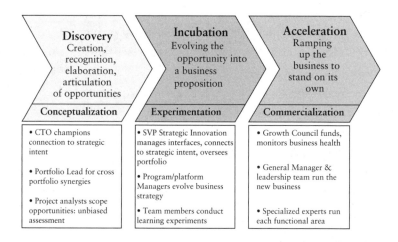

FIGURE 4.1   Roles Across Discovery, Incubation, and Acceleration

or people are stretched across multiple roles. But we have come to realize that, in fact, there are distinctive responsibilities not only across discovery, incubation, and acceleration but also within them. When those responsibilities are not acknowledged or assigned, a capability for strategic innovation is less likely to survive in companies, and that means the probability of successfully commercializing breakthroughs is low. We formalize this insight in Table 4.2, which introduces nine innovation roles. Each column corresponds to a specific competency area: discovery, incubation, and acceleration are formally recognized in this framework as different, requiring different talent, decision criteria, and metrics for success. Also, the three rows correspond to a level at which the strategic innovation portfolio must be addressed. In that way, the framework recognizes that projects take place within areas of strategic intent, and those combine to define the company's strategic innovation portfolio. Clarifying these roles will help a company maintain strength in strategic innovation.

In addition to these innovation "line" responsibilities, there is a host of crucial staff roles that support the creation of new business platforms, but are not involved in the project commercialization effort per se. These include innovation process facilitators, strategic coaches and advisory board members, partnership developers, and the various contributors from the human resources and organizational development community. The entire group is overseen by the chief innovation officer with his second

TABLE 4.2   Nine Roles for a Strategic Innovation Function

| | CHIEF INNOVATION OFFICER ORCHESTRATOR | | |
	Discovery	*Incubation*	*Acceleration*
Level 3: Portfolio	D-3: Director, Discovery	I-3: Director, Incubation	A-3: Innovation Council
Level 2: Platform	D-2: Opportunity Domain Leader	I-2: New Business Platform Leader	A-2: General Manager, New Business
Level 1: Project	D-1: Opportunity Generator	I-1: New Business Creation Specialist	A-1: Functional Manager

in command, the orchestrator. We recognize that the full complement of talent a company needs to develop expertise in innovation can seem a little overwhelming, especially since companies have not formalized innovation groups this way to date. Following are a few of the concerns expressed by managers when they first see the framework.

ARE YOU KIDDING?

We know . . . you can't believe it. When we present this idea at conferences, people are incredulous—ready to dismiss us out of hand. No one wants hierarchy or increased role complexity these days! Companies are moving *away* from formalized organizational structures and charts. The flat organization is in. Hierarchy and formalization are *out*, especially for innovation, where the culture of openness, fluidity, and creativity reigns supreme. You are probably wondering if we've lost our minds.

We don't think so. People tend to equate hierarchy with bureaucracy, but they are not the same. Bureaucracies are organizations with tight divisions of labor run by administrative officials who may not be expert in the subject matter itself and tend to impose multitudes of procedures that many consider unnecessary. Hierarchies may become bureaucratic, but they need not. Their purpose is to enable coordination of many parts toward a common objective. Organizations require hierarchy in order to make decisions that affect multiple units within them, including decisions on resource allocation, strategic direction, and planned change of any sort. Without hierarchy chaos quickly ensues. Everyone sets their own agenda, and no one can galvanize the troops. Others are beginning to agree about the importance of formality and hierarchy in organizations.[3] Without some order, communication suffers and individuals tend to misuse power as a result of confusion over roles. Perhaps most relevant for us, innovation suffers.

Strategic innovation, by its very nature, requires change across many parts of the company. We are not talking about random acts of innovation. We are talking about harnessing the resources and power of the large company to effectively commercialize new-to-the-world products. Those decisions must be coordinated. Individuals need some structure and hierarchy in order to effectively drive innovation.

Our framework for innovation roles will clarify the work to be done and how it is best grouped according to specific skill types. Role clarity helps institutionalize innovation as a function rather than leaving it up to the whims of the current leadership. By institutionalizing innovation we mean that it becomes an ever-present activity in the company. Investments can be increased or decreased as the organization's capacity allows, but the function itself should always be maintained. Historically organizations have started breakthrough innovation programs and then defunded them just as quickly. They become the program du jour, rather than part of the organization's fabric. We need to move from pinning our hopes on breakthrough innovation to developing a strong competency in strategic innovation.

Since these role descriptions outline the types of activities necessary to move strategic innovations forward, they can become a tool to help those occupying them feel safe engaging in the types of activities that are the norm for innovation but largely unacceptable for the ongoing operations part of the business: experimenting, prototyping, trying new partnerships, and pivoting if necessary. By understanding these roles, we establish a culture of innovation such that people can operate without fear of reprisal. Clarifying the skills and responsibilities associated with each role will also provide a talent pool that can successfully move up through a career path associated with strategic innovation as needed. It's a bit counterintuitive for sure, but it is just what our research shows. When you think it through, we believe you'll agree.

You will see that we are not advocating overly rigid roles. As one person told us, "Give people a fence for where to play, but then it's up to them." What we're offering is a blueprint for organizational design. It's a place to start that has been distilled from research and observation. Once that blueprint and its basic principles are understood, the way it plays out in practice must fit the context of your organization.

Right now you're likely thinking about how or if these roles would work in your organization. You're not alone—we went through a fair bit of iteration with the companies we worked with and audiences we spoke to at innovation conferences, workshops, and other events.

Your concerns likely mirror the list we received all throughout our journey. Here are the most common questions we received, along with our thoughts:

Are you actually suggesting that we add nine new roles in our company? We can't afford to fatten our costs this way!
We have two responses to this reaction. First, you may already have people performing these jobs but just don't realize it. Many company representatives, after thinking about it for a while, acknowledge that they can identify people in their organizations who play these roles but just aren't formally recognized as part of an innovation function. They may not all reside in R&D, and they probably don't report up through the same lines or even collaborate with one another. Certain individuals may be fulfilling multiple roles, as we noted in Chapter 3. Upon reflection, though, you might conclude that, at some level, even if it's informal, the bare-bones infrastructure of what we are proposing is already there.

Second, if we don't acknowledge these roles and their associated tasks and responsibilities, innovation outcomes are compromised. Clarifying the three competency areas of discovery, incubation, and acceleration allows leaders to specify the correct selection criteria for the type of talent needed. We know they're different, and ignoring this distinction promotes the kind of role ambiguity plaguing companies today.

Finally, we know that these roles conflict with the typical Hay System for determining an individual's managerial level in the company, since innovation teams are typically small and have meager budgets compared with ongoing business platforms. Explicitly defining them provides an opportunity to attract and retain the best talent to the innovation function, and not risk losing it from the company.

If, after reflecting for a while, you believe your company lacks personnel in any of the roles shown in Table 4.2, we'd ask you to consider how satisfied you are with your organization's strategic innovation outcomes. Even if your company does have innovations coming into the market, and even if they are making money, how "breakthrough" are they?

We believe the framework will bring clarity to what you already know through experience, help you design a more effective innovation function, and be able to capitalize on the investments in R&D and open innovation that your company has made but from which it has not fully benefited.

Do we need three layers of hierarchy? Innovation is supposed to be fluid, creative, and collaborative. Hierarchy implies a top-down decision-making approach, and this suppresses innovation.

It's true that our three-tiered design is completely counterintuitive, and it flies in the face of recent trends. The inclination is toward flat organizations and reducing hierarchy, toward task teams and circle structures. But if we dig in to understand more deeply, we see that organizational design philosophies are evolving to one with which we are completely aligned. The holacracy movement,[4] adopted recently by a number of fast-growing companies, claims to be a new way of running an organization that removes power from a management hierarchy, eliminates the need for a "micromanaging boss," and unleashes innovation and responsiveness to customers.[5] The online retailer Zappos was highly publicized as one of the first companies to adopt holacracy as an organizational design. But when approximately 14 percent of their workforce quit, citing too much ambiguity in their roles, the movement quickly claimed that, in fact, this approach to organizational design provides even more structure than a simple organizational chart. Carefully defining the responsibilities required of each role, those to whom that role is accountable, and the deliverables and outcomes expected are key aspects of a holacratic design. It recognizes the need for authority and autocratic decision making.[6] So, again, it's bureaucracy that people do not want; they can deal with hierarchy and structure because it can bring the clarity they need.

Pundits claim that holacracy may work for smaller, newer companies, but that large, mature firms simply need a reporting structure that aligns strategies with the overall organization's direction, and this requires hierarchy.[7]

We agree with both perspectives. If innovation tasks and responsibilities could be more clearly articulated, companies wishing to build such a capability would be better off. Internal networks and communication flows would certainly be made easier rather than more difficult. But hierarchy is needed to ensure alignment of the innovation function with the company's strategy for its future. Large companies have many options for growth, and allowing everyone to chart their own course can easily sub-optimize the potential of an organization in its quest to create new business domains. *Hierarchy* need not mean *bureaucracy*. It can provide clear decision-making and strategic guidance, and it arises from the need for different types of expertise and responsibilities. The key is to have people with the right qualifications at each level.

Why are we suggesting three levels? First, because our research suggests that three meaningful levels actually exist. We also observed that if companies do not address all three levels of new business creation (projects, platforms, and the entire portfolio of new businesses), they tend to fall into one of the following failure traps.

Incrementalization Trap.   When companies fail to distinguish between projects and platforms, and essentially ignore the middle level of the hierarchy, the outcome may result in new products but most likely not new businesses. One VP of R&D explained his company's experience in this way: "We have breakthrough projects that are incrementally executed." In other words, one low-hanging fruit, an obvious product deriving from a breakthrough, may be quickly developed and transitioned to a business unit for market launch. However, the opportunity to create an entire new business—a product family—is not cultivated. Another company we studied issued a request for proposals for breakthrough ideas, and the ideas poured in. However, they were considered too small, too isolated, or too far removed from the company's mission. One company's representative told us that its innovation oversight board vetted many ideas, and they all seemed great. Innovation portfolio leaders had trouble discriminating among the ideas since each was viewed as an independent project, and no one could foresee which among them had the highest likelihood of achieving blockbuster success. When that happens and a company invests in many small independent projects, there is no system for cross-pollinating them, or for considering how they might fit together to create a bigger opportunity. Each slowly fades away, underresourced and lacking a strategic contribution to the company's future. Companies need to consider business platforms rather than smaller independent projects, and platforms need strategic leaders to guide their strategic development.

Project Evaluation Trap. Another problem associated with ignoring the platform level of an innovation hierarchy has to do with the definition of *failure*. The "failure rate" of strategic innovation projects is high, as we know. This can bring trouble to project leaders who become associated with failure more often than with success. By using projects as experiments to build a competency in a new business/technology platform, companies remove the threat of failure for risky projects. DSM's strategic innovation portfolio is typically composed of no fewer than four emerging business areas at any point in time. GE's Advanced Development Programs are the same way. Each is managed as a business platform, with multiple business model projects and forays into the market taking place. Who knows which customer partner, which technological direction, or which new market will catch hold first? Who cares? The point is that they are experimenting on several fronts simultaneously. These experiments are all projects. If any is shut down after a business experiment, others are continuing. At some point, DSM will have several new business platforms, but for now we don't know which of the four will succeed, or how they'll play out. Individual projects are evaluated not only on project objectives but also on the learnings they generate. The platform's progress is evaluated based on the learning across projects that allows the new business's strategy to clearly emerge.

Bottlenecked Decision-Making Trap. Nothing breeds more frustration among innovators than slowing the pace of decisions. As business opportunities grow increasingly complex, one needs a middle management level to streamline coaching and decision making. A leader of one strategic innovation platform we observed claimed she needed a midlevel director because the team had surfaced many applications, partner relationships, and multiple forms of technical solutions. She could not keep up with all the possible opportunities and choices the team had to make. She told us that she had become a bottleneck to the team's progress. Her request for a middle-level manager was denied. In frustration, she left to join another company's innovation hub, and within one year the promising new business platform had fallen prey to the conventional management practice. It was shut down.

Putting All of Our Eggs in One Basket. Portfolios are typically diversified, and that is why they are viewed as mechanisms for mitigating risk. Yet when one considers a portfolio of truly strategic innovations, with breakthrough potential, they're all risky! How does one diversify to mitigate that risk? The answer is by targeting several different domains of strategic intent: new business areas of the future that rely on different types of technology breakthroughs and that will create a diverse suite of markets. If firms don't distinguish between platforms and portfolios, then the likelihood is that the company's portfolio is too thin. Too much dependence on one or two platforms and the probability of success declines. In one of our cases, the strategic innovation group developed two promising platforms and was told to stop there, rather than develop a more robust portfolio. Within the four years that we observed them, one of the two platforms devolved into a more incremental opportunity than expected and was transferred to one of the operating units, where it contributed incremental revenue in one of the current lines of business. When the second platform hit some technical roadblocks, the company's leadership balked, and the entire breakthrough innovation infrastructure was disbanded. In contrast three other companies we studied had five, six, and twelve emerging business platforms, respectively. Each company has sunsetted one or two of those opportunities, and several others have been recognized as incremental innovations and transitioned to the most obvious business unit for commercialization. The others sustained, and the diversity of those companies' portfolios has helped each company succeed with launching several new businesses. Platforms are exciting and strategically important, but they are not sure bets.

Opportunism vs. Politics vs. Strategic Intent. Without a senior-level person or top management committee to guide the portfolio, choices of platform investments may be made on the basis of individual political ambitions or simple opportunism rather than serious discussion about the company's future profile. The presence of a portfolio leader is necessary to ensure its size, pacing, and diversity are in a healthy state. In one of the companies we studied, the lack of a senior-level portfolio owner allowed for lapses in articulation and constant reexamination of strategic intent, resulting in a "throw it on the wall and see what sticks" approach to platform evaluation. The organization is losing patience and asking the breakthrough innovation group to move closer to adjacent spaces, since they lack portfolio-level leadership to maintain the corporate executive team's alignment with the "big vision." High-growth ambitions require someone to harmonize/integrate the company's efforts to develop new competencies with existing core competencies, values, and thought worlds.

While companies may elect to streamline their innovation function to two levels for appropriate reasons, just being aware of these traps can help avoid them . . . hopefully!

My company is too small. How can we modify the framework?
The three competencies of discovery, incubation, and acceleration are necessary, as we've described. So, too, is a distinction between the project, platform, and portfolio levels. However, depending on the size, scope, and degree of diversification in your organization, one person may span multiple roles. As long as the innovation leader, the chief innovation officer, understands the framework and institutes the principles behind it, we recognize that it may require modification to fit the company's context. We call these modified approaches "Squishing" and "Squeezing," illustrated in Tables 4.3 and 4.4.

Squishing. When the technology and industry areas are constrained, and there's not much choice in applications, companies may focus on one product area and try to hit it big. There's only one killer app. Under those circumstances, product variety within a platform is not a natural consequence of a breakthrough innovation. Instead, one product changes the game of an entire industry. Examples include small modular reactors that will allow nuclear power plants to be built on a small scale, the first cell phones that allowed individually addressable calls, and desalinization technologies that will ensure we have plenty of drinking water. While there can be many follow on products and styles, and continuous improvement in the technology, there is only one major market application, and it's big enough to warrant investment.

TABLE 4.3   Squishing the Strategic Innovation Function

| | CHIEF INNOVATION OFFICER ORCHESTRATOR | | |
	Discovery	*Incubation*	*Acceleration*
Level 3: Portfolio	D-3: Director, Discovery	I-3: Director, Incubation	A-3: Innovation Council
Level 1: Project	D-1: Opportunity Generator	I-1: New Business Creation Specialist	A-1: Functional Manager

Squeezing. Some organizations are not as interested in the extreme levels of game-changing innovations that disrupt existing markets and create new ones. Even adjacent product offerings are new enough in many organizations to cause trouble. When an organization's objectives are closer in to the core, discovery and incubation may not be as long or involved, and the uncertainty levels may not be quite as high on all four dimensions—technology, market, resource uncertainty, and organizational uncertainty. It may still be organizationally necessary to originate and nurture the projects outside the business unit, because even moderate levels of uncertainty cannot be tolerated. In this case, as shown in Table 4.4, "dincubation," in which discovery and incubation are handled by the same team, may work. The novel ideas may build on some of the organization's capabilities and networks. Experimentation is more directed and clear-cut, and the incubation process, in particular, is shortened. Examples include IBM's move into cloud computing, Moen's MotionSense faucets, and Corning's Willow Glass.

As long as people understand that the dincubation roles are stretched to include both discovery and incubation roles, and as long as the expectations for people filling those roles are realistic, the management system can be successfully aligned to accomplish the objective of "adjacent" innovations. Also, as long as those people understand that they are part of one function and are well integrated with the other roles in the innovation management system, the likelihood of the management system producing its intended types of innovations is high. While this sounds obvious, the management system can be well designed, but if they are not populated

TABLE 4.4   Squeezing the Strategic Innovation Function

	CHIEF INNOVATION OFFICER ORCHESTRATOR	
	Incubation	*Acceleration*
Level 3: Portfolio	D-I-3: Director, Strategic Innovation Portfolio	A-3: Innovation Council
Level 2: Platform	D-I-2: Platform Champion	A-2: General Manager New Business
Level 1: Project	D-I-1: Project Champion	A-1: Functional Manager

with strong personnel in these roles, the innovation function does not operate like a well-oiled machine.

One of our companies' innovation management systems originated at one of its largest US sites, and was geographically proximal to the US R&D center. The company's global headquarters was in Europe. The US group, led originally by Bob, took up the challenge of finding and developing potentially breakthrough opportunities, including those that strayed from the company's current operating models and markets. In other words, they worked on the early stages, or discovery. When Bob retired, Jay, who'd worked with him in the discovery group, took over. Jay was excellent at motivating his young idea hunters but had neither the desire nor the know-how to manage the organizational politics with the innovation function's epicenter in Europe. It wasn't more than two years before his group was disbanded and the discovery activity was concentrated into the European group. So, while Jay performed his job and led his discovery teams well, he committed a grave error. He allowed his group to become an island, separated from the rest of the innovation function. He allowed them to become dispensable, and that is just what happened. He was disconnected, and eventually the group was shut down.

Jay was in an institutionalized role but allowed himself to become detached from the rest of the innovation organization. Once Jay's predecessor left, no one maintained or worked to strengthen the relationship with the innovation function in Europe. The moral of the story is that companies cannot institutionalize just one or two innovation roles. We are talking about institutionalizing an entire system, and it has to all work together.

Everyone in my organization is supposed to be responsible for innovation. Why assign the responsibility to a single group?
We hear this a lot. In some ways it is a valid point, but it also creates a vacuum for a lack of accountability. Of course everyone in an organization is supposed to be innovative. Everyone is also supposed to be marketing and quality oriented and customer focused. But organizations have marketing roles, sales roles, and quality control roles, so that the ultimate responsibility for those outcomes is assigned, and people are held accountable for accomplishing the company's objectives in those areas. Likewise, companies need innovation roles—people who are experts at the process of new business creation in unknown territory: the world of strategic innovation.

When we dig more deeply into this issue with managers, we hear another angle to it, and that is one of elitism. How will people who are *not* part of the innovation function react? Innovation, in many respects, is viewed as the more glamourous side of the company. It draws management's attention and is the fodder for the company's public relations and branding campaigns. So the rest of the people, who work day in and day out fulfilling orders and keeping customers satisfied, say to themselves, "What are we . . . chopped liver?" Why should innovation be the responsibility of a few people?

The answer is one you'll recognize: "If everybody owns it, nobody owns it."

While we certainly want everyone to be innovative thinkers and creative problem solvers, commercializing strategic innovation requires a distinctive set of skills and abilities from those associated with running the core business. In addition, the processes used for managing potential breakthroughs are different enough from those for more incremental innovation that they need to be managed separately. So, no, everyone cannot be involved in strategic innovation, and even if they could, they should not.

If they did, the company could not survive. No one would be managing for today's market, today's customers, and today's products.

We need someone and some group in the company to be tasked with the mandate of strategic innovation. And the company's leadership needs to make clear that the strategic innovation group is just one of many contributors to the company's health. Everyone's contribution is important. We address this again in Chapter 9, when we talk about reward systems for people filling innovation roles.

Small numbers—is it worth it?

Interestingly, company executives move from one side of the argument to the other as they wrestle with the proposed framework we are suggesting for an innovation function. The first reaction is that nine new roles is way too many. But by the time they work through it, they realize that this number is, in fact, quite small for today's large established multibillion-dollar operations. Corning, for example, has teams of two generating projects within each of their platforms. For four platforms at any given time in discovery, one might have eight people at the project level, two platform leaders (one person overseeing two platforms at such an early stage), and one discovery leader (perhaps the CTO or someone in advanced research who reports to her).

In incubation, one platform-level manager can oversee three to five projects in early incubation. Similarly, one first-level incubation specialist can work on two to three projects at the same time. It could be a small core team, maybe four to six, who conduct experiments for each platform. For four platforms, that's approximately another twenty-five people or so, including the platform leaders.

Acceleration is a different animal, and it requires strong investment, but by then company leadership has determined they want to go all in. So between discovery and incubation, for four to five platforms, we are talking a core of thirty new business creation people plus a chief innovation officer. These are the commercial people. They'll need R&D partners as well as a complement of others as projects begin to show promise. But those people report to their functional leaders. The core team in the strategic innovation function is composed of people with discovery and incubation business/entrepreneurial skills.

Is thirty people across a company of many thousands of employees worth designating as a function? If it's so small, how will it get the attention it needs from the HR group? Should we lump them in with R&D?

Again, the answer is no, we should not. This group, though small, is too unique to be assimilated into other groups. Companies have small, specialized departments for other disciplines, including legal, tax, government relations, and licensing, for example. Strategic innovation is generating the businesses of the future for the company, and it needs to be considered its own function.

DIGGING IN

In the next several chapters, we thoroughly examine each of these roles. We describe the people we've met who are performing these jobs, the activities they engage in, and their backgrounds and experiences that have prepared them. We also consider metrics for evaluating their success given the typical high "failure" rate associated with breakthrough (now referred to as "strategic") innovation. Chapters 5, 6, and 7 address discovery, incubation, and acceleration, respectively, and each handles the project, platform, and leadership roles within those competency areas. You may recognize yourself among them, or you may recognize a role you'd like to hold. We certainly have. The roles themselves are interesting, but those who fill them are inspirational.

In this chapter we take up the discovery competency and the roles within it. Many people equate discovery with research and development roles. They're not the same. While the acts of invention and creation are at the heart of it, building a discovery competency for strategic innovation involves a great deal more. Here, we examine each of the discovery roles through the stories of the people we've met. These are the folks engaged in the frontline work of attempting to generate, create, and articulate opportunities; elaborate them into robust platforms of possible applications; and oversee the portfolio of multiple opportunity platforms that align with the company's vision of its future self. Companies do not practice discovery in the exact same manner, but by bringing the practices we've observed together here you should see a way to augment, adjust, or revamp the way in which your people perform this foundational competency within strategic innovation.

The launch of a strategic innovation initiative often leads to the question about how to prompt really big ideas that could be springboards for new businesses. One common approach is to collect and consolidate orphan projects from around the firm into bigger, more visible projects that have sufficient critical mass to make an impact. Other companies attempt to stimulate new opportunities through idea fairs and jams. While both of these actions might seem like a great step toward getting breakthroughs, in reality they are not unless managed as part of a larger complement of discovery activity. The former just gives you a collection of the current corporate options. While the latter might create some initial excitement and noise, the ideas from jams and fairs are just that—undeveloped ideas—not opportunities. Many are small and unrelated to the company's intentions. The sheer number of ideas that are generated creates a burden to respond, and can demoralize those who submitted them if their ideas are not accepted. The result is a backlash and nonparticipation in future calls. To develop true opportunities you need an organization and culture with commercial and research expertise designed to develop ideas into true strategic opportunities. Ideas can bubble up from a crowd, or they can be proclaimed from the top. Both work, so long as the rest of the discovery competency is operating. Before we distinguish the different discovery roles from one another, we first share some of the broader organizational designs of discovery groups in companies like Sealed Air Corporation and General Electric. We begin with a narrative about a move from DuPont to Corning.

When Joe Miller moved from his role as chief technology officer at DuPont to the same role in Corning, he brought some interesting practices along with him. One that is most relevant for our purposes was the institution of business+technology teams of two, whose job it was to explore a particular opportunity space for growth and to scope those opportunities into new business concepts for the company. At DuPont they were called inbound marketing teams. At Corning they were known as exploratory marketing and technology teams.

When Corning started that practice in early 2000, three such teams were identified, each directed to a specific domain area that Corning leadership thought had the potential to be an important growth platform for its future, but in which it did not participate at the time. The team members were midcareer people with long tenure in the company, who were quite familiar with Corning's inventory of scientific prowess. Though each team was composed of a "marketing" lead and a "technical" lead, each member had capability in the others' domain. In addition, the marketing member of the team typically had had some experience trying to build or grow a business within Corning in the past, and most had started out with a technical background and migrated into the business side over the course of their careers.

The teams of two were expected to be out on the road collecting information through lab visits, discussions with potential new market partners, and "lead customer" meetings. They were required to produce at least one white paper per month depicting an opportunity for Corning. Each of these reports was to be replete with enough evidence through their field and desk research to make a compelling case for the possibility of it becoming a new product family for Corning. Given that each team was assigned a fairly specific "fertile field," as they called it, the accumulation of twelve opportunities over the course of a year could potentially build enough evidence that indeed, that fertile field was an investment worth making and could become a whole new platform of business for the company.

Of course, the opportunities weren't always compelling. The space may have been too thin—too sparsely populated with opportunities as these hunters nosed around—or the space may not have aligned with Corning's competency or strategic investment objectives. In those situations, the platform was sunsetted and the team would be repurposed onto another potential domain.

The directors of this exploratory marketing and technology group, Deb Mills and Daniel Ricoult, operated in the same manner. Deb was the strategic marketing expert, and Daniel came from a technical background. Both were long-term, visionary, possibility-oriented thinkers, who were not shy about networking with people they did not already know. They began to see patterns in the white papers that were coming in and could scope how those initiatives might potentially accumulate to a real strategic platform for Corning. They worked with Joe Miller and the Corning Technology Council to determine where the company's "Tomorrow and Beyond" investments should be allocated.

Sealed Air Corporation had a different overall design. Throughout its history, this corporation had followed a long process of identifying opportunities that resulted in merging and integrating with other companies (including W. R. Grace, Cryovac, and Diversey, among others). When we began following them in 2000, the discovery activity was called Technology Identification Program (TIP). It was a committee composed of R&D directors and one or two midlevel new business development personnel who reported in to the two largest business units. The new business development committee members' primary responsibilities were to scout new customer segments for these large business unit's products.

By mid-2010 Sealed Air evolved from using a TIP committee to instituting a full-time dedicated team called the Strategic Innovators Group. The group was directed by the vice president of global business development, Gareth Crain, who reported to the corporate vice president of strategy and business development in that role. Gareth was a long-tenured Sealed Air employee, having come up through the sales and marketing ranks of the organization, but he had spent most of his senior-level career in new business development. For instance, he had participated on the TIP committee.

His strategic innovators team was composed of six people fully dedicated to this role, whose mandate was to find opportunities for Sealed Air in the "white spaces"—that is, areas between Sealed Air's current lines of business. The group was colocated, but was separate from R&D, in contrast to the earlier TIP team. Three of the team members were business development / commercial people, and the other three had technical backgrounds. In contrast to Corning, some of the team members were new to the company and fairly early in their careers. They were responsible for scoping out market possibilities that existed but were not part of Sealed Air's current scope of business. They were engaged in monitoring megatrends, emerging technologies, and drivers of market behavior of the future. They were investigating ways that Sealed Air could participate in big challenge areas such as alternative energy, fresh water shortages, and others.

Similar to Corning's requirement that the exploratory marketing and technology teams generate one white paper per month, Gareth set expectations for what his team needed to produce. He did so through a process: a sixteen-week cycle made up of two phases. In cooperation with his senior leader counterparts, within each cycle he chose one domain area for his team to explore. All six people worked 100 percent of their time, all day, every day, on understanding and ferreting out opportunities in this space. They were to consider ways that Sealed Air—with its current technological capabilities and those the company may be willing to invest in—could address those problem areas. There were three such cycles each year. The end result of each cycle was the generation of three well-elaborated business concepts within one strategic domain that could create a new business platform for Sealed Air. That set of three ideas was then handed over to a program manager for development, or, in our lexicon, incubation. And the strategic innovators team would start again.

Finally, let's take a look at GE. When Jeff Immelt took over for Jack Welch he initiated a change in their approach to discovery. Immelt determined that the company's strong stock performance was in jeopardy owing to a lack of investment in organic growth initiatives over the company's past decade, and he initiated GE's Advanced Technology Programs. Prior to this change exploratory research initiatives were rarely commercialized and only in an ad hoc fashion unless there were obvious connections to a current line of business. Immelt changed the direction and appointed Scott Donnelly as the new senior vice president of R&D. Together they initiated the Advanced Technology Platform program by issuing calls for proposals from among their R&D community.

After culling through and combining the best of the twenty-one proposals they received, the two decided on six such programs. In time, Michael Idelchik was appointed vice president of the Advanced Technology Programs, and worked with CEO Immelt and the leadership of GE's business units to strategize as to how those opportunities might play out as businesses as the R&D investments were surfacing commercializable options.

Each of these stories highlights people working in discovery among our participating companies. Each of these accounts provides a sense of variety of the people, their roles and activities, and different levels in the discovery hierarchy. Not every company we studied approached discovery in the same way, of course, but in tracking them over time, the ones who ended up with a pipeline of strategic innovation projects evolved to the point where there was systematic development of business concepts and platforms that were on the radar screen, in one way or the other, of the company's top leaders. It's not easy, and probably like you, our companies struggled with how to assign people to the tasks of opportunity scoping and how to measure their performance.

To clarify an approach best for you, below we provide details about discovery roles at the project, platform, and portfolio levels. We refer to them by the labels in the figure at the beginning of the chapter. We describe the responsibilities, tasks, performance metrics, and selection criteria for each of the three roles in the hierarchy. We intersperse quotes and stories from our interviews, so that you come to know some of these people. Chapter 6 takes up the same topic for incubation, and Chapter 7 addresses acceleration. We focus on our insights about what does work, and also highlight practices we've seen where it is glaringly apparent that they do not. Why repeat others' mistakes? You'll see that we focus on particular companies in each chapter. No single company was strong on all the roles we identify in the framework. That's the point. We highlight the strengths of each one, and, together, this allows us to piece together the whole infrastructure.

D-1: OPPORTUNITY GENERATOR

A person serving in a project-level position in discovery, along the first row of our matrix, is responsible for identifying and elaborating new business concepts that could change the game in an industry, and for articulating those in a manner that aligns with the company's strategic intent or areas of interest for the future. Opportunities can be sparked either by the declaration of a field of interest or by a scientific result, but they are not simply "aha" moments. Work is needed to flesh them out and gain some confidence that they're real. "I kick the tires and see which ones kick back," one D-1 told us. Thus, although DuPont eventually put inbound marketing teams in place, many of its breakthrough innovations have been initiated by lab discoveries. One that we studied was the electron emitter technology, in which a scientist that was characterizing a fibrous material found to his surprise that electrons were emitted from that material forty thousand times more easily compared with other fibers that were known at the time. Of course, this opened up many possible opportunities, but where does one begin?

Opportunity developers must be able to start from either place: the market or the lab. Thus, DuPont's "inbound marketing" teams were resident in R&D, and hunted there to be aware of what was happening in the labs, but also attended conferences, visited companies with whom

DuPont was not currently conducting business, and monitored technology investments of governments, both domestic and foreign. In this way they sought opportunities to apply their vast reservoir of knowledge and technical prowess to problems heretofore unsolved. Corning's exploratory marketing and technology teams did the same thing, always seeking "keystone" opportunities that provide combinations of technologies to enable a system of solutions, or a platform of opportunities, to be developed for an entire industry.

The appropriate number of Opportunity Generators is likely to be driven by the breadth of the company's declared strategic intent. If a company has identified several key domains of interest as future grounds it intends to plow, one discovery team on each such domain may be sufficient. In addition, one discovery team may be assigned to scope opportunities that are outside the company's strategic intent, to allow for serendipity and opportunism that frequently generates the greatest breakthrough businesses. You don't want to overly constrain the company's exploration of new futures.

Responsibilities

Opportunity Generators identify, develop, and elaborate opportunities in big problem/strategic areas. They articulate strategic options for the company to consider as new growth platforms. Corning calls them keystone components. A director of new business development in GE called them "care areas." "We shape and imagine the future," one such person at Bayer MaterialScience LLC (now Covestro LLC) told us. In addition, they facilitate idea development of others. Opportunity developers become known as the place to go for people with wild ideas, and they spend a fair amount of time hearing those and helping others articulate their ideas properly and with discipline. "We have to put a limit to crazy visions," one mentioned. Opportunity developers serve as translators for R&D's discoveries and identify market gaps and potentially company-relevant applications for those R&D discoveries. One D-2 Opportunity Domain Leader labeled his D-1 team as "sandbox managers."

Beyond coming up with ideas and opportunities or helping others vet theirs, however, D-1s are responsible for identifying a path forward for the opportunities they scope: technology gaps that need to be addressed, application areas to consider, and potential connections to maintain strategic relevance. They must elaborate and develop the opportunity a bit before we know if it's worth pursuing. It's more than coming up with a whizbang idea off the cuff. Gareth Crain at Sealed Air Corporation expressed the high level of discipline and analysis necessary for a successful discovery capability this way:

"Scoping opportunities is difficult every step of the way—it's very interesting to talk about white space, and you think of the world as your oyster as you look at that, but then what do you do? Well, what we challenge them to do first is to look at the world and look for mega trends, emergent technologies, significant influences that we believe will be drivers of market behavior in the future.

For example, alternative energy could be one of those things. Use of water may be another one of those. I mean, those are the things that everybody sees coming, right? So to look at those megatrends and say, what does that mean? By studying those markets and understanding what are the drivers, what's happening geographically, what's happening with the technology within those markets, we start to get an impression. With water, for example, we ask questions like, "When is water going to become monetized and what does that mean?" . . . so beginning to understand the markets and the drivers and the unmet needs, to understand the implications of those megatrends and those things that are going on in the world.

The opportunities are so vast, you have to have a process of culling those things that ultimately are interesting and those things could well go into a traditional business development or market development funnel—so that front end is very difficult to find the right place to go. So that is a challenge, but then as you move through that process, I want my team to assess value, whether it be volume, market size. I mean, you know, addressable market. If you find a really compelling great sounding solution in, let's say, wind energy, but then after you do the market research, you find that the entire market would buy $500,000 a year of it, and it's not interesting, right?

So that learning curve at the front end is very difficult. It becomes a question of understanding the customers, understanding the needs, and understanding the value of incumbent solutions, if there are incumbent solutions, and then understanding our ability to address those incumbent solutions in a financially competitive way.

Key to Gareth's description of the D-1's responsibilities are these points: that: (a) the learning curve is steep for every project, since each one is a new, potentially nonexistent market, requiring novel technology, and, (b) while market size is important, it is the market of the future that is most important. Therefore, coming to understand the potential value this opportunity can bring to the market, the benefits it can offer, and the drivers of market behavior in a space requires understanding in detail how those problems are currently solved today. The rest is imagination at these early stages.

Finally, D-1s are responsible for informing managers up the chain of command about strategically interesting opportunities, even those that may not fall within their assigned domain area. One D-1 who is technically oriented told us his job was to "tell the company some potentially interesting products we could make, rather than waiting for marketing to tell us." Indeed this fluid relationship between technical possibility and market scoping is what can lead to opportunities of a more breakthrough nature, since we know that traditional market research tends to yield incrementally new ideas.

Tasks/Activities
Opportunity Generators tend to work as self-directed small teams. They fill their time with desk research and reading, but also spend a fair amount of time traveling to visit sources of opportunities or those who might benefit from them. They talk with idea generators and inventors, domain-relevant people in companies, professional societies, and universities. They monitor external technology and social trends via conferences, readings, and interaction with think tanks. They find interesting novel science and technological discoveries from inside and outside the company and search for company-relevant applications.

To capture ideas from others, D-1s arrange and facilitate idea workshops (the idea cafés, jams, and fairs we described in the beginning of this chapter), and coach others as they vet, build, develop, and elaborate their ideas into strategic opportunities.

Opportunity Generators go beyond idea generation, and must develop and elaborate opportunities that appear exciting, by providing evidence of the concept's importance, its ability to solve big problems, and the technical hurdles it must overcome in order to provide that solution. Similarly, they must be able to identify the holes in the current market structure and organizational setup within the company and clarify next steps for investigating those should the company elect to pursue the project. To do this they leverage internal networks to get information needed about the company's capabilities and brainstorm the business concepts with others. They get some initial market and technical validation by developing a proof of concept to determine that it's technically feasible and worth pursuing. They rely on R&D partners to help develop mockups or conduct modeling and analyses to ensure that the concept could, in theory, work. In one of our companies there was a D-1 person whose job title was manager—innovation opportunity modeling, in fact. Finally, they present these data to potentially interested parties to gauge market enthusiasm.

An important part of the Opportunity Generator's job is to establish new networks as needed by reaching out to new potential customers or market partners to test out and elaborate ideas into business concepts. One director of discovery required his team members to attend two conferences each year, but not the same conference two years in a row. The idea was to continuously meet new people and gain exposure to new types of knowledge, to stimulate their creative thinking and constantly enrich their networks. In another case, a scientist presented his discovery at a technical conference and was delighted when, after the conference session, he was approached by a counterpart in R&D from another company, who indicated that his company needed the solution that he had just presented. Unfortunately several companies we have studied do not support having their scientists present or publish their work, choosing instead to focus on gaining the competitive advantage that secrecy and being first to market might bring. While that approach is important for heavily competitive, short-life-cycle products, the arena of strategic innovation requires a different approach. When working to create new markets, as opposed to competing in existing ones, collaboration is required. Single firms do not create new markets by themselves.

D-1s must also write up their business concepts in a way that is compelling for the platform leader, and then work with the platform leader to hone the concepts into presentations or documents that identify the links to the company's future and next steps to be taken.

The output required of the Opportunity Generator is a steady stream of possible and highly innovative new business opportunities for the company, usually in the form of white papers or well-documented presentations. These documents articulate the opportunity and provide evidence of its potential based on analysis and research into trends, with area experts, and by piecing together disparate bits of information that build a compelling case for the opportunity. Each D-1 person or team may be required to submit a certain number of such opportunities annually, to feed the pipeline of options for the company. The appropriate number will differ by company and industry. Companies that we studied noted that between six and twelve per year per team allowed for adequate research while also maintaining a rich pipeline.

Performance Metrics

Senior managers in innovation roles told us that Opportunity Generators are evaluated on "how they handle being given a blank sheet of paper." To be viewed as successful, D-1s must meet the following performance standards:

- S/he must find and articulate the required quota of opportunities, in the form of white paper descriptions or presentations.

- S/he must take the actions necessary to find answers to the questions that arise about the opportunity space that s/he's working. It cannot all be done through Internet research. It's a proactive, listening-oriented role. The D-1 must be able to get access to the people who can answer the relevant questions, engage in productive conversations with them, enhance the understanding of the scope of the opportunity space, and report results to the team in a timely fashion so the team can develop insights based on their collective learning.

- The quality of the opportunities identified will be judged by the breadth and robustness of the opportunity space, connection to or influence on the company's strategic intent, and the willingness/ inspiration of others to advance them.

To some, these metrics may seem impossible to meet. But to others, they can be a very enticing set of goalposts.

Selection Criteria

What does a manager look for when recruiting an Opportunity Generator for strategic innovation? Here we'll examine the personal characteristics, skills, expertise, and some of the background and critical experiences the Opportunity Generators we met showed, and how others described the idyllic D-1.

Personal Characteristics

Opportunity Generators, as with most roles in the strategic innovation function are described as "motivated to be a part of creating something new." The primary descriptor our company representatives used for D-1s is that they are "lovers of information." They thrive on learning rather than on reordering the known and familiar. They can find answers, ask the right questions, and learn in any field. They are keenly motivated by the opportunity to operate in a new domain every few weeks or months. Here is the way several of them described themselves or other D-1s.

So my view on it is that you need a kind of information lover for Business Intelligence. Normally they have pretty good analytical skills and they're smart thinkers. You know, they see cross connections. (discovery and incubation platform leader at John Deere)

What's different (from my old position) is that it's a completely different business every time. So now I work with the x business, I work with y business, and I work with z Business. And they are night and day compared to the BU that we used to support. (R&D scientist in discovery work at GE).

What excites me every day, it's not just doing the job, but it's as though I'm constantly learning. There's always something new to learn. Anybody who has that mind-set can do this job. (marketing/strategy person in discovery at GE)

To do discovery work in an area, you don't have to be an expert in that area. (HR / organizational development director, DSM's Innovation Center)

Some Opportunity Generators can be perceived as prima donnas, challenging the status quo in the organization or in the technology domain. Most of the time those challenges are offered in a healthy, productive way, but not always. They can by cynical about organizational bureaucracy, impatient, rude, and even self-serving, seeking credit for every idea they generate. This is the exception rather than the rule, but we've come across enough of them to make an impression. Most discovery managers believe these people are so smart that it's worth tolerating them. If that is the case, the petulant D-1 may require extra coaching to help him or her understand the boundaries of the domains the company is trying to cultivate, and the contribution he or she is expected to make. Sometimes, we believe, it is simply not worth the effort. It may be better to counsel him or her out and incorporate a team player. Strategic innovation is not for rogue pioneers.

Finally, although Opportunity Generators thrive on ideation, they must also recognize the fact that many of their ideas will not ultimately become businesses for the company. A high churn rate of projects is the norm in any strategic innovation portfolio, given that the opportunities are leading edge and may not be feasible from a technical, market, resource, or organizational fit perspective. This may be discouraging to D-1s, and even cause cynicism or disillusionment in some. For this reason we suggest identifying people with a high level of resilience for this role, those who will not be personally affronted if each project is not selected for investment. You need individuals who realize the value of their contribution is in finding and elaborating *potential* robust business concepts. In addition we encourage a career trajectory that recognizes their creativity, ability to network, and their well-honed skills of articulating possible futures for the company. Like any other career assignment, a position in level-one discovery that lasts too long can lead to stagnation, which can be exacerbated further by the fact that most opportunities will fail.

Skills
Discovery opportunities are not product ideas. They are system-level, game-changing opportunities. Opportunity Generators must be design thinkers,

taking into account all the potential aspects of this complex problem, to determine if there is a case for an opportunity. This implies that they must be able to think both deductively and inductively, allowing for creative leaps based on bits of data and partial evidence they accumulate in their travels. Experienced D-1s are systems thinkers about possible business options. They are able to see the relevance of certain combinations of technologies or market needs that might elude you and me, and understand how those combinations enable an entire ecosystem of products. Scientific prowess is needed to create or evaluate novel technology or combinations of technology and foundational knowledge. However, the ability to learn about new technologies and be fungible across them outweighs deep experience and knowledge in any one single technical arena. One of our discovery leaders was perplexed about how to populate the technical side of her teams: "If I put a physicist on it, it'll be a physics problem. If I put a chemist on it, it'll be a chemistry problem." The head of the innovation group in another company made a similar statement when he said he needed "technically neutral" teams. Acumen for understanding and a natural curiosity about scientific, technical or business solutions along with insight into how those add value are what we need in D-1s.

The same applies for market knowledge. Some of our companies regretted hiring people with networks in specific markets because if the project was shut down, the company was forced to lay off the new employee. Many companies used consultants for specific market contacts and knowledge, and the permanently employed Opportunity Generators worked in partnership with them.

To be able to learn about markets in this manner, D-1s need to excel at deep listening, keen observation, and an ability to connect different bits of information together. One discovery level-two Opportunity Domain Leader explained these necessary skills for the D-1 group:

You need people who understand what our core competencies are and what's possible . . . some technical people on the team that can dream and imagine and say, "Yeah, we can do this. We've got the technology and skills sets to be able to figure out how to do that." And you also need that marketing and business sense that can sum up customer opportunities as they're out listening to what customers are telling you. They're purely listening. They're not trying to solve a problem; they're not trying to sell them anything. They're trying to understand what the needs are, and maybe even hear things that customers don't even recognize as needs or maybe they see things that customers don't recognize as needs. So they're trying to capture all of that and boil it down, so they can say, "This is why we think this is a win."

Another company representative contrasted the type of marketing skills required of a discovery team member with traditional marketing roles:

We are an R&D-based marketing group. We're only focused on understanding articulated and unarticulated customer needs in the context that we can solve them through technology or innovative business models. So we're not doing marketing flyers. We're not worried about websites. It's very much around that early stage of marketing, and understanding needs, or in some cases, creating needs.

Beyond breadth in markets and across technology domains, D-1s are less likely to be specialists on either side, even though, as in the case of Corning, a team member is assigned the lead responsibility for one and may come from a background more steeped in one or the other. The most successful and productive D-1s are described as "not market, not tech . . . but both." So they are able to move from one market space to another, from one technology domain to another, and see opportunities.

In addition to an eagerness and ability to learn new technologies and new market spaces, capable D-1s can see patterns based on contextual interactions. They can be excellent situation-specific learners, in addition to just applying what they know to whatever setting they find themselves in (which is what most of us do). These folks are adept at both. In other words, D-1s can draw conclusions about their current projects based on facts and insights collected in previous situations, but they also have the ability to be zero-based learners. They can begin with the evidence and patterns they've seen in their investigation of the current project and draw conclusions only from it.

To be able to learn so quickly, we mentioned that Opportunity Generators must create new networks on a regular basis. That means they must be facile at accessing information from sources with which they may not be familiar. While most of us are great at leveraging our current networks, Opportunity Generators are skilled at creating new ones, both inside and outside the company. The ties among those people in each new network may not be strong, and they may not be used for a long time. One research scientist involved in the Advanced Technology Programs at GE referred to the need for internal networking as follows:

For these new programs, you might not have a relationship built up front (with the relevant BUs). In traditional R&D, you know the BU's management and technical people.

Unfortunately, the skill sets needed to create such "weak ties" are not necessarily valued by companies. Companies, particularly those steeped in technology, promote people based on their deep knowledge that is re-inforced by a strong network interaction. The idea of being "a mile wide and an inch deep," which may be necessary for early stage discovery, is anathema to most corporations since their focus and systems are set to le-verage current competencies rather than evolving new ones. These require-ments mean that D-1s must be adept at interpersonal communication: to get the attention of people inside the company and in other organizations who may not be interested in answering a cold call or e-mail.

Several of our discovery personnel described the ability to imagine the possible as a key skill of their D-1s:

It's a lot about creativity, technical insight, and very good listening and sort of people skills with customers. That's what really good [D-1] people do. And they also have to have the ability to inspire their management, other people on their team, to see things that aren't right in front of your face,

So the people that are really good at [early business development] can paint a pic-ture of a dream of something that doesn't exist today, and also have the technical knowledge and insight to know what is actually possible and what is not.

The move from the possible to generating the next steps is important. In other words, D-1s are not just dreamers; they are executors. They are "able to envision possibilities where gaps exist, but to be realistic and not operate on unfettered optimism." They apply a healthy skepticism and are able and motivated to hunt down answers or creatively design methods for getting answers. They develop models and visualization techniques to array a set of options, and they work with ranges rather than point estimates to incorporate the uncertainty of the opportunity. They conduct all this analysis to ensure that an opportunity is scoped broadly enough and is robust enough to be of business interest to the company. The director of Enterprise Advanced Marketing at John Deere described them as able to "generate the world of the possible and move to something that can be tested."

Critical Experiences

When we examined the Opportunity Generators we encountered in our research, we found that they come from all sorts of backgrounds. Most have a technical background as a starting point, but that neither guarantees their success nor is it required. For instance, consider the following story of one Opportunity Generator from Sealed Air and her circuitous, "nontechnical" route to the role.

Denning Saum, a D-1 from Sealed Air, holds a BA with a double major in Spanish and political science from a small private college in the southeast United States. She spent a year abroad in Argentina in college, and then leveraged her school's alumni network to land an internship in Atlanta, at the Southern Center for International Studies working in their research library. The center served global companies trying to gain access to US markets, and Denning was exposed to business strategy and new business development concepts there. She moved to the Hispanic chamber of commerce, where she increased her involvement with large companies headquartered in Atlanta.

After several years Denning entered an MBA program at the University of South Carolina. The program emphasized international business, and through that she spent eight months in Brazil working for the US Department of Commerce, doing international policy work and issue advocacy for US companies. She dealt with a broad range of issues, from intellectual property to customs control for product imports. Ultimately she decided to make a move from the public to the private sector and went to a consulting firm specializing in clients from Spain and Latin America trying to grow their US business base. Every client was different, of course, so she gained an understanding of multiple industries, including clean water and renewable energy. "There wasn't any one particular segment necessarily that was my specialty, just the strategy overall, and the implementation of new business development is what I worked on." She remained connected to her MBA colleagues, one of whom worked for Sealed Air and who mentioned the formation of the Strategic Innovators Group. By that time Denning had amassed a wide enough set of experiences across industries to attract the attention of the group leader, Gareth Crain. So the combination of her networking skills and broad industry background helped her land the job. She told us:

When I read the job description for strategic innovator, I thought, you know, this is exactly what I'm doing in a lot of ways. I mean, it was like, I couldn't have written something that seemed more perfect. And I will tell you, I probably will never have a job that's as much fun as that one. Gareth was just building the team. So I was the only one that was completely external to Sealed Air, so I came in with zero knowledge about packaging, nothing—extrusion was completely new to me, but that was by design, and I think Gareth really wanted that for most people to change—you know, take you out of your paradigm, so you're not encumbered by what we do today.

Other companies we've studied have also used the D-1 position as a way to onboard people from outside the company, in order to gain their fresh perspective. At Bayer MaterialScience LLC, Ray Yourd evolved from hiring technical people with three to five years of experience at the company to seeking out newly minted MBAs for their Creative Center. A parallel organization, the New Technologies Group, was populated by young PhD scientists who were exploring novel areas of material science. The people in the Creative Center were only expected to stay there a couple of years, monitoring market trends and scoping opportunities, before they moved into one of the business units onto a more traditional career track. While that worked out well for them, it was difficult for Ray. He appreciated their fresh ideas and great energy, but was concerned about finding them their next job within Bayer.

Another one of our companies' innovation hub adopted the founders of small companies that the parent was acquiring as key members of their discovery team. The entrepreneurs' skills at opportunity recognition combined with their healthy Rolodex of connections enabled them to identify a number of possible business opportunities for the company once they understood its technological capabilities.

DuPont, Corning, and GE used experienced strategic marketing and technology pairs to identify opportunities. Grundfos used a mix of PhDs and young people trained in technological innovation management from a business school setting as their D-1 mix. There are different ways to configure the group, but it's clear that companies preferred a mix of backgrounds in the Opportunity Generator group. For example, in one of our companies, a discovery manager mentioned that one of the best guys in her group was a seventy-five-year-old who'd been with the company for forty-seven years and then quickly followed that with another strong player on the team, who was a "young guy who will rock the boat, is great with user experience, and asks the right questions."

We cannot claim to have found patterns in the experiences and backgrounds of Opportunity Generators. Some have a lot of experience; some have almost none. Some have a broad background; others, young in their career, are simply curious and smart. The patterns among D-1s are more obvious in their skills and motivations. They seem to be able to make up for any gaps in their experiences by their shrewd smarts, incredible curiosity, and willingness to talk to anyone to move a project forward. One D-2 manager described finding and hiring his team members this way:

We've got a lot of different types. We've got one that comes from a traditional marketing background. The other folks come from more technical disciplines. And as we interviewed people—these folks just rose to the top. And so what they didn't know about our marketing process, you know, was offset with their technical understanding, with their attitude about innovation, with their motivational fit with what we do here. And so we brought them in.

D-2: OPPORTUNITY DOMAIN LEADER

Opportunity Domain Leaders are more noticeable by their absence than by their presence. Without domain leaders in discovery, the strategic innovation initiative can easily become a pipeline of eclectic, smaller projects, championed by individuals who leap into them without strategic scrutiny and that therefore are subject to a high degree of political manipulation. Domain leaders shape the myriad opportunities their team members present them into larger business platforms, and keep a focus on the domains of strategic intent to the best extent possible. Since they will review all the D-1 teams' ideas, they may see opportunities for combining ideas from across their teams or, for that matter, across time. Companies who maintain a rich memory of ideas that have been "shelved" can leverage those with current ideas to build blockbuster opportunities, so long as there's someone to recognize those combinations.

D-2s become domain experts because they are steeped in the area and are exposed to many dimensions of it, including possible market applications, codevelopment partners, and business models. They are the ones who can get a sense as to whether or not this domain is actually coming to fruition or whether it will remain a figment of the company's imagination. They screen, evaluate, and combine opportunities to make sure they're big enough and strategic enough. They define and articulate the "opportunity landscape" of the domain that is emerging through their team's work. In contrast to D-1s, their past experiences and backgrounds are a crucial part of their readiness for this role. In particular the D-2 must have the organizational credibility to gain and hold leadership's attention as a new platform begins to emerge. Obviously, new business concepts never emerge as expected, so the D-2 gets involved in some interesting facilitation activities, both within her team and upward, to help the company determine if and how to invest in incubating this new business opportunity.

Responsibilities
The Opportunity Domain Leader has three primary responsibilities. The first is to ensure her team identifies and elaborates opportunities that have the possibility of becoming viable business platforms in the company's future. The second is to vet the opportunities softly with people inside the company who will eventually need to be involved in commercializing those businesses. Finally, the Opportunity Domain Leader recruits people into the D-1 role and develops them so that the discovery capability is institutionalized beyond themselves.

D-2s tend to be the glue of discovery. They carry organizational memory and internal networking responsibilities, and they coach and develop the level-one discovery team's business concepts. In this manner they advance innovation opportunities. They have the authority to reject discovery ideas that are weakly researched or justified. Ideas that are clearly out of line with the company's strategic intent may be culled out or raised to higher organizational levels as potential emerging domains of interest if a domain leader sees the evidence beginning to build from multiple discovery teams.

Depending on the size of the company's strategic innovation appetite, D-2 personnel may be assigned one or several platform- or domain-related teams, so that they are bounding their review work within a domain or two. The advantage of this election is deeper expertise and knowledge within a given platform, but the tradeoff is letting go of the potential to link opportunities from across them.

Finally, D-2s have the task of scoping opportunities in such a way as to fit the organization's willingness to stretch its current businesses. As the D-1s within their domain work to scope the opportunity, its boundaries and extreme points become apparent. The D-2 integrates this information to form a picture of the landscape of possibilities that the domain offers. Identifying an organizationally acceptable approach to considering this potential new business platform is part of the discovery role, and its early vetting falls to the Opportunity Domain Leader.

Tasks/Activities

The D-2 manager is uniquely positioned to accomplish the first area of responsibility. By constantly engaging with her opportunity development teams, coaching them, and helping them elaborate opportunities, the domain leader is exposed to a broad spectrum of information over a significant period of time about the domain. One R&D director compared the Opportunity Domain Leader role with that of a traditional R&D manager, noting that the former handles an expanded volume in her portfolio, with a higher attrition rate and a greater breadth of projects. We agree completely and realize that, in fact, this difference allows the D-2 manager to perceive the weak signals that are not obvious to others but eventually lead to the tipping point of a new market domain's emergence. One D-2 manager described the power of sticking within a strategic domain for a while as a way to hedge against uncertainty, since there are so many novel aspects to each domain:

I think it's interesting to explore markets of the future, because there's no right answer, but it's about that journey of discovery. You don't know. Nobody knows what the future's going to bring. But the more you amass understanding, within a realm of uncertainty, the more likely you are to have a feeling for what's likely to happen. So you get involved. The more you involve yourself in markets and spaces that are emerging, but unclear, the more you get a feel for what's there and what's not.

By working with the D-1 Opportunity Generators in the domain, and coaching them to elaborate those opportunities to become true strategic innovations, the D-2 manager envisions possible futures that others may not be in a position to see. After all, they're in the catbird seat. D-2 managers constantly think about the possible, and they consider all of the myriad combinations of technologies and markets that can play out in that domain, based on the concepts that their team is presenting them. We call this output the opportunity landscape. It's a positioning map of possible new product/service lines that the domain might enable. No one knows yet if any of them are viable, but having that landscape is useful input to an incubation team as they start their work. One D-2 told us the following:

The way I've been thinking about that all cutting edge technology is that it is actually a recombination of existing technology. And it's just understanding how things recombine. So part of my role is to think about that mental map. How do improvements in one space in technology benefit another? For example, the battery program we talked about, I think is a completely new business. We've never been in that space before. But it's thinking about the technology in a new way. The fundamental chemistry is not new. But what is new is the way we think we can manage it. If you look through history, the Japanese just had some batteries catch fire using this technology. The Swiss, who were making the same battery technology five or six years ago went bankrupt because they couldn't make it work. So what are we bringing that's new? Well we are bringing this company's expertise in manufacturing, and modeling and understanding how to make it successful. So that recombination, even though the technology's fairly tame and old, can be breakthrough when you bring all of those pieces together.

Another example of the task of envisioning possibilities and the power of collective memory comes from a team of three R&D directors at another one of our companies. These three sifted through ideas that had come in through various channels. (They did not have a D-1 team in place at the time, so ideas arrived by happenstance.) The fact that the same three individuals did this every month allowed for their collective memory to see combinations of ideas that, when taken together, could provide wholly new opportunities for the company. They were able to augment and elaborate the ideas and help shape them in a manner that became not just interesting but interesting *and* worth pursuing.

Clearly D-2s spend time ruminating, putting pieces of a puzzle together, considering alternative futures and how this domain can contribute and add real value. They connect ideas they've been exposed to through time and across geographies, industries and technological solution areas.

But there is more to their job than ruminating. D-2s are responsible for screening, elaborating, and critically thinking. All of this is done with an eye to articulating the idea internally, both upward and outward to partners in the business units. It requires active engagement, through their D-1 teams, with the market. One D-2 voiced his concern at becoming pigeonholed as an analyst in his role: "We're moving more towards becoming scouts, or trend watchers—but I see a little bit of danger in that all we do is scouting . . . We need to be creating action around the scouting."

Besides guiding market interaction, interfacing with the business units is critical since the idea often does not come from them, but it may require change to their operations down the road. In other words, the Opportunity Domain Leader needs to vet the opportunities as part of the strategic intent of the organization, and remind those parts of the organization that will ultimately be affected should the opportunity take root and grow. For this, they spend a fair amount of time facilitating discussions upward and to key BU leaders to ensure the arena of strategic intent that was committed to early on is still in play. As one told us, it's a way to improve the chances that his job has ultimate impact:

When you retire, how are you going to feel if you can't point at anything that you did in a thirty-year career that ever made it to market? What if everything you ever worked on never got out of the lab? Would you say you were innovative? I don't care how much you can see the opportunity about this, that or the other. If we can't get better at identifying things that make a difference, and if we can't get better at linking with the rest of the organization to make these things reality, it's not innovation. It might be invention. It might be creative. It might be all those kinds of things, but it sure isn't innovation. And so I try to facilitate those discussions.

Another one of our D-2s assembled a council of all the chief marketing officers (CMOs) of each business unit. One of the items on their regular agenda was to allow our D-2s to test out ideas with them that were brewing in discovery.

To do their jobs well, D-2s, as managers, need to attend to their team. Domain leaders told us that they spend significant time finding people whom they can properly develop, who are interested in working under conditions of ambiguity, and who can dig into and elaborate opportunities. Bruce, an innovation process facilitator at Corning, described their discovery domain leaders' responsibilities in this way:

Obviously Deb and Daniel were picked because of their experience and subject matter expertise in early stage marketing and technology assessment. But part of their role is hiring people who have an interest in doing this work as opposed to ongoing product line marketing kind of work. So they, in addition to having real platforms that they are doing work on, trying to cultivate the next five-hundred-million-dollar opportunities for Corning; you know, they are at the same time developing a group of people to have this ability. They are trying to clone themselves.

D-2s engage and inspire their teams, and keep them connected to the company's declared strategic ambitions. They coach D-1s by asking insightful, challenging questions to ensure they're looking at all dimensions of the project and not ignoring aspects with which they may be unfamiliar. D-2s work with their teams to combine opportunities and elaborate and develop them in such a manner that the platform can be described in a compelling way and attract leadership attention. They also help identify potential strategic directions and next steps to pursue.

Of course, this is easier said than done. D-1s can become committed to their projects and may struggle to express the evidence behind their strong opinions. One domain leader described it this way:

So the innovative people around here would like to think that they just shouldn't be questioned once they're moving forward with something, because if they were an entrepreneur, they wouldn't be (questioned), right? If they were an entrepreneur, it would be their own money at risk, their own marriage and their own house. They're risking my marriage and my house now, right? So we have to sit down together and talk all through it and say . . . what value do you think this is going to create? What can we do to understand customers better? What can we do to understand technology better? And how can we do that in such a way that we've got some options . . . It has a lot to do with getting the right people around the table and understanding some basic questions and then, you know, you make an option play. And what we find is that people don't necessarily come in here mentally programmed for that. And so we have to try to work through it. They don't like to be challenged when they're in the middle of something. If they see something that they think is a great idea, and you ask them to complete a process step, it's like you're killing the innovation.

Performance Metrics
Domain leaders are successful when the business concepts they and their team present are perceived by company leaders as highly innovative possibilities worthy of pursuing. The opportunities are presented in a manner that makes them seem possible, albeit stretch goals, and that provide evidence as to how their business potential could possibly be achieved and the next steps needed to begin the exploration. Preliminary contacts in the market will have been made, and some form of enthusiasm will have been demonstrated by those external to the company. In addition, the opportunities offer a rich list of applications and potential product lines, possibly for different target markets. In other words, if one branch of the opportunity tree breaks, there are many others to pursue. It's a platform or family of products, rather than one product. Ultimately, you need to

deliver a domain full of opportunities that are insightful, nonobvious, well-researched, and compelling as strategic plays for the company.

Selection Criteria

As with any function, the selection criteria for roles that are higher in the chain of command presume the presence of some of the skills and expertise of those below them, but not all. The same applies here. So in this section we will describe only the characteristics, skills, and critical experiences that the Opportunity Domain Leader must have in addition to those of the Opportunity Generator. In cases where those characteristics actually differ, we'll point them out.

Personal Characteristics

Beyond the creative, inductive thinking patterns, penchant for associative thinking, and love of learning that D-1s exhibit, we find that D-2s are more organizationally savvy. They have typically been with the company for a while. To be able to connect opportunities to strategic intent of the company and communicate upward and outward, D-2s must be well networked.

One new business development director we encountered was located in corporate R&D, and spanned both discovery and incubation. He was well known throughout the company, and was a somewhat controversial character given his intense drive for innovation and the company's minimalist appetite for it at the time. However, his willingness to reach out to anyone in the company was legendary. Anytime he made a phone call, people answered. "We employ thirty-five thousand people across the globe. I am sure to find someone who knows the answer to any question I have," he told us. He was credited with trying many new things and succeeding on a few of them. That was enough to earn him the respect of his colleagues and superiors, which opened the door for other opportunities he scoped to be seriously considered.

So beyond the ability and willingness to network, D-2s must also have credibility with their peers and leaders. They need it since they are challenging the company to change through strategic innovation. Having organizational credibility is key to getting those meetings and gaining the attention of the appropriate business leaders. One of our companies did not have D-2s for their inbound marketing people (D-1s) and found that the D-1s had too little organizational credibility with the BUs. The D-1s could not get senior leaders' attention to those opportunities, and the business unit went forward with its own product planning, refusing to take seriously any initiatives from this part of the Strategic Innovation Group. So D-2s need to have internal selling skills and organizational credibility.

Opportunity Domain Leaders may appear impassioned by a particular opportunity given their latent understanding of the domain and commitment to an opportunity after having studied it for so long and becoming so involved in the emerging market space, but they value their credibility and do not risk it. They are well prepared with evidence or at least clues to the broad emerging opportunity space. One way to summarize D-2s is as associative thinkers who know when to focus. As one person told us, the D-2 "can't be a shiny object person," meaning flipping from one idea to the next. Their job is to craft the suite of ideas into a strategically relevant, robust business platform with potential for bringing real value to the market.

Skills and Expertise

The Opportunity Domain Leader builds on expertise as an Opportunity Generator but must add to the skill set in a manner commensurate with the increased strategic responsibilities associated with the position.

Yes, he's a lover of learning and is agile in learning new technologies and markets. We noted that D-1s tend to exhibit a breadth of knowledge on various topics, and depth in a few, but shallower knowledge where appropriate. Organizational development experts call these types of people "M-shaped."[1] They are the connective tissue between experts. By comparison the D-2 tends to focus on those areas of deep expertise that she has developed within the domain area, because she is steeped in it. She sees the synergies across the opportunities presented to her by her team.

Organizational psychologists call the D-2 a T-shaped person, meaning he has one major depth area of expertise, and is broad as well. But the meaning of depth has changed. Rather than depth in a technology or a market, the depth is in the strategic domain. He'll know all the opportunities, how they're connected to one another, and what each might require to implement. The "domain" is the area of depth now, rather than an initial technology or market. We've redefined the boundary of expertise.

We noted that D-1s are systems thinkers. They stitch together disparate pieces of information to see relevant combinations of technologies and market applications for potentially breakthrough opportunities. D-2s do this as well, but they're not in the field as much. Rather, they're connecting the opportunities that D-1s bring forward to the company's possible capabilities. So, it's necessary that they have a market vision capability—meaning they can articulate opportunities in a manner that clarifies their value to internal constituents, and possibly to potential customer partners and value network partners.

Additionally, strategic insight is needed to clarify how the opportunity enhances the firm's position relative to its future objectives. D-2s spend time connecting the opportunities that D-1s bring forward to the company's possible capabilities. The D-2 is building in the complex dimension of the organization's willingness and ability to organize and deliver on the opportunity should it appear promising as it is incubated. Whom should the D-2 connect with for help? How should they think about a possible organizational arrangement? Which business unit might sponsor this and how do we get their attention? These are the considerations of concern for the D-2. Opportunity Domain Leaders are recognized as having judgment regarding the degree to which the projects emerging within the domain are compelling enough for the company/portfolio, and the company's ability to digest it. He can express the value propositions and vision for the platform and its connection to strategic intent in a way that inspires the team as well as the company's leadership. Her words can attract enough attention to create the context for a proper strategic vetting of the opportunity at hand. Suffice it to say, the Opportunity Domain Leader has strategic visioning skills.

D-1s are evidence based, and good D-1s are agnostic to the opportunities they surface. If, as they investigate further, the market is not responding with any enthusiasm, the D-1 moves on. The D-2, however, may be more committed. Since the D-2 is seeing many opportunities within the platform, he may be able to see the promise where others cannot. As he becomes more deeply involved, it may require more effort to examine all options and determine that the pursuit is not worth the investment. He sees too many combinations, too many possibilities, to let go so easily. Evidence is important, but intuition born of deep experience in an area is added to the mix at the level of D-2. The balance between overcommitment to a domain owing to passion alone and intuition based on reading cues is a difficult line to draw.

D-1s, we noted, have deep listening and keen observation skills. They're able to connect disparate pieces of information together due to these intriguing abilities. The D-2 has those as well, but with the added feature of experience, typically a fairly long history of it. The D-2 is no longer primarily in the field, and relies on the inputs from her team members. She is a deep listener to them, and serves more as a provocateur, asking "what if?" questions to help the teams elaborate and enrich the opportunities they bring forward—to kick the tires and sense if it is "big enough." One of our D-2s described his experience, and others like him, in this way:

The good (Opportunity Domain) managers are the ones that say, "OK, even though you think you've closed this off, have you thought about this?" And it's not necessarily asking you to open the door and spend more time beating your head against the wall. It's like, OK, make sure that you're not just trimming it off because you want to move on. Make sure that you have at least considered what might be behind Door Number 3. And I think the really good managers are the ones that create more opportunities . . . And I think it's a gift, it's a skill.

When we tracked the coaching skills of successful D-2s we learned that they're viewed as managers who don't over constrain their team. Rather, the D-2 frees them and encourages them to think more broadly, to elaborate further and develop the opportunity space. He's used to uncertainty and is willing to prolong it to ensure the team is exploring all aspects of an opportunity space. He helps them formulate the critical hypotheses they'll need to test to determine if the opportunity is worth pursuing into incubation. By separating what is evidenced from what is still unknown, he helps them plot a path forward. His approach is motivating because of his deep listening and working with the team. He is a clear thinker and effective communicator, and is concerned with developing the talent and skills of those working for him. But he holds them accountable for high-quality work.

Finally, we noted that D-1s are skilled at creating new networks for situation specific learning needs. The networks may not be used once a domain has been explored, but they serve a purpose and help the D-1 learn quickly. D-2s will need to continue to leverage that skill set, as they help coach their teams and work on the opportunities to build them into platforms. But in addition, the D-2 maintains strong rich internal networks throughout the organization that can be called on to check information and gauge organizational response to an opportunity as it is evolving. She knows the company well, and knows where to find pockets of talent and specific skills as needed. She knows how to leverage the knowledge and resources of the large organizational setting.

Table 5.1 summarizes some of these additional skills that the domain leaders we observed tended to exhibit over and above the D-1 Opportunity Generators who operated at the project level. It's pretty clear that an automatic career step from a D-1 to a D-2 is unlikely. There are a num-

TABLE 5.1   A Comparison of D-1 and D-2 Skills and Expertise

D-1 Opportunity Generators	D-2 Opportunity Domain Leaders
M shaped, broadly curious with expertise in a few areas. Fungible across domains. Lovers of learning.	T shaped. Deep expertise in developing business concepts. Breadth across technology domains.
Systems thinkers. See relevance of combinations for technology and market.	Systems thinkers. See relevance of combinations for technology and market. Also sees connections to the company's possible capabilities. Considers ability for organizational system to reorganize and deliver.
Evidence-based.	Evidence-based. More willing to sell/influence because of commitment to the domain. More passionate due to increased latent understanding over time and resultant ability to sense opportunity.
Deep listeners. Keen observers. Able to connect disparate pieces of information.	Deep listeners. Keen observers. Able to connect disparate pieces of information. Not a collector of primary data. Operates more a listener, reader and coach. Poses provocative "what if" questions.
Creates new networks.	Creates new networks. Also has strong rich internal networks that s/he can call on to check internal political response to the opportunity.

ber of differences between the two roles, and so an aspiring D-2 needs to gain experience in a variety of settings to be prepared for this next move.

Background and Critical Experiences

In contrast to D-1s, the Opportunity Domain Leader's past experiences and background are crucial. In particular the D-2 must have the organizational credibility to gain and hold leadership's attention as a new platform begins to emerge. A number of them that we've encountered have saved the company from big technical disasters a couple of times or contributed strategically in big ways. They do not usually come in from outside. Our D-2 respondents have fairly lengthy histories inside the company—ten to fifteen years on average—and have usually experienced at least three or four assignments, in both the technical and marketing functions of the company. If they've had product line experience so that they've "felt the pain of being responsible for revenues"—so much the better. If they come from a stronger R&D background, our respondents told us they need to have a track record of both successes and failures, or "war stories to share." They may even have worked in multiple business units within the company, and experienced cross cultural assignments as well. Every one of our respondents believed the D-2 should have some subject matter expertise to evaluate opportunities, and also have had previous experience with customers to be able to have an "outside-in" view to help them understand if the opportunity facing the is truly a big idea.

This multifaceted, rich experience base enables the domain leader to take a broad perspective, not only about the opportunities facing him in his domain area but also about the company's capacity to make the most of them. The experience base builds his legitimacy so that when he makes a case for moving a project area forward, it's credible. He has a view of the business side issues the company faces and the experience to back it up.

D-3: DIRECTOR OF DISCOVERY

The third and most senior level in the discovery hierarchy plays two important roles: one is internal to the discovery function, and the second navigates between the discovery function and the mainstream organization. In some of our participating companies, this role was played by the chief innovation officer, who managed to identify and scope the domains of strategic intent and assign D-2s to examine them. More often, the duties were assumed by the CTO or someone who reported to the CTO, chief strategy officer, or president of a growth businesses division. In these cases, the position's label varied from vice president of advanced technology programs, to director of product technology and innovation, to senior vice president, advanced research, to vice president of global marketing and business development. While the director of discovery's level in the overall organizational hierarchy varies today, it is emerging as a strategic role.

Responsibilities
The overarching remit of the D-3 role is to seed the company with possibilities for game-changing new businesses and ensuring they have the right climate to grow. To be successful, she must address two categories of responsibilities. The first is the set of duties within the discovery organization. Second is managing the interface between discovery and the rest of the organization. In that capacity she is responsible for ensuring that the purpose of the discovery group is understood and valued throughout the company, and she works with the chief innovation officer to inform the choice of domains of strategic intent that the company commits itself to realizing.

Within the discovery organization, he educates. He must ensure that the discovery team and their close partners, the R&D community, understand the language of innovation: how it differs from invention, how it differs from R&D, and how the management approaches to strategic innovation are distinguished from those associated with more familiar new product development projects. It is so easy to slip into traditional R&D practices and phase gate vocabulary that lead to the traditional types of output that companies produce. To fight this instinct the D-3 must constantly support the company's strategic innovation mandate by reminding those in discovery that the bleeding edge, the far out, the breakthrough space is where they need to be. Even if they don't get there, the effort to stretch beyond the known will lead at least to evolutionary innovation. Uncertainty and ambiguity are crucial elements of the vocabulary. While R&D scientists may be used to this from their educational backgrounds, their industrial R&D experience may have dimmed those memories. Certainly the commercial personnel, feeling pressure to produce, may tend toward closure when they instead need to continue to expand their horizons. Education and constant reminders of their mandate from their leader are an important part of this process.

A second component of the education process is to set the proper culture for strategic innovation and hold people accountable for delivering, even though they're operating in a fuzzy environment. The director of discovery sets and maintains a culture that recognizes strategic innovation as one of the many responsibilities that the company must fulfill, and reminds the organization that this mandate requires both a longer time frame and a sense of urgency. The culture protects the innovation function from the tyranny of today's pressures, but couples that protection with an expectation of discipline and accountability. One of the discovery managers we interviewed described that culture this way:

One of the basic principles we applied to the formation of [our discovery] team was that they have to be 100 percent focused on innovation. They don't have the tyranny of today to deal with customers and emergencies and other—meetings around this building, so they are a team who is entirely focused on innovation. They're colocated in a facility away from here to remove them from the distractions of day-to-day activity. They're in one large room. There are no walls or no cubicles. One of the things that I think is a learning from being in that environment is a very intense level of accountability. By that I mean we have meetings today and we all leave saying, each one of us is going to go do something and we get back together . . . We agree what we're going to do. We go sit back in our chairs and we get working on it, and when we get back together, I have absolute accountability to deliver what I said I was going to deliver.

Finally, the D-3 is charged with determining which among the myriad opportunities within and across each platform are presented to the innovation portfolio board. She draws on her familiarity with the portfolio of opportunities to identify and execute cross-domain synergies. She evaluates which platforms, or combinations thereof, are worth pursuing and which should be fast-tracked to the lines of business or shut down completely. "Knowing when to say stop," as one of our D-2s told us, and advocating for those with promise is a key part of the D-3's responsibility.

While not the sole decision maker, the D-3 has insight into the growing (or shriveling) technological promise, the availability of potential partners, and the robustness of the opportunity space in each domain. This also means he advocates for a platform rather than remaining neutral. Again, knowing when to say stop and advocating for those with promise is a key part of the D-3's job.

As to the second set of responsibilities, the director of discovery plays an important role in constantly negotiating the integration of the innovation function and the mainstream organization. He supports the chief innovation officer in his efforts to champion the need for sustained investment in strategic innovation by describing promising opportunities and progress made within each domain area and instilling excitement about future growth prospects. He interacts with business unit and corporate leaders to gain their support for or to reshape emerging opportunities as his discovery teams uncover new potential directions for each platform. If there are ways to leverage some of the opportunities quickly, he alerts the appropriate business leader, but also considers with them whether quick commercialization of an obvious low-hanging-fruit opportunity is strategically the best course of action for the company.

Tasks and Activities

The director of discovery communicates the company's strategic intent inward to her platform leaders, and keeps them in check. The market may be prompting one course of action or another, but those must align with the company's ability and willingness to deliver. Domain leaders may find every avenue exciting, and continue to encourage their teams to explore them all, but at some point they may become too far removed from the company's intent and need to be reminded. Worse yet, D-3s who fail to push upward for an articulation of strategic intent do not provide adequate guideposts for their teams. We saw this at several of our companies.

In one, the discovery personnel believed that every idea they had was of immense value. Most had been highly rewarded for patentable ideas, many of which had no commercial value. They'd become the prima donnas we mentioned earlier. Unfortunately, the director of discovery failed to ascertain any input from senior leaders on selected strategic domain arenas of investment for the future, leaving the portfolio evaluation board to assess each project on its own merit. The discovery team members rebelled, since most projects were rejected as being too small, and the director was eventually fired from the role. Had she instead pressed her leadership to engage in conversations about the future direction of the company and investments in domains of strategic intent, she could have guided the discovery talent within those boundaries. At present, the innovation function in that company has been completely dismantled.

In another case, one of the Opportunity Generators complained about the lack of leadership this way:

I've been somewhat vocal with (my boss) about it, but I don't think there's much strategic direction about where the company wants to go, and so because of that, our new business portfolio is really scattered . . . We have a very loose model of how the innovation team chooses projects.

Beyond setting guideposts for business concepts and platforms, the director of discovery prompts D-2 Opportunity Domain Leaders to be thorough in clarifying the domain's potential directions, by exploring beyond technologies and markets. The strategic, organizational, and business model options that confront a potentially breakthrough new business may be more threatening to the company than the enormous technical and market challenges it faces. Moving from a purchase to a lease model, or from a product delivery to a service model, or from large capital expenditures to a high volume of transactions are all characteristic business model changes associated with the digital economy that is pervading every industry. These changes threaten organizational infrastructure and people's jobs, as wholly different skill sets are required for the two scenarios. While most of these experiments occur in Incubation, the discovery director helps seed the conversation at the senior levels of the company, as the domain leaders begin to suggest these opportunities with their peers within the company's lines of business.

Michael Idelchik, the vice president of the Advanced Technology Programs at GE spends a tremendous amount of time in conversations with senior leaders, talking with the BU presidents, about strategies for leveraging each of the advanced technology platforms with the most clearly aligned business unit. Before any products are identified, or business models are considered, but when promising opportunities begin to reveal themselves, these discussions are happening . . . at very senior levels.

The person fulfilling this role engages in and stimulates intellectually challenging, strategic conversations with discovery personnel at both the project and platform levels to learn from their explorations and to describe imaginative opportunities. From that understanding, he helps develop a vision of the future that feeds the company's innovation strategy.

Together with the chief innovation officer, the D-3 must push for the senior leader conversations and meetings that focus on the far future. If left to their own devices, corporate executives typically attend to nearer-term problems.[2] But the discovery team cannot be successful without a commonly held view of the company's future direction, where strategic innovation is needed.

The director of discovery's involvement in those conversations is not to simply listen. These meetings require research, preparation and thought. Part of his role is to educate the leadership team about the unexpected opportunity spaces and weak signals that are emerging in the technology community, the company's discovery activities, and elsewhere. So he raises new emerging opportunities that had not been considered, as they arise in the natural course of the exploratory work that is happening within the discovery teams. In that way he may advocate for a new domain of strategic intent to be identified as a focus of investment for the company. He works with senior leadership to develop and revisit the company's strategic intent (i.e., the company's ten-year-plus agenda) with respect to innovation on a somewhat regular basis.

Finally, the discovery leader coordinates with the director of incubation to ensure the portfolio of innovation opportunities is healthy and balanced across the company's domains of interest. Monitoring the churn rate of discovery opportunities will be key to measuring the quality of the ideas provided by the discovery personnel. Additionally, this person represents the company externally on matters of innovation policy. She may be involved with influencing governmental policy regarding industrial funding of exploratory research and other aspects of building and enriching the innovation infrastructure of the company's key economies in which it operates.

D-3's *metrics* flow from this long description of responsibilities and tasks. A compelling, inspiring set of strategic intent domains that have been shaped and influenced by the discovery leader's strong understanding of science and technology trends and what their combinations will enable is one. A motivated discovery team who is working to explore those areas that the company has outlined as its ambitions for breakthrough new businesses of the future, is a second. A flow of potentially game-changing new business concepts that the chief innovation officer and innovation portfolio board finds believable is a third. Finally, a strong understanding throughout the company of the importance of scoping imaginative new business opportunities and excellent partnerships with R&D and senior leaders is also an important indicator of the D-3's performance.

Selecting your Discovery Leader

Directors of discovery should comprise a brilliant combination of technical minds and business acumen. Unfortunately, in our observation, that combination is the rare case. Perhaps because this role is so informal, and not actually recognized by many organizations, it's primarily staffed through volunteerism. In fact, it's often this role that initiates the formation of a strategic innovation group in the first place. They're often R&D directors who want to see their companies reach farther, be more innovative, and leverage the reservoir of great internal R&D talent for the world's benefit. So, many of them are very well networked inside the company and extremely well respected, but they don't have a strategic business bone in their bodies. Many of them are quite enterprising, great problem solvers, and extremely personable, charismatic leaders. But they need more to successfully carry this role.

Beyond being great technical problem solvers, D-3s need to understand the new business creation process from beginning to end. They must speak in business/strategy language, in addition to their technically visionary skills. Some sort of new business creation experience helps.

One of the D-3s we studied was initially handling the D-3 *and* I-3 roles. In fact, we've seen many leaders in this situation. While he did not make progress in incubation, and was eventually succeeded in that role by another person, he claims that the exposure to incubation caused him to lead discovery differently from the way a typical R&D director would. He indicated to us that, as a result of that experience, he does the following:

- Makes sure the R&D and discovery business people are all educated regarding the language and frameworks of breakthrough innovation.
- Thinks more strategically about the possible directions a project/business opportunity could take, and how it ties to the company's future.
- Ensures that experimentation with new business platforms is happening, rather than claiming a specific direction and business model for each new platform.
- Requires the use of learning based project management tools as opposed to tools that prioritize monitoring and controlling.
- Knows how to help his people design technical, market, and organizational strategy experiments that can be executed as quickly and efficiently as possible.
- Motivate his team better than he could prior to his incubation experience, by communicating the purpose of the strategic innovation platforms and their fit with the company's overall strategy better.
- Remains involved in coaching the project teams because he recognizes the strategic implications of their choices.

Wow . . . that's progress!

DISCOVERY'S ROLE IN STRATEGIC INNOVATION

Without the creative, disciplined, systems thinking people, the ideas that bubble around in companies are random, and may rise to the attention of leadership through happenstance. Discovery is necessary to flesh out new business possibilities before we start to invest too heavily. To do this well, companies need specific types of people on the job. The skills and attitudes common to all levels of discovery personnel include a willingness to try many approaches, tolerate failures and an ability to endure rejection when an opportunity one favors is not selected. There is a high need for people with the ability to restart and look at problems in many different ways. A lack of bias is important. Let the evidence speak for itself, but the Opportunity Generator must know how to find the evidence, the Opportunity Domain Leader must know how to stitch it together into an opportunity landscape, and the discovery portfolio leader must be able to articulate the opportunities across the portfolio in a manner that compels senior leaders to realize they cannot afford to ignore them.

Discovery is the beginning. Incubation is the long road. The relationship between the two is critical so that the portfolio constantly renews itself as incubation experiments result in the need for renewed attempts and a continuous flow of business concepts, generated in the discovery portfolio to fuel the pipeline of potential new platforms of business . . . potential breakthroughs. Discovery personnel are a special breed. In Chapter 6 we learn of another group of important contributors to the innovation function: incubation experts.

Incubation is like a business laboratory where technology, market, and strategic considerations coalesce. It is the part of the innovation function that houses the company's ability to experiment. The experiments, though, are business experiments. The objective of incubation is to nurture the portfolio of opportunities identified in discovery, which have uncertain outcomes but immense possibilities, and to test their potential for helping the firm realize its strategic intent, or to stretch the firm into new domains not yet considered. Many opportunities generated in discovery may look promising, but as the experiments take place in incubation, most of them will wither. Those that blossom may do so in unexpected directions that require reconsideration since they may veer off course from the firm's strategic intent. Company leaders must make allowances for failures but hold expectations for continued pursuit of new frontiers as they evaluate the incubation portfolio. A healthy incubation function raises strategic conversations about choices the firm must make for growth into frontiers that do not currently exist.

Incubation is the most underdeveloped of the three competencies needed for a healthy strategic innovation function. It is the place where difficult decisions and smart actions about technology, market, and business strategy truly meet, in a fog of ambiguity and among markets that may not yet exist. People with incubation expertise are rare birds in large company settings. Given all of this, companies don't know how to value the contributions of incubation professionals.

Chapter 6 is designed to help. In this chapter we introduce you to some of the people we've met who work in incubation. We describe the roles within the incubation function and provide some insights surrounding the skills, aptitudes, and experiences of these uniquely talented people. Readers can assess the extent to which they may be current or aspiring incubation experts themselves, or be better prepared to build and improve the incubation capability in their companies. To start us off, we'd like to introduce you to a couple of the New Business Platform Leaders we encountered and show you the challenges of managing incubation through their experiences.

FAIL FAST, FAIL OFTEN, HAVE A BACKUP:
LESSONS FROM PEPSICO

When Indra Nooyi stepped into the CEO role at PepsiCo in 2006, she was determined to transform it from a company known for sugary drinks and salty snacks to one that provided nutritional benefits in its products . . . a Herculean task.

As CEO, Nooyi made her strategic intent explicit. She reclassified PepsiCo's products into three categories: "fun for you" (such as potato chips and regular soda), "better for you" (diet or low-fat versions of snacks and sodas), and "good for you" (items such as oatmeal). She moved corporate spending away from junk foods and into the healthier alternatives, with the aim of improving the nutritional content of even the "fun" offerings.[1] The company had been acquiring healthy brands, such as Tropicana and Quaker Oats (including Gatorade), but as CEO, Nooyi wanted an internal capability to develop and commercialize healthy snacks.

To achieve that transformation, she had to build an infrastructure for innovation and develop the necessary talent pool. One of her first moves as CEO was to hire Mehmood Khan as chief scientific officer in late 2007 and double R&D spending. Mehmood's job was to build a corporate R&D group composed of nutritionists and other life sciences experts. Previous to joining PepsiCo, Mehmood had been president of global R&D at

Takeda Pharmaceuticals, where he helped commercialize a number of new products. He had also been a faculty member at the Mayo Medical School in Rochester, Minnesota, so he knew his stuff, at least from a technical point of view. In 2011 he was also appointed CEO of the Global Nutrition Group, a new business unit that housed the "good for you" brands and a new ventures division that was one of the various vehicles PepsiCo implemented to incubate and commercialize their game changers.

It wasn't long before Mehmood sought out Dondeena Bradley. Dondeena had joined PepsiCo just a few months earlier after having been recruiting for more than a year. She decided to leave her role in strategic planning for Johnson & Johnson's McNeil Nutritionals group and join PepsiCo in mid-2007 as vice president, global nutrition R&D. "I really believed in what they were doing in terms of top down and bottom up change," she told us. She spent her first couple of years working with Mehmood to redesign the global R&D organization, and in July 2010 she assumed the role of vice president of nutrition ventures, with the purpose of helping incubate some of the promising research coming through R&D as well as acquiring other opportunities. The nutrition ventures group was one of several innovation models that PepsiCo was experimenting with to accelerate its portfolio transformation goals, and it was to be focused on building a business platform targeted toward women's nutritional needs. In our lexicon, Dondeena is an I-2, New Business Platform Leader.

Dondeena's career was driven by one overarching passion: creating nutritionally rich, healthy foods. She held a PhD in food science and had fifteen years of experience in R&D, business development, and marketing strategy for several large companies, including J&J McNeil Nutritionals, Campbell's, M&M Mars, and Stepan Company. "I've always been at this intersection of health and nutrition, and making it actionable. That has really driven me to take on a lot of different types of roles, so I could ultimately be in the role that I am in now, which I absolutely love."

Dondeena had a talent for translating the science into something that marketers could talk about every day. She found herself getting pulled into strategic projects early in her career because she "was the scientist that people felt that they could work with." She grew to recognize this as a unique skill among the scientific community in which she operated. She was able to simplify the message in order to communicate the value of healthy foods. She honed that skill during the several years that she had a consulting business to help R&D groups in client companies develop strategic marketing plans for their research investments. She took some business courses in finance and marketing along the way to learn the principles more formally and became the first R&D Scientist at J&J to move into marketing, launch a new brand, and hold profit-and-loss responsibility. That experience provided her with an appreciation for the commercialization process, including the uncertainties and urgencies associated with it.

When Mehmood asked Dondeena to start the ventures group, she and her team were tasked with pioneering a new category of healthy food products targeted to women that provided solutions to women's issues that did not yet exist in the market . . . a real breakthrough opportunity for PepsiCo.[2] Dondeena loved the role, and extolled her boss's vision and sensitivity to the need to provide the ventures infrastructure. "I'm like a floating island between long-term research and the Global Nutrition Group," she told us. She did not report to the Global Nutrition Group, however, because of their profit-and-loss responsibility and shorter development cycles than organic new business creation requires. She reported directly to Mehmood in his capacity as chief scientific officer and expressed appreciation of the runway the team was given to prove the value proposition. "You've got to really make sure that the intent of that science actually works out in a real relevant setting with the consumer. You don't have time to do that with brands."

Having led a potential but doomed game changer (a veggie-based snack product) in one of the business units earlier in her tenure at PepsiCo, Dondeena appreciated the protection and clear mandate that the ventures group was given. She told us that Mehmood understood the iterative nature of incubation, as well as the need to make some of those business experiments very visible and others not so visible. She also appreciated the independence she was given to formulate her own business model and organizational structure as the business platform's proof of concept was tested. While she could not divulge much about the specific new business, Dondeena told us she'd been funded to develop a brand name, had provisional patents in place, and had the go-ahead to use a distribution channel that, at the time, was foreign to the company. "We've created a venture inside the company because we want to control the direction of it, and leverage what we learn onto other brands," she explained.

When asked to describe her team (those we'd consider I-1s, or New Business Creation Specialists in our matrix), Dondeena depicted them as "lean and mean." She hired three full-time team members, all from outside the company, who had expertise in areas that she and the company lacked. One had worked on a breakthrough innovation in another consumer products health food company and had excellent new business creation, market experimentation, and project management expertise. She came in at the senior director level. The second was a social media expert, and the third was Dondeena's assistant, whom she called "the glue" for the project, preparing statements of work for external contractors, managing the travel schedule, and maintaining communications on the team. She hired each as a contract employee for six months first, to make sure they'd established their names within the company and could find another job should the project fail. The rest of her budget was used to hire external consultants (industrial designers, chemical formulators, and product developers), since it was not yet clear that the new business platform would succeed. Finally, she relied on internal PepsiCo staff expertise for long-term exploratory research, technology scouting, legal help, and procurement support. The use of internal experts helped her socialize the project, and ensured that internal decision makers knew about its progress. Dondeena checked in regularly with Mehmood, and she updated CEO Nooyi as the project progressed. She made sure to "socialize it enough" since, if the new business began to gain traction in the marketplace, it could become an entirely new growth platform for the company.

Ultimately we learned that the new business platform did not succeed, although many of its foundational elements were taken up in other PepsiCo product ventures. This is not unusual given the unknown market size and dynamics, the pursuit of technical and scientific challenges that may not be solvable within the desired cost constraints, and organizational strategies that may be shifting. But the problem in this case, as with many others we've seen, is what happened to the people. Rather than leveraging her learning into the next venture at PepsiCo, Dondeena left the company.

Professionally she did well: as of this writing she serves as the global head of innovation at Weight Watchers International. PepsiCo, meanwhile, parlayed the learnings from the ventures group into other innovation activities, including a venturing and incubation unit that has since been created as part of its North America nutrition business.

As they continue to evolve their capability, PepsiCo and many other companies are recognizing the need for a portfolio approach to strategic innovation that allows them to repurpose innovation talent on to other potential emerging business opportunities as any specific initiative's promise begins to dim. Retaining such talent is a priority concern for companies that have experimented with different models to execute Strategic Innovation.

STAFFING A NEW BUSINESS PLATFORM AT GRUNDFOS

Like Dondeena, Fei Chen, a new business program director for Grundfos's Rethink Decentralized Water Treatment (RDWT) platform, provides a common story of the challenges associated with incubation . . . one of managing a team of people who need a lot of guidance while also trying to demonstrate steady progress to senior leaders.

Fei earned her PhD in chemistry and began her career as a scientist at the National Environmental Research Institute, affiliated with Aarhus University in Denmark. After five years she moved to a medical devices firm in Denmark, working in new product development. She left to join a start-up that provided online analysis of milk samples to dairy farmers. There she developed the working prototypes, the advising system for farmers, and built the team. After nearly four years Fei moved to a larger company in the same industry, this time in China, as a general manager. Personal reasons brought her back to Denmark two years later, this time as senior manager of new business development for an enzyme producer. Before two years was up she was pirated back to the medical devices company, this time with the responsibility for building a technology scouting capability for the company. Soon after, Grundfos sought her out to lead the RDWT incubation effort. In our lexicon of innovation roles, Fei held an I-2 position, New Business Platform Leader, when we met up with her.

She spent the first six months at Grundfos developing a strategy for the new business platform, and soliciting buy-in from senior leadership

and the company's executive committee about the direction she wanted
to take. She recruited people onto her team, whose total size was about
twelve at the time we met with her. She structured it to include four people
who'd explore new technology ideas within the platform, and four who
could run the incubation learning experiments. In addition she had one
"coach" to help guide the learning experiments, one person in charge of
finding and managing strategic partnerships, one in charge of acquisitions,
and one assistant.

Fei learned a great deal from many of her early hiring decisions. Of
those she selected to conduct learning experiments, only one had experience in doing so. The others had great potential but ultimately she found
them to be "too academic." They were excellent scientists and/or consultants but were not execution oriented. They were uncomfortable making
decisions in the face of little information. In relaying her experiences to us
she was mimicking the difficulties of dealing with "the fog of incubation"
we noted at the outset of this chapter. The projects that she expected her
team to take on were "complicated," she told us. She described a big part
of her role as having to motivate her team, and to be both systematic and
entrepreneurial.

In recounting her initial organizational design, Fei realized a different
structure might aid in achieving the execution she desired. She had too
many direct reports and spent too much time developing and mentoring
them. She had no time to "think strategically, manage the internal stakeholders, or coach the incubation experiments." Taking a self-critical view
(perhaps unfairly), Fei felt she had become the bottleneck for the program's
progress. She was unable to shift the team quickly enough, and progress
on the platform was too slow. Ultimately, Fei left the company to become
the vice president of innovation at another organization of similar size in
a different industry. She would apply her lessons learned at Grundfos to
her new situation. Unfortunately, the business platform was shut down ...
too much money spent for not enough progress.

Both Dondeena's and Fei's stories provide direction for those of us trying to manage and build success through the fog of incubation. Innovation
of all kinds is beset with failure; it is inevitable. Fei felt this and so did
her Grundfos colleagues. Hers is a tale about hiring and design. Talented

people abound in the innovation space, but not everyone fits every role. From Fei we learned about the need for folks who are both technically competent but execution oriented and comfortable with ambiguity so they don't need to check every detail with their boss. Experience clearly helps in incubation. We also see how a flat organization can create bottlenecks . . . there is a need for hierarchy in innovation as a new business platform evolves. Finally, the need to pace the learning experiments within an emerging business platform to match the ability of the platform leader to absorb them, understand their implications for the emerging business, and chart the path forward given the new information is evident in her story.

PepsiCo truly provides a proxy for the incubation structure we saw throughout our research. Dondeena's and PepsiCo's story is one of many that, taken together weave a pattern of the roles and responsibilities for incubation. Level-one new business project leaders and participants work away at investigating applications of the new business platform opportunities that D-2 personnel develop. The I-2 oversees those experiments and charts the strategy for an entirely new emerging business platform, both within the market and within the firm. I-3, the head of incubation, ensures that each emerging business platform is making progress and, if not, determines what to do with it. But this only works if we're able to re-purpose people onto new projects and new business platforms as they cycle off those they're testing and finding lack the originally expected potential. There are so many opportunities that appear exciting at the outset that, on their own, don't measure up. The people working on those opportunities should not be punished when their work demonstrates that the company should not continue to pursue them. They've learned how to engage in incubation, and companies need to find ways to deploy them on the next possibility. Experience that is earned in this manner is highly valuable.

As we saw in all of our interactions, incubation is the part of strategic innovation where companies are the most vulnerable and most underdeveloped. This is a bit ironic since it's the incubation capability that mitigates risk, incorporates learning, enlarges opportunities, confirms strategic commitment, and actualizes business models. Only by going through the fog of incubation can a potential new business platform's growth potential become clearer. In the remainder of this chapter, we dig into the details of each of the roles of incubation, all of which are crucial if a company expects strategic innovation outcomes. We begin at the project level of incubation.

I-1: NEW BUSINESS CREATION SPECIALISTS

The I-1's job is to take an identified opportunity from the discovery portfolio and test it from every angle of the opportunity landscape to decipher whether and how it may contribute to a significant new business platform for the company. Level-one incubation projects may require a rather lengthy period of time given the sea of unknowns and working assumptions that must be tested. The output of the level-one incubator's work will be either a complete business proposal, a recommendation to abandon the opportunity, or a suggestion to fast-track opportunities that ultimately appear to be incremental innovations to the company's Stage-Gate® process for development and launch. The hypothesis testing for incubating opportunities is accomplished through a lengthy process of clarifying a host of technical, market, resource, and organizational uncertainties to arrive at an economically justifiable and competitively exciting business model.[3]

Responsibilities

We have seen I-1's responsibilities allocated in two different ways. Some support all the I-1 projects in the portfolio on an as-needed basis, by providing a specific expertise. Others are dedicated to a project and operate as part of the "core team" that nurtures the project through incubation.

As exemplars of the first type of responsibility, at John Deere, DSM, and Moen we encountered dedicated market analyst/desk researchers who staffed multiple projects as needed, identifying (a) potential codevelopment partners with specific types of expertise, (b) start-ups with a needed technology, (c) first customers, (d) sources of supply and costs of materials, or (e) optimal locations for a first physical plant. Once that groundwork was completed, the I-1 core project team members then visited those companies to vet them more carefully and arrange for next steps.

As an example, the leader of the Bio-Based Products and Services EBA (Emerging Business Area), a new business in DSM's portfolio, wanted to know where to build the first factory for a certain application. To start the search, several researchers found information on a number of unanswered questions across several locations they might consider, including the availability and cost of needed chemicals and raw materials, trade barriers, governmental restrictions, strength of the local competition, likelihood of customers to switch, and a whole host of additional information the team would need before they could even start talking to people if they wanted to form a partnership for manufacturing in a region.

New Business Creation Specialists may also work in teams, each of which is led by a new business project manager, an I-1 role itself. At Corning, for example, multiple teams of I-1s on the new business platform that ultimately produced Corning® Gorilla® Glass were each composed of a technology commercialization specialist, a sales and marketing person, and an R&D person. Each of those teams was assigned a different market segment or field of use in which to test out the value proposition and business model options. Another company identified level-one project managers who all assembled their own teams with the relevant skills to tackle a part of the long list of unknowns as designated by the I-2 New Business Platform Leader. One was working on a lightweight shipping container that had the potential to change the dynamics of long-haul transportation. To experiment with different materials, an I-1 project manager assembled a team of people from R&D, manufacturing, marketing and sales, and regulatory analysts so that the proposed materials for the new containers could be tested in the market, in the factory, and in the regulatory environment as well.

I-1 new business project leaders are responsible for guiding the team through the cloud of uncertainty. They articulate those technology, marketing, resource, and organizational uncertainties, prioritize them, and take the actions needed to test them out. Traditional project management tools, such as Gantt charts, don't apply when the resolution of one uncertainty guides the next set of actions. Rather, a learning-based project management approach is needed, and a priori planning just isn't relevant. One of the most experienced I-1s we encountered illustrated how different managing an incubation team is from other project management experiences:

Well, you can easily recognize the people who will fit. The people who have that skill, they love me as a boss, but the people who don't have those skills, they hate me as a boss. They think I am a lousy boss because I don't help them enough and I ask questions that are too complicated. I explain it as they need a kind of fence, so I create that fence, and then I say, "OK, guys, you are going to do some business development within that fence." The people who don't like me as a boss need more of a fence. And so they think that I don't create an environment for them to do their jobs. And then they get frustrated—I don't need a fence myself. I can work without a fence. I create my own fence and then say, I'm going to work here. And if I want to move the fence, I move the fence. And people who also have that capability, they are very happy with me as a boss. But other people feel very insecure if they are in a position without fences.

The New Business Creation Specialist needs to be empowered to make decisions to change a team's direction or "move the fence" as they learn from the results of their experiments. The normal hierarchical decision processes used in companies is too slow to be effective in the experimentation environment of incubation. Figuring out what hypotheses to test, experiments to conduct, how to execute them, and then doing so are the I-1's key concerns. Responsibility for interpreting the results is shared more broadly with the New Business Platform Leader and, at times, a broader set of strategic coaches.

Tasks/Activities
To accomplish those responsibilities, I-1s spend their time carefully designing experiments to test the most critical assumptions, and then executing them as efficiently as possible. They make sure they're asking the right questions and not getting too narrow a perspective. The experiments must be designed to provide insights to the specific questions posed. Ambiguity in the question or the experiment's design amplifies the normal "fog" of strategic innovation. Evidence is their guidepost, nothing else. We can give you a perspective of how an I-1 spends his time by picking up on the story of the lightweight shipping container project we mentioned earlier. The excerpt that follows is from the I-1 who led the project:

We had a joint development agreement with this logistics company to develop a lightweight container, and we came to the conclusion that we could not do this with the standard materials. We have to work on finding new materials. OK.

So we need to develop materials, but now also we have no crew and no idea, so we needed an external company, so it becomes a whole new world to discover. And also, all the business models can be different. The business model on these lightweight containers can be different than that of containers made from other materials. And originally we were talking only with this one joint development agreement partner, so most information on the model we got from them. But what is good for them might not be completely valid for the whole market. So our exposure was far too limited.

So I proposed to go the industrial trade show with our developer. At that time, we were discussing a joint venture partnership, and my boss asked me two months before we were scheduled to go to the trade show whether or not we could withdraw from it. And I told him, well, you know, if there is one time we have to go it is right now. We need new partners, we need new input. We need a response from the market. We have to do it. And now everybody is very happy that we did it, and now with a lot of new contacts, we got reconfirmation of the market. Our CEO and the chairman of the supervisory board are going to visit with one of the biggest shipping companies in the market to discuss these containers.

My boss asked me not to go to the trade show because he was not so sure that we could make this project a success. You know, this relationship with the joint development partner is still very difficult. Our chief innovation officer is not sure about it, and I am also not that sure. They did a wonderful job for us. I think they were an excellent partner in the joint development, but they are not a very good partner in the commercialization. And that is, indeed, producing a lot of tension.

To this I-1, and others like him, everything is an assumption to be questioned, to form a hypothesis about, and to seek evidence that will help test it. He is always questioning, always monitoring the technical, market, resource, and organizational/strategic uncertainties. Everything is a hypothesis to be disconfirmed.

Two important principles guide their experiments. I-1s test the most critical uncertainties first! They learn to prioritize experiments and attend first to those that, if not confirmed, could kill the project. Most project leaders gravitate toward proving out the technology and investigating market issues. They work within a given set of resource constraints without questioning them, and typically don't consider organizational structure or strategy challenges at all. But we find that, in fact, the most critical assumptions that cause strategic innovation projects to fail are related to organizational commitment and resource issues. Of course, these are the least comfortable for most project managers to tackle, since they are so highly political.

The second principle is that the experiments should be designed to maximize the learning gained per dollar invested. This "good enough" principle recognizes that in a world of ambiguity, precision of an experiment's results may be less important than the directional cue they provide. "I ask a lot of stupid questions," one New Business Creation Specialist told us, "but we focus on the showstoppers." Another elaborated by contrasting the "good enough" approach with the one that's traditionally used:

I think one of the challenges you have with incubating businesses within a large company is inherent biases that come from the divisions. So, for example, our largest division is all about selling one or two products to a bunch of different customers. You want it standardized; you want to tighten specifications. I mean, it's just a well-run machine. You want to narrow in on things. Here, we don't know, early on, what the specification is. It turns out the specifications are much more loose, which means, I don't want a really high quality product, I just want a product that's good enough in order to get meaningful feedback. That goes very much counter to what's engrained in people in the divisions. Rather than what I call total quality, just give me something that works and it's cheap, for now.

I-1s may conduct initial analytical modeling to consider value propositions of possible opportunities, and to determine parameters that the opportunity would have to meet in order to be perceived as offering significant value to the marketplace. Then they seek out the relevant people to talk with to test out their ideas of how this opportunity could deliver that value. Getting meetings with the right people is more important than getting a lot of meetings. Through these interactions, I-1s find the path of least resistance in the market, meaning segments or fields of use where the value proposition is the most clearly apparent. It doesn't matter if that application market is small, so long as customers or partners perceive game-changing levels of benefit. Markets grow and fields of use multiply as the market comes to understand the innovation. So I-1s iterate, test, moderate, test, until they're convinced that they've got a real value proposition and have a proposal for how it can play out in the market . . . or not.

Performance Metrics

Given the complexity of what they're doing and the ambiguous outcomes likely to result, the way our companies evaluated I-1s was based on just a few metrics. Developing and communicating nonintuitive learning and insights about potential business models and directions for the opportunity was most important.

Executing their experiments in a disciplined, timely manner, with a sense of urgency and judgment about focusing on the most critical uncertainties first and executing via the "good enough" principle was also a crucial evaluation criterion. Overengineered experiments are viewed as wastes of time. Using a learning prototype, or a "klugey" prototype to get market reaction is more important than refining the prototype for the look and feel of it. Disciplined experimentation requires clever thought and focused action.

Finally was their ability to "communicate what they are actually doing, including failure," we were told. Masking the results of experiments whose outcomes were not positive in order to appear successful was not tolerated by I-2 New Business Platform Leaders. In several companies, leaders depended on the I-1s to tell them when a project should be closed down. That meant, of course, that the I-1 felt secure enough to do so, and didn't fear the pink slip that we've seen so many receive when their project was defunded. We return to this topic when we share practices and our thoughts for innovation personnel development and retention mechanisms in Chapter 9.

Selection Criteria

We label I-1s *New Business Creation Specialists* for a reason. They should have a technical background or acumen to be able to understand the technical domains of interest and exercise adequate judgment during the incubation process. However, we find that many I-1s did not spend a lot of time as technical specialists. Beyond technical skills, successful I-1s need business savvy to address the strategic and business model issues that arise as their projects evolve.

Personal Characteristics

I-1s are described as having a "start-up mentality," but in fact are greatly motivated by the idea of working in a large company because it allows them to shoot for "big bets" that most start-ups do not have the resources or networks to consider. One I-2 described why his team is motivated by the role:

The career is challenging and interesting because it's about taking something off of a blank sheet of paper and making it happen. The people we've recruited . . . they see that and they also see the scale and scope of an organization like ours as giving them an opportunity to make it happen . . . and not like a little start up where it might go nowhere. I'm a start-up within an organization, which gives it a lot of possibility of going somewhere.

The most prominent characteristic of I-1s is their willingness to admit that there is a lot they don't know and their drive to seek the truth through evidence. One I-1 told us, "My job is to get an answer, even if it's no, and be resilient and move on." Another respondent who works with I-1s told us, "They don't need a recipe to start working. They don't wait for clarification . . . they act to bring clarity."

While they are on the hunt for evidence to reinforce or disconfirm their hypotheses, I-1s don't let ambiguity get in the way of progress. They're described as unafraid to make decisions in the face of little information, and are mature enough to deal with the fact that "stuff doesn't always work." They are comfortable changing direction rapidly as new information becomes available. They are goal-oriented learners and "like being the driver."

In addition, I-1s are viewed as diplomatic. They make sure to maintain their legitimacy in the company, and they work to clarify the strategic relevancy of a project they're working on and of the incubation group itself. They're persistent without burning bridges and know when to stop pushing boundaries, although on occasion they may need a little extra coaching to help them navigate some of the organizational challenges they tend to encounter.

Skills

Whereas D-1 personnel are excellent *systems thinkers*, I-1s are *integrative thinkers*. Systems thinkers can visualize the big picture of the future new business platform and the potential ways in which it could unfold, including the complexities of all of its markets. *Integrative thinkers*, by comparison, synthesize new information from each experiment into the current picture and draw the implications for their project's next steps. They are able to let go of their most recent view of the business opportunity if new information comes in that debunks it. Rather than committing to one vision and sticking with it, I-1s pivot as needed, constantly assessing its fit with the larger new business platform of which their project is a part. One I-1 described it this way:

You have to have a pretty broad mind. I can live on two levels. I can live in the detail level, so I can focus and zoom in and really nail down some of the steps. But I can also easily step out and look at what I see and see if it matches with what I want to achieve.

I-1s must be able to identify latent assumptions—those that we believe to be true on the basis of folklore rather than evidence. That means they need to question conventional wisdom at all times and in all contexts and recognize that, oftentimes, what has been accepted as fact are actually strongly held beliefs. Their logical, unbiased thought process helps them decide which of the long list of uncertainties are the most threatening, and tackle those first even if the experiments needed to test them are not as obvious or comfortable.

They are creative problem solvers, finding the easiest and most practical way to test each assumption, using the "good enough" principle. At the same time they need to critically assess the credibility of the information they're getting, sorting out the wheat from the chaff. Their persistence helps them endure the long and winding road of incubation, and they must be resistant to closure so they can continue to generate and investigate options as various aspects of the value proposition don't prove out and new ones appear.

Like D-1s, I-1s must have a high degree of interpersonal skill, since they develop new networks for each project. They should enjoy contacting people they may not already know, including potential partners, customers, and professional organizations. Whereas D-1s are excellent at deep listening and gaining information from these organizations, I-1s must be able to go a step further and persuade potential partners to engage in codevelopment arrangements, extended use trials of a prototype, or other experiments that will test out the value proposition and other hypotheses.

Finally, I-1s must be capable of managing and using external experts well, since domain-specific knowledge may not be available in the company or on the team. In several cases we saw that as a project evolved, more than half the team was composed of external consultants.

Incubation project team *leaders* require a few additional skills beyond those of the I-1 team member. They must be able to pick up on the discovery team's opportunity landscape and conduct a "landscape assessment," meaning a scoping exercise that outlines all the possible applications within the opportunity space and determining where to begin to test within it. This assessment guides the sequencing of application areas the team explores, at least at the beginning. Of course, in incubation, plans change at a moment's notice. But having the catalog of fields of use and a plan to address them ensures they are thorough and strategic in their pursuit of understanding the opportunity and developing a strategy for the new business. During this time, I-1 project leaders must be able to keep the team motivated while maintaining a common understanding of the redirection as course corrections inevitably arise.

As part of the landscape assessment, incubation project leaders can discern when the team is focused too narrowly, or is too dependent on a single source for their information. As the example of the lightweight freight container project showed, I-1 leaders challenge their teams to open up the problem by questioning assumptions and the sources of data that the team uses to draw conclusions. Striking the right balance between broadening and focusing the problem is a critical I-1 skill set. As one of them told us, "I try to create new directions for the project, because in this kind of project, you never know if you are on a dead end street or not because you don't know what is around the next corner."

Critical Experiences

Whereas D-1 personnel come from a wide variety of experience bases, there is a more predictable pattern for New Business Creation Specialists. They have been involved in starting or growing businesses in the past. Some, though not all, have worked in start-ups or small companies along the way, and a fair number come from entrepreneurial families.

I-1s don't join the company from outside. Most are quite senior in their level and have at least ten years with the company. All the I-1s we've encountered have held positions in other parts of the company, so they understand the culture and political dynamics in which they're operating. They have typically held project management roles in an operating unit and experienced the pressures associated with profit and loss responsibility. But they don't like it. Most have sought out projects "on the fringe," finding bosses who are starting something new and joining those teams. However, the need to maintain credibility in the company forces I-1s to cycle back to traditional roles in between their "fringe" experiences.

A number of companies allow R&D scientists to travel with a project into incubation, and lead it at the I-1 level. No matter how talented these people are in their R&D roles, company leaders tell us it is a mistake to name them as incubation project leaders. One chief innovation officer articulated this perspective and broader thoughts about the need for general business development experience first:

In this role you are sort of a general manager type and that is also why you have to be quite experienced. Traditionally, people tend to put very talented R&D people on it, but in our view that is a mistake. If you have already worked in a running business and you know how that works with customers, with manufacturing, with complaints, with logistics, with SAP, with sending bills, with having working capital and everything that comes with running a business, you know where you are headed. Most of the R&D people have no clue. They are technically capable, they are usually very clever, but they have never even sold a nail polish to anybody or negotiated a deal.

People can learn those skills but then you make so many mistakes before you have it right, it takes too much time. That is one of the reasons why many start-ups never get to the point that they are successful. They burn money like crazy because they do a lot of things wrong.

I-2: NEW BUSINESS PLATFORM LEADER

The New Business Platform Leader is central to our matrix, and shoulders a crucial role in the innovation function. I-2s position the emerging opportunities to be built into robust new businesses that will reinvent the company over time. That means they are frequently in positions of conflict, since companies can be schizophrenic about change. On the one hand, they know it is important. On the other hand, change is hard for most people, and certainly for established organizations. Since the New Business Platform Leader is introducing a change in the organization, he butts up against pockets of resistance on a regular basis.

Responsibilities

I-2s have one overarching responsibility, and that is to explore the potential of a business concept that the discovery group has identified and develop an evidence-based proposal for how it could play out as a new business platform for the company. That means clarifying its strategy, its value proposition, its addressable markets and applications that may or may not yet exist, its business model, the technical solution, and its relevance and connection points to the company based on the experiences of their I-1s. I-2s maintain the big picture of the new business platform for the team. They decide, with input, on the next directions to pursue and pivots to take as the team's learning experiments are conducted and choice points arise.

The New Business Platform Leader's role is strategic. As one told us: "I can't place bets on one thousand things that might not work out. My job is to shape this opportunity as a big strategic program." They must balance the need for a sense of urgency, on the one hand, with the need to fully explore the opportunity landscape, on the other. They begin in a context that requires starting from scratch on almost every issue, and they deal with organizational resistors that are almost always sure to emerge. As one New Business Platform Leader described:

The difference with strategic innovation occurs when you recognize that if this works, it's going to disrupt some other part of your business. And how are you going to manage that, and how are you going to stomach it, and how are you going to make sure that if you're wrong, that you're not putting the company in a bad position? That's when you know the difference between whether you've got an incremental or even a series of incrementals that add up to something big versus something that's really breakthrough. And it's at that point that you need leadership support from the top down, and you need to have a group of people that are getting some special care and feeding.

It's quite a job.

Tasks and Activities

To accomplish these responsibilities, I-2s work a complicated matrix of activities, managing inward (their team and ongoing project experiments), outward (to the relevant business unit and support staff personnel, as well as external partners for needed resources and coordination), and upward to senior leadership to monitor and maintain the emerging business's alignment with the company's strategic intent. They manage with aplomb: challenging with respect, but arbitrating, negotiating, mediating, brokering, collaborating, and influencing as the emerging business begins to take shape. There are many degrees of freedom to choose how a new business model could evolve. As such, an I-2's time and energy is spent on the strategic guidance of his team, and also managing a complex web of relationships to gain buy in and commitment with important influencers as decisions are made.

I-2s guide the design of creative experiments that their team can pursue quickly for effective learning and risk mitigation, and then help interpret the results. An experiment may be a traditional lab test to learn more about the technology's robustness under varying conditions, or it may occur under specific usage conditions. But experiments also include tests of the company's willingness to venture into new business models and partnerships, and those are tested through internal discussions with a number of stakeholders, reviews of potential collaboration agreements, and proposals for commitments of investment. Discussions with possible partners to explore possible business models are other sorts of learning experiments that provide insight into how the market may structure itself as it emerges. Through all this, New Business Platform Leaders ensure that the most critical uncertainties are being addressed, and require teams to pursue the discovery platform's options through multiple experiment paths since it's never clear if an experiment will yield useful information. They work to mitigate the risk of inaccurate interpretation or lack of relevant information as best as they can. As one I-2 described it:

I would say we try to have a different culture about, you know, how I go about contingencies. I always have at least two or three paths to every problem I'm trying to solve because, for us, it's, I've got to deliver something in two years. I don't know how I'm progressing to get there, so I'm buying time. If what I've learned in one path doesn't work, I have a backup. That's really how we operate.

I-2s distinguish their work, and that of their teams, from marketing roles, claiming that new business creation is strategic rather than tactical, and execution oriented rather than planning oriented, as these two I-2s from different companies explained:

We're only focused on understanding articulated and unarticulated customer needs in the context that we can solve them through technology or innovative business models. So we're not doing marketing flyers. We're not worried about websites. It's very much around that early stage of marketing, and understanding needs, or in some cases, creating needs.

My job incorporates operational marketing, meaning execution. I need to make it happen.

As each of the I-1's experiments generates new information, the New Business Platform Leader works with the team to determine their next steps. She encourages them to broaden the opportunity landscape rather than honing in on a relatively small but definable solution too early. In other words, she makes sure they examine all aspects of the opportunity landscape before converging too quickly on one application or one perspective of the business's strategy, since those tend to incrementalize the opportunity. It's a tough challenge, since there is constant pressure to show progress. Yet to achieve an entire new business platform rather than one or a few products, the team must refrain from closing in on one single revenue stream too soon.

In addition to managing their teams of I-1s and overseeing those experiments, the I-2 allocates time to managing other company constituents. Stakeholder engagement is a crucial part of the I-2's role, not only to pave the way for acceptance of the new business into the mainstream organization when it's ready but also to leverage the organization's resources as needed. I-2s engage the business units to either gain their cooperation or to defend against resistors—usually both. They pay homage, constantly, to other types of innovation initiatives and processes in the company, to prevent an "us vs. them" mentality from developing. They work hard to reduce fear on the part of those who'll bear the consequence of the new business' success. I-2s learn to recognize hidden barriers and deal with them explicitly. One told us:

You can't take an idea,—develop it in a central innovation role, throw it over the fence at one of the business units and expect them to say, oh, my God,—we never thought of that before. Usually what the reaction is, is nah, thanks, but no thanks. We're really not interested. There are a zillion different reasons why they come back with that response. So the lesson there we learned was that, when you have something that you want ultimately a business to pick up, you had to get them very involved in the very early stages of the identification of the idea as it morphs into whatever it turns out to be then as a project and a business case that you want to build or put together for a business it actually owns.

Unfortunately, it's not always that easy, as pockets of resistance can pop up from many angles, and no amount of discussion will help. The emerging business will likely threaten the old order, and the I-2 is right in the middle of it. They can't shrink from this part of their responsibility, but it takes incredible political diplomacy and reliance on the commitment to the domains of strategic intent that senior leaders have declared, which the I-2's emerging business platforms are attempting to realize. The temptation to suboptimize the emerging business's scope in order to align it with the company's dominant business model is sometimes overwhelming, and it must be avoided if strategic innovation is the goal.

New Business Platform Leaders also spend time forging relationships with corporate support functions such as purchasing, legal, R&D, and

PR, in order to leverage those assets. I-2s tend to identify specific individuals in the company's purchasing and legal functions, for example, who understand the need to create different protocols for negotiating deals or selecting vendors that are more specific to the new business creation context. While much of this relationship management occurs formally at the I-3 level, it was the I-2s, in our observation, that really worked those relationships and educated their counterparts . . . or suffered the consequences.

Finally, I-2s spend time managing upward, in order to maintain organizational support and fend off resistors. As strategic thinkers, they must constantly consider how the new business that is emerging will contribute to fulfilling the company's strategic intentions, and how the business might be resourced and run given the company's current structure or willingness to change. Constantly checking in with leadership to ensure their continued commitment is important. We have seen I-2s who operated too independently for too long, allowing the business model to unfold in a manner that did not work for the company, and the New Business Platform Leader was left standing on his own. Savvy I-2s make sure that strategic alignment is there, or that there's a plan for achieving it over time. They should have a good sense of what to keep, what to shut down, and what to spin out, and when that decision needs to be made. That doesn't mean they don't advocate for a new business platform that may be veering away from the expected business model, but they know when to raise that issue. One described the importance of having a committed senior leader to help advocate for the changes that emerging businesses may introduce:

I'm a project director. I'm happy to be project director, but I also need a project owner. I've no problem with putting a lot of ownership in the project myself. That is my standard value of operation. I want to do that, but there is a role of the project owner, and he should really want the project. If the project owner doesn't want the project, then what am I doing here? I'm working for our company. Everything I do, I try to create benefits and added value for the end user. And if my owner doesn't recognize that, or my owner has other ideas, then please let me spend my time on other projects.

Ultimately the I-2 manages all of these relationships for one purpose: to allow a promising new business platform to take root, grow within the organization, and become tomorrow's cash cow.

Performance Metrics

The ultimate goal for an I-2 is to generate a working business model for the emergent business, including first revenues, partners, a market entry strategy and follow-on applications, an operating model, and a proposal for the organizational setup within the company. That's if it's a successful experiment. It may not work out, and that result may or may not be associated with the I-2's performance. Technical showstoppers or value proposition glitches pop up, and many times they're just not solvable. The New Business Platform Leader's job is to ensure the experiments are designed to provide maximum learning and are executed well. They need to guide the emerging business development in a way that examines the options efficiently and determines if it warrants significant investment. The answer may be no. Most of the I-2s we have encountered, like Dondeena Bradley at PepsiCo, develop their own metrics together with their bosses, and the metrics depend on the challenges facing the new business platform that year. I-2s are trusted soldiers. They've typically proven themselves in other roles in the company. But they appreciate and need guidance from senior leadership, including the I-3, most importantly, but from the Innovation Council as well, to ensure their emerging business is unfolding in a way that the company can run with it. Those objectives help guide their activities. The most dangerous situation an I-2 can find himself in is when he gets so excited by the business's prospects that he disengages from internal stakeholder relationships, and ends up developing a new business area that the company refuses to fund through acceleration.

Selection Criteria

As far as personal characteristics, I-2s are the quintessential corporate entrepreneurs who take opportunities and build them into business platforms. They're achievement oriented and driven to build. They chart a course in the fog of incubation, and do so with disciplined execution and strategic savvy. In that respect I-2s are a real enigma. As much as people think of intrapreneurs as crazy, wild champions, we find that New Business Platform Leaders are self-disciplined and well organized. As one told us:

Being self-motivated, proactive, and able to structure yourself are key elements in this whole innovation area; otherwise it fails. And that's why we play a very important role in a conversion of an idea to something more. There are always many opportunities, so, the biggest failure risk for an emerging business is to focus on too many things. You have to get things done first before you embark on something else.

Part of their self-discipline is an ability to balance passion with a willingness to walk away. They can escape the stigma of failure, and do so over and over because of their excellent execution skills and history of results. They're passionate about innovation but agnostic about the project. In other words, they don't allow themselves to get too committed to one project to the point of coloring their interpretation of the results of learning experiments. They're brutally honest. Sometimes their honesty points them in a direction of advocating for a project even when others do not see the promise or when the obvious, typical evidence is not yet supporting their recommendations. That spark of intuition and deep understanding drives them through the long course of incubation.

An I-2's honesty is also apparent when they face organizational challenges. They're blunt and bold, and have the moxie to express opinions about how the company is supporting or inadvertently sabotaging the opportunity. They know which battles to fight and when, and become frustrated when they cannot make progress on the organizational front. Those that lose this perspective or don't have an excellent I-3 to help them navigate these political challenges end up taking leaves of absence . . . or just leave. It happens. Frequently.

Even with the long incubation time periods and concomitant frustration about lack of promotion opportunities (which we address in Chapter 9) and organizational challenges, we find that New Business Platform Leaders love their roles. They can become discouraged and demotivated when occupying a role that doesn't involve novelty and upside potential for their companies. One told us:

I guess my strength is, I can take an idea and concept to something that's real and tangible, and I've got good business acumen, but I would want to hand it off to more of a general manager to scale it. I'd have oversight to the vision of it, but then I'd probably want to start over again.

Skills and Expertise

Perhaps the I-2's most significant skill, over and above those we described of an I-1, is the ability to visualize and communicate the big picture of the emerging business while simultaneously plotting the course for getting there. She's not rigid about either. New information is incorporated in real time and guides her next steps, including directional change if needed, and including updates to her leadership. She can deal with the fact that reality doesn't always work according to the plan. I-2s manage expectations by talking about ranges rather than specific outcomes.

I-2s are able to balance the cues picked up from the market and the lab about ways the business model could take shape, with cues from the organization about how far it is willing to stretch to incorporate these variations. Successful I-2s work within and sometimes around current organizational constraints. Many work through their I-3s to influence significant organizational structure and strategy changes. Emerging businesses are required to pivot many times over the course of their development, and may not align as neatly with the company's business model by late incubation as originally expected. Kodak needed to move from film processing to digital technology. IBM's dominant business model has moved from large capital expenditure plays in mainframe computing to licensing or fee per use models for cloud based computing. Internal R&D may be replaced by in-licensing. Energy storage may become moot as real time energy capture becomes easier. Large plants in the nuclear industry will be replaced by small modular reactors, enabling nuclear power in smaller communities. All of these business model changes cause enormous ripples in companies, and it's through incubation of new business platforms that those options become obvious and difficult decisions are faced.

As one I-2 told us:

I have to be able to work well with my primary sponsor. This is a change project so I will be taking bullets. I cannot work for consensus or nothing will get done. I need his support and help.

In order to effect change, they invoke their people skills. I-2s are described as people who influence others in the company with their ability and willingness to convince, challenge in a healthy way, debate and unify at the same time. Those we've met have been highly respected by their colleagues, have a history of solving problems, and have reputations for being very good at what they do and for their unbiased approach to new business creation.

Background and Critical Experiences
We mentioned that I-1s have typically been involved in starting or growing businesses in the past, and may have held several project management roles. They find "fringe" projects to work on, but also center themselves in the mainstream to ensure they retain credibility.

I-2s mirror that experience but have also been involved in projects that cause them to be considered change agents in the company. They're more visible than the I-1. Their credibility comes from perhaps taking one of those fringe projects, or one they worked with as an I-1, and moving it further than incubation. In other words, they have been part of a new growth platform, whether resident in a line of business or on the fringe, in the past. Most of the I-2s we encountered held director-level positions, so that they could wield influence as necessary. They've been in situations that have resulted in trusting relationships with their sponsors, which causes the strong reputations throughout the company that most of them enjoy.

The training and experience base of the I-2s we've studied indicates they've been successful in business as well as technical roles. They understand how R&D works but have also held positions that provide experience in articulating business propositions in a manner that convinces others of the need, and have been in roles where they had to respond to the urgent demands of the marketplace.

We also note that I-2s have been exposed to a broader range of industries than many of their counterparts, and are experienced across multiple business units, divisions, or even companies. The breadth of experience across industry and company settings enables the I-2 to develop and hold onto that larger vision of the emerging business opportunity.

Many of the I-2s we encountered tell us they've been building their careers carefully with the ambition of becoming a general manager of the company. But when we look back at those we studied, they're not running the largest or most dominant business units these days. They're running the new growth businesses, either in the companies they were with when we met them, or in competitor companies.

One I-2, reflecting on his many different career experiences, had this to say: "New business creation has always been in my career. Normally business development is something people do for a few years, and then they get frustrated, but for me, it's my life."

I-3: DIRECTOR OF INCUBATION

The senior role in incubation is a complex one. Depending on the size of the portfolio, the I-3 may take on responsibilities for managing the portfolio of new business platforms that the company is incubating, overseeing the health of the entire strategic innovation management system, and managing the link between the strategic innovation function and the mainstream organization.

The first of these is the responsibility of the incubation director, and the latter two are those of the chief innovation officer (CNO). In many companies, the role is played by one and the same person, and that makes perfect sense. Incubation is the most challenging and the most absent of the three competencies. At the same time, it is the connective tissue of the strategic innovation capability, leveraging discovery activities into workable businesses, all in service of the company's strategic intent and value creation in the marketplace. The leader of incubation is the strategic owner and facilitator of these relationships and, understandably, is concerned with the health of the discovery and acceleration competencies. But in some companies, those roles are played by separate people. Here we address the I-3 incubation director responsibilities, and we take up the larger strategic innovation management system responsibilities of the CNO and orchestrator in Chapter 8.

Responsibilities

The incubation director manages the portfolio of emerging businesses—that set of new business platforms that could change the game in the market and for the company, as they are wending their way from a concept to a real demonstration of business value. Her primary goal is to make sure the incubation group is "working toward big plays." She guards against "incrementalization creep," the tendency to only fund those avenues of a new business platform that have a familiar, and therefore more certain outcome, but which may also have a rather small impact on the market. As we noted in Chapter 4, sometimes companies fall into the trap described by the quote, "We have breakthrough opportunities that are incrementally executed." What that person meant was that the pressure to commercialize is so great that the team finds the easiest, more familiar application first and transitions it into a business unit where the fit with the current business model is perfect . . . ignoring the rest of the opportunity landscape. This happens all the time, owing to the ongoing organizational barriers to change.

The incubation director works to legitimize incubation's unique purpose in the organization by making sure the emerging business platforms truly differ in scope and purpose from those that could be carried out within the company's business units. They're strategic, but they're oftentimes uncomfortable. One incubation director described this concern as follows:

So your strategy can be to start in a small area that we think can grow, right, but you always have to have the vision that this is going to be big. Anything we do in new business development, if we don't have the vision that it can eventually be in that range of half a billion dollars of annual revenue, we shouldn't be doing it. And anytime we think that it's not, we really start questioning, "What are we doing here," and "Do we need to change the program or do something different?" Otherwise, we'll be hitting singles and doubles and we need home runs at the right frequency.

Another told us:

I make sure it's big enough. We have to articulate the value of the innovation in a global context, and think about global brand development and global strategic development, and the category innovation that's involved.

As part of this, the incubation director is responsible for advising and developing those New Business Platform Leaders and teams, and for removing internal barriers. In this capacity the I-3 becomes aware of opportunities for cross platform synergies as she's working with each one, and may need to press the New Business Platform Leaders to leverage them.

Finally, the I-3 is responsible for selecting which new business platforms within the incubation portfolio should receive continued resource investment, and which to defund, spin out, or send to the business unit if they're not emerging as truly strategic innovations. As one described it, "We have to be sure that we are getting the resources right, that we are asking the right questions, and that, indeed, we are building business models that are important."

Tasks and Activities

In their capacity as incubation portfolio leaders, we saw that I-3s spend their time in the following ways. First, they communicate continuously with the members of the incubation platforms and others as opportunities arise. Beyond the specific opportunity at hand, they continuously speak about the nature of strategic innovation and how it differs from processes and outcomes associated with traditional project management. They spend time educating and setting expectations internally about vocabulary, time horizon, and appropriate project management processes for strategic innovation.

Reflecting on how he was developing the people in his organization, the incubation portfolio leader at DSM told us:

Well, first of all, I communicate a lot about what we need to bring as an organization. So recently, we had a group gathering with the whole global team where we explained to them what the mission and vision of the group is, and how the decision processes are run within the organization which is pretty complex and is not always easy for people.

I-3s monitor the portfolio of new business platforms, and use the political power of the position to break down barriers and advocate for the right talent and partnerships on those platforms as necessary. As one told us:

I coach them. I give them advice. I make connections for them. I do high-level sell-ing for them . . . I help populate the teams . . . You know, I basically try to remove their barriers. Whether they're barriers they bring to me or the barriers I think they have, I try to remove them. So I'll do whatever I can in the office of this position to help remove their barriers. And their barriers range from—you know, they're telling me, we have to move our lab. We can't stay where we are, you know, and this is going to disrupt the program, so then I will pick up the phone and call the facilities people and say, "What are you guys doing?" You know, is there another solution? Whatever is hurting that team or slowing them down, it's my job to help them.

Another of the I-3s we spoke with advocated strongly for the need to develop in-house competencies in electronics, even though the indus-try had traditionally been mechanically based. She began with external contractors, and it took two years to convince the company that the new platforms they were working on were all going to require electronics ex-pertise. Ultimately the company agreed to develop a stable of electrical engineers that have since been kept very busy, and the first platform she advocated for returned record-breaking sales.

Besides advocating for specific platforms, I-3s must allocate resources across them. One compared this portfolio-level role with previous roles he'd had as a project manager, and pointed out that the degree of moni-toring was at a much more strategic than tactical level:

It's not digging into each individual project, but trying to get a sense of, if I look at these as mutual funds, which one looks like it's performing well, has a lot of prospects, which one should I feed and which one should I starve a little bit. And so that's a different model. You can't really evaluate each individual project.

Another I-3 described the challenge of dosing funding appropriately within each platform. Too much is just as bad as not enough:

We titrate resources at the right level, because if you over-titrate, if you get too much, then it's not good, and if you don't get enough, it's not good, so we just want to get the perfect amount of resources at the right time to these programs.

The I-3 works hard to create the context in the company for change. In that capacity he helps the new business platform teams clarify their strategies as they learn, and then vouches for them at the executive levels of the company. One I-3 described his time spent in this way:

It used to be a lot more operational, just get your customers and get things done within the current context, whereas now we are creating our context. It's a huge difference. A lot of my time is spent on stakeholder management internally, so does this really fit with the thinking of management in the company and try to see how we can convince them. There's a lot of storytelling to be done. And typically, also a lot of messaging work of lobbying, trying to talk to the right people with the right message at the right moment.

And threatening doesn't work. It's really trying to understand the thinking process at the top. Also reducing all of the detailed content, so getting rid of the details and building the story line which I think is understood, which fits with the thinking, but slightly stretches because—we are seen sometimes as a pain in the ass because by definition, innovation is about changing things which not necessarily everybody is convinced that we need to change, since they are measured on short term performance.

We are, by definition, longer-term thinking than the rest of the organization, which means that it always goes at the expense of today, so we also have to think about, well, who should I turn to for the message because, well, certain people will not be open for that type of massaging, so it's really—it's always what I tell my wife . . . I say, I'm more psychologist nowadays than the hard chemist.

Performance Metrics

In her role as the incubation portfolio leader, the I-3 is measured on her ability to bring new business proposals to the company that have been vetted and demonstrate market enthusiasm, an operating model that works, and has some level of internal commitment behind it. While many tell us in discovery and incubation that failure is OK, if, at the end of the day, no new options are presented, the director of incubation gets questioned. Is she making the same mistake time and again? Are the processes they're using too loose? Are they withdrawing from opportunities too early, without scoping the whole landscape? Do they know how to operate given high uncertainty? Investigating options, some of which don't yield fruit, is understood in the strategic innovation context. A venture capitalist's portfolio, however, typically depends on one of ten investments succeeding and paying for the others. A strategic innovation portfolio should yield a higher percentage of options that the company can choose to scale up. Why a higher percentage? Because of the power of a portfolio of platforms that are tied to the company's strategic intent, meaning they are experimenting in the same ponds over and over. The company also can leverage the strength of the brand, the wealth of internal competencies and knowledge, and access to external resources that only a large, established organization enjoys.

Selecting the Director of Incubation

In terms of personal characteristics, the I-3 is described as a person who "sees innovation as his work." He sets a culture of learning, and can allow for ambiguity for a period of time. He advises with a real options mentality, constantly weighing the multiple directions a business model could take, and is very clever about imagining alternative arrangements for an emerging business. He thinks without constraints first, letting the platform leader bring issues forward and then considering their implications and possible courses of action. At the same time, he's loyal to the company and concerned with the long term possibilities that strategic innovation can offer, and how to engage the executive team and other stakeholders in dialog about those options. Skill sets that the incubation portfolio leader has over and above New Business Platform Leaders are the ability to think and operate at the portfolio level and across many market and technology domains, and to cleverly help guide business decisions among the platform leaders. He brokers and negotiates on behalf of the emerging new businesses, and takes great care to ensure that the platform leaders feel valued, given that their job is so difficult and frequently frustrating.

To handle the broad ranging platforms, an incubation portfolio leader must have experienced new business creation from beginning to end, and have had a wide variety of disparate experiences. One that we encountered started in an R&D role as a PhD research scientist but quickly moved to the management career ladder. She moved again before too long to a business unit to become a program manager, then a general manager within that unit. She has run a corporate ventures unit and has launched several businesses. On reflecting on her career moves in preparing for the I-3 role, she told us the level of complexity in experimentation increases and you need more professional experience in your backpack in order to grow it.

Another held a master's degree in chemistry and had twenty-seven years of experience with his company. "I think I've been in innovation all my life, even trying to commercialize when I was in research," he told us. His first ten years were spent as a bench chemist. He moved from there to custom manufacturing in one of the business units, and then held roles in new business development, marketing and sales, supply-chain management, and sourcing. In ten years he had changed positions five times to experience all sorts of activities and believed he'd received an excellent education in general management through those career moves. Once he moved into the company's innovation function, he managed projects, then innovation processes, and ultimately platforms, before assuming the incubation portfolio director's role. The I-3 role requires significant preparation, and those who aspire to it should carefully design their career paths to ensure they're prepared. Incubation is a long, winding road. It takes perseverance, discipline, and intuition to recognize the weak signals of a preemergent market and follow them through. Those platforms that show promise must be advocated for. The evidence that accumulates in incubation provides the currency leaders need to develop the courage to commit the substantial investments required for ultimate success. Clearing the fog of incubation to find this evidence and commitment is what allows leaders to accelerate strategic innovations and to compel the company to change in order to incorporate these emerging new businesses as part of its mainstream operations.

Next we take up the set of roles for the final competency, where commitment of resources is the highest, and we move from uncertainty to real risk: acceleration.

7   ACCELERATION ROLES

Acceleration is the capability to scale a business that appears to have great promise and a demonstrated path to profitability but does not necessarily conform to the culture and operating routines required of any of the company's ongoing businesses. It's the exciting time of growth in a business that should be viewed as one of the bright stars for the company's future. Acceleration typically requires intensive levels of investment in capital equipment, personnel, and marketing. We've moved beyond exploring and experimenting to focusing and responding to the market and scaling production. New types of uncertainties plague the business now . . . those associated with an ability to scale. In addition to uncertainty, now we face greater risks as well, given that higher levels of investment are on the line. That is why incubation is so crucial; if done right, it provides us with the confidence needed to undertake acceleration.

An accelerating business has been incubated to the point of having first customers, and is likely experiencing inquiries from other potential customers as the market begins to understand the value the innovation can provide. They are delivering product in small quantities, primarily for the purpose of confirming the value proposition and identifying new performance attributes that the market finds valuable. The new business platform now moves toward becoming a full-fledged business and needs leaders of each function (i.e., heads of engineering, marketing, sales, purchasing, etc.) and a general manager. As one innovation veteran described it, "In a project, you can still have project organizations. But the minute you sell to the market, then all the functions of a regular business are needed."

Innovation is still happening in acceleration—breakthrough innovation, in fact. But rather than focusing on the product and features, focus tends to shift to operational process and organizational innovation. Important challenges accelerating businesses face include reducing costs, increasing yields, debugging systems, instituting financial and IT systems that enable the new business's operating model, scaling the number of personnel, and confirming how and where this new business will fit within the company's current organizational structure.

We have seen the value proposition change completely during acceleration, because sometimes the process innovations that occur as the emerging business is scaling enable new functionality or unexpected cost-performance outcomes. Alternatively, scaling presents so many new problems that the company decides to halt its investment. The point is, there is still risk and uncertainty in acceleration. For this reason we caution senior leaders against incorporating acceleration into the ongoing lines of business, but instead to take it seriously as a capability within the innovation function and recognize that it still needs to be managed differently from traditional new product introductions.

To illustrate, we start with a story that illustrates the risks that exist with strategic innovation, specific to this most crucial and expensive acceleration phase. The story focuses on decisions and assumptions made within an emerging business team as it faced somewhat typical acceleration challenges.

THE EVAPORATING VALUE PROPOSITION

Today we buy fresh, washed lettuce, cut and ready to use. Remember not too long ago when heads of lettuce were the only option at the grocery store? The move from one to the other had to do with the properties of the packaging that enabled produce to remain fresh and healthy while it was housed in a plastic bag. The market has shifted nearly completely to these convenient bags, but it was an interesting journey from the perspective of the companies that were leading the way. We focus on one of them here.

Nate, a packaging expert with a PhD in chemical engineering, numerous patents in the packaging and plastics domains, and years of experience in developing packaging processes for consumer and industrial goods, found himself named as one of the experts on the team being formed to scale a new business platform that would change the fresh produce aisle in the grocery industry. Food scientists in his company's R&D labs had developed a breakthrough technique that would allow packaging experts to customize oxygen and water transmission parameters in packaging film to fit the needs of the foods it housed, from lettuce to broccoli and everything in between. Different types of produce require varying rates of permeability in their packaging because of their unique rates of respiration. Nate's colleagues in R&D had not only demonstrated the ability to customize packaging films, but had just received FDA approval on their test data, indicating their process and materials were safe to use. This meant that lettuce could be prewashed, cut, and bagged, improving the convenience factor for consumers, and shelf life for grocers, and establishing a new form factor for fresh produce that was expected to dramatically increase sales of the category.

Initial commercial attempts were very promising. All the early adopters in the growers' market were signing on, and the new packaged form of lettuce was selling at a brisk pace in the grocery stores that had agreed to test it. Nate's job was to make sure the film could be made in high volume at a price the food growers were willing to pay, since grocers could not increase the price too much and expect consumers to adopt.

One of the design assumptions, based on long-standing market research, was that consumers wanted packages to look full. Bags or boxes of chips, crackers, or, in this case, lettuce that were half-empty were perceived as overpriced by consumers. In setting their parameters for transmission rates of oxygen and water, this design feature was viewed as critical, and determined the number of layers and chemical content of the film used to create the packages to hold prewashed lettuce. The development team could also modify their parameters depending on the respiration rate of the food, and was proud that they could target those rates very accurately. The sales force and application engineers were trained to work with growers to determine the best fit of films, and the market perceived that this company had the most sophisticated technology to achieve the closest fit within the required safety guidelines.

Nate told us, "Things were great for a while. As produce companies were switching over to this new format, we were way ahead of the market. We even bought a company because we needed more extrusion lines. Early adopters were using our film and we thought this would really be the next big thing. We priced the film to get higher margins as the first entrant—we'd invested a lot of capital and needed the margins that specialty materials and deep technological expertise warrant."

But then disaster happened. The market was growing so quickly that competitive packaging producers were attracted by the opportunity. They questioned whether the bags needed to actually appear full in order to attract consumers' interest. If the surface area of the packaging was increased relative to its contents, a lower permeability film could be used. Now a single layer and other more simplistic approaches to producing the film were acceptable, and still met FDA safety standards. The company's competitive advantage evaporated and gross margins plummeted. Today, the company is barely visible in the business, even though the research that its food scientists conducted, and its pursuit of FDA approval, enabled the product category to emerge and become established as a new model of convenience in fresh grocery products that we all enjoy today.

What happened? From Nate's perspective, it was a failure to question every assumption:

We didn't have enough capacity with our existing production lines. We had our own proprietary technology, but ended up buying turnkey systems to increase capacity. That should have been a signal that our proprietary extrusion technology was not a significant part of the value proposition. All of a sudden, we realized that our "proprietary technology" was of little value if we could expand by purchasing off the shelf technology. And once we realized that the film could be a simpler technology because the surface area to content ratio was increased, our secret sauce for making multilayered film was once again confirmed to be of little value for this application. We had been an inward-looking team . . . We believed there were no other competitive solutions.

Once the market learned about the technology, it responded soundly. Is this a problem with incubation? Potentially, yes. The team did not question every single assumption. In addition, they might have looked for other applications. Surely multilayer films that used the R&D team's "secret sauce" would be useful for something . . . films and coatings are extremely important in many industries.

But as Nate reminded us, when you are in the moment, it's impossible to see some of these things. Once a new category is initiated the technical solutions and business models that ultimately win can leapfrog the original approach very, very rapidly. New markets for breakthrough innovation can happen slowly, or they can happen like a flash in the pan.

Our point is that acceleration is (a) chaotic, (b) urgent, and (c) still risky. It requires specific skills, talents, and backgrounds that differ from incubation roles and also that differ from those in the ongoing lines of business and conventional new product development processes. And it must remain connected to incubation so that, when the first entry application fails, we can remind ourselves that there are other fish in the sea. Acceleration is not the last step in a three-phase process. It's a capability that we invoke as needed.

Another failure mode for acceleration that we've seen involves macro-level strategic positioning enacted by a company's senior leadership as investment requirements grow and commitments falter. Accelerating businesses in operating units is challenging. The big dream articulated in statements of strategic intent early on is constrained by the pressures that the receiving operating unit faces. Alignment and oversight across all metrics between the emerging business, the operating unit that receives it, and corporate leadership's long-term, strategic intent is necessary. That way, when the time for investing in acceleration comes, the internal commitments are there.

All of the companies we highlight are prosperous organizations who have thrived on innovation for decades. However, strategic innovation can be challenging even for the most successful companies. As such, you may be wondering if acceleration is ever successful.

Yes, absolutely, it is. DSM's Innovation Center is seven hundred employees strong. Most of them are part of three accelerating businesses that are producing revenues and destined to become new business units for the company. Moen's move into smart plumbing products is another case in point. The MotionSense™ kitchen faucet was incubated through its strategic innovation group by a key team of leaders that consisted of a marketing director, a technology director, and a technology scout, all reporting to the vice president of global strategic development. MotionSense™ has broken records for unit sales at the company, and the platform technology is being perpetuated through many products in that family now, with MotionSense II™ and follow-on Dolphin, a smart shower. The marketing and technology directors worked long and hard to ensure that new marketing materials, new educational approaches, new packaging, and new relationships with vendors were laid down. They stayed on the project as it transitioned into the business unit. Moen's strategic innovation (SI) team is small and its portfolio is very lean, but the technology-market platforms they are cultivating have wide application. Having the SI team nurture the first products of that platform through acceleration helped ensure that they would get over the finish line, and the record setting results prove that out. It is now up to the SI group to incubate other dimensions of smart technologies for plumbing in the home.

So, how did DSM, Moen, and others organize their people to aid in successful acceleration? Again, we look across all the companies we worked with to better understand the roles required to make acceleration work. In this chapter we describe the three levels of acceleration roles. As with Chapter 5 on discovery roles and Chapter 6 on incubation roles, we address the responsibilities, activities, and success metrics of each, along with criteria to consider in selecting them. Then we address their personal characteristics, skills, expertise, and critical experiences that aid in their performance of accelerating a breakthrough based business.

The top level of acceleration, as we've noted, isn't a singular role: it's an entire board of senior-level people in the company, since that is where the decisions are ultimately made to invest big money for scaling a new business. So we don't have as much to say about the individuals . . . we'll talk more about the composition of that group. We begin with the A-1, the functional managers of an emerging business.

A-1: FUNCTIONAL MANAGER

A-1s are people with deep knowledge and experience in operations, marketing, logistics, engineering, or finance. The A-1 team is comprised of representatives of all of the required functions of a mature business. To be successful in the acceleration world, though, they must be creative problem solvers, since problems (actually, crises!) arise as emerging businesses grow, and those problems can be expensive or politically difficult to resolve.

Responsibilities

The functional managers of an accelerating business are on the hook for delivering. "We have to ground the business from a practical experience perspective," one told us. He elaborated that his job was to move from "pie in the sky" experiments and expressions of market interest to real products and real customers. By way of comparison, late incubation requires delivering a real product to a real customer, but acceleration means delivering in higher volume, and driving for repeat purchases from those customers or referrals from them to others. In other words, we need to know that the value proposition we thought we could deliver on is realized in large scale.

Process development is a critical concern for each of these managers. They must understand how the core business works *and* how the market is directing their emerging business model. Sometimes, indeed oftentimes, it is necessary to stray way beyond the operating model that the company uses in its current product lines. New supply chains need to be built and accepted. New revenue models may emerge as those most appropriate for the market. Kodak needed to cannibalize film processing for digital photography. Moen needed to add smart technology to its products, requiring all different kinds of service agreements than they were used to delivering. Figuring out how to align the new business with current operating models and convincing the operating units who will ultimately house the new businesses to augment and modify what they do are key parts of the A-1 team's responsibilities in support of the A-2 general manager. Their priority, though, is the emerging business. Their job is to design processes that fit the emerging business and its partners in the value chain rather than adopt those that the core business has fine-tuned. Then, within each of their functions, they find the important stakeholders in the company and convince them to partner as the emerging business gets up and running.

Tasks/Activities

A-1s work together as a team to solve problems associated with rapid growth. The marketing and sales groups are expanding sales by learning about and solving customer problems as they arise, and fielding inquiries for new uses of the technology. They're busy educating and responding to the market. Operations is working to fill orders and find ways to improve efficiencies and quality. They work on yield by developing processes that are optimized at large scale, so they can demonstrate a path to profitability. Sometimes, as in Nate's case with the produce film and bags, surprises happen.

There's a sense of urgency associated with acceleration that is heightened compared with discovery and incubation. A-1s, who are trained in the world of operational excellence, have to let their six sigma mentality go at times, and instead prioritize getting the most important, breakthrough attributes delivered into the market to claim the space. One manufacturing manager compared his experiences on an accelerating strategic innovation project with more typical new product launches:

So when I look at the three-year product plan, as soon as we put the stake in the ground, my team is responsible for executing to that product plan. Especially the first two years, we're set in stone, and our whole group is marching toward that deadline. And so when issues come up, it's hard for us to sit there and think about ten different ways to make it better. Even though there's ten ways to make it better, we've got to come up with one or two best solutions so that we can meet our timing and meet our commitments to deliver the product. And after that, we can clean up all the nitty-gritty stuff that we have missed because we need to launch it fast. So a lot of times, we—even though it may not be a best cost model, we do it. And then we come back and by doing sustaining innovations, we convert that material for a better result over time. We get it out to the market at as high a quality as possible, even if it is not at the lowest cost.

A product development engineering leader described the transition of a project from incubation into acceleration:

So when we started that project, the incubation team described their research and showed what the possible approaches were . . . and then our team started laying down our plan. How do we execute that into our product plan? At times we come back to that team because we still need their technical expertise as we refine those solutions. It's no longer about making one part. Now we've got to make thousands of parts. You know, it's very easy to make one working part, but trying to make the half a million parts within the expected time frame and making sure all the parts fit and work just right—it's challenging.

A-1s spend considerable time developing the new operating processes for the business. A sourcing director, for example, described how he developed a protocol for identifying and qualifying sources of supply for a brand-new set of components by arraying forty potential vendors on a two-dimensional matrix: capability and strategic alignment. Two were chosen, and they were different from the partners with whom the team had worked in incubation.

Sometimes the processes aren't necessarily new or different but need to be institutionalized anyway, just because the business itself is new for the company. One A-1 expressed frustration at having to get down into the details of operational issues that he'd taken for granted when he'd previously worked on more established lines of business in the company:

The frustration is that—and—I have to tell myself it's normal, but it's constantly that you have to spend time on things that you took for granted in the bigger businesses. Very simple things like having to write all of the specifications for products. All these things that are absolutely necessary to run the business, you have to start from scratch . . . and those are not always—let's say, the most exciting things to do, but that comes with the size of the business.

Essentially, the team is creating a new business, and trying to align as much as they can with the company's needs, but responding most closely to market demands. It's a time of crises, ad hoc problem solving, and completely new experiences, mixed with mundane tasks of developing and codifying operating routines as the business begins to scale. A-1s describe their experiences as some of the most exciting times in their careers. They *love* this stuff:

I joined this emerging business against other people's advice, and it turned out to be much longer than I thought—I was with that business for twelve years. I witnessed the business going from a small operation somewhere off site in an industrial park to something like a business unit, and that was tremendous. Talk about experiences; this one determined my direction. It was very important for me to experience the growth and the difficulties and the struggles that you face constantly to get the business going and growing.

We had to go up against the big companies like DuPont and Honeywell, who were our biggest competitors, and we weren't taken seriously. We were the laughing stock of the industry. Then they noticed, "Whoops—they're here to stay." And in the end, some of them we clearly overtook. That whole process, being able to witness that and go through that whole phase, was a tremendous experience. It was very rewarding.

Performance Metrics

A-1s are measured on their ability to innovate new processes and solutions to the problems of scale. How do we institute a production capability? Who will our steady state partners be? How do we penetrate our first entry niche market and determine the next one to enter? How do we create routines and reliable processes that will allow the business to grow and scale? They are not about managing by exception. They solve the exceptions and turn them into routines.

We find an attention to quality in acceleration. This focus requires trade-offs on financial metrics for a time. And that is critically important, since the objective of acceleration is to grow the business to a critical mass. The primary metric is winning in the market, which means ensuring the value proposition is delivered on and building sales volume. Cost economies are a concern, and that is why process development is important, but they are not achieved during acceleration. When A-1s are measured on the basis of profitability rather than growth, the business can become stunted. There are still too many unknowns, and delivering on the breakthrough attributes to attract a loyal customer base is most important. One of the A-1s we encountered described their interaction with leadership as follows:

We have regular project reviews with our leadership, and we give updates on what's going on with the project, so they know all the problems and issues that team is going through, including cost or quality issues that we're overcoming. And, you know, their expectation is "do it right." We have to protect our consumers for products that we ship, so doing it right is what everybody is working towards.

Selection Criteria
Functional specialists are an intense bunch. Those with a passion for innovation are intense and creative at the same time. To accelerate an emerging business platform successfully, selecting the right team is crucial.

Personal Characteristics
A-1s are focused on execution but are willing to make decisions without full information. They fixate on a problem—be it manufacturing innovations, executing on a market entry and growth plan, or building their organization—and they work it. They don't allow themselves to be distracted. One marketing leader on an A-1 team working on a new performance material told us:

It has a lot of applications. But what we needed to do was focus because, with this material you can do many, many things, but you'll have a shotgun approach. And it takes so much hard work to get one thing really successful that you should not try to do too much.

As far as motivation for the role, A-1s are truly gratified by growth and the upward trajectory of the business itself, and their place on the team in helping reach those outcomes. As one mentioned when asked about what he liked about his role:

What I really like is building the business and all the, let's say, unexpected events that happen outside, not knowing everything exactly, but working with a team, with other colleagues to achieve that. That, for me, is a really fun thing.

Another described the reward of hard work based on a series of mistakes and failures. These guys tend to like intensity:

The success itself is not just only success. It's a series of failures, as well, and mistakes and problems that you face, both organizationally, because you have to build an organization from scratch, and market wise as well, because, in our case anyway, we were up against some very well-known companies at that time, who were well entrenched with these potential customers, and we were the new kid on the block. It was hard work. Every day hard work, and you have to know your business. You have to know the people. You have to know your market, extremely important. And then just by extremely hard work, you're able to get to where you want to be. And even then it's not a guarantee that you'll get there.

Skills and Expertise

A-1s require deep expertise in their specific function along with creative problem-solving capabilities. Rather than T or M shaped, as we referred to earlier, A-1s are more likely to be I shaped, where their depth of expertise is true specialization. As specialists, they prefer to be on the leading edge of developing new processes and solving problems that arise. A Marketing director serving in an acceleration capacity told us:

I'm passionate about marketing. I like the challenges of it. I like the ambiguity of it. I especially like wholesale marketing because there are many influencers and the path is unknown. You don't have a customer telling you what to do, calling all the shots. I like trying to solve the problem and figure out where we should potentially go with things.

The skills required are similar to those of many high-growth businesses, that is, to rapidly respond to opportunities and challenges that crop up and to comply with the plan for growth in terms of timelines and budgets as much as possible. These individuals have to work across functions within their team and also within the company to solve problems that may not have been anticipated, but which inevitably occur given a rapidly changing market and technology landscape. Technical leaders must be able to evolve the technology to a point where it will function reliably in its final form and under expected use conditions.[1] Marketing and sales personnel will have developed the collateral material, communications plan, and channel relationships and incentives. Finance will have developed the traditional chart of accounts for the business and identified the areas of concern for the business's future financial health. All other support functions will be preparing to run at a small but steady volume and anticipate growth.

So they're expert, and they're problem solvers, but A-1s are also viewed as able to operate in chaotic conditions, manage expectations well, and retain focus. We lurked on LinkedIn and found the following recommendations posted for one of our acceleration technical directors:

John has great balance. He inspires his teams because of his experience and knowledge, but he also creates confidence among his peers because of his ability to communicate effectively. He can make difficult challenges seem manageable by applying tools and processes that help mitigate risk and make results more easily predictable. He's very strategic in his development approach and he understands how to rally people around his vision. People love working for John. Those who have would say that they learned more than they realized, and developed true technical skills and tools that will propel their careers forward.

Another echoed the same sentiment:

I consider John to be one of the strongest R&D/Engineering leaders I know. He has the unique ability to strike the right balance between engineering reality and strategic and visionary thinking. If it can be done, John and his team will find a way to make it happen.

Critical Experiences

A-1s need to have a deep appreciation of both the strategic innovation and operational excellence worlds. While they don't necessarily need to have been involved in generating new business concepts and incubating them, they need to understand or be familiar with the practice of incubation. They need to recognize that many experiments have taken place to get the business to where it is so that they can take it to the next level. Having had interaction with incubation teams, then, is an important critical experience.

But more important is experience within an operating unit, in particular with a high-growth business, since the ambiguity in acceleration is associated with how the business will operate at scale, not as much about which markets it will serve. Experience in a high-growth business will have provided the test bed for them to practice solving problems within their area of expertise, under pressure. One A-1 manufacturing lead we interviewed, a mechanical engineer, spent several years as the director of new products manufacturing for the company's largest business unit, where he had to convert engineering designs to manufacturable products in their pilot plant, and then scale those processes. Similarly, the A-1 project manager for Moen's MotionSense™ faucet was selected because of his previous experience with Moen's first digital in-home plumbing device. His boss told us the following:

He launched that project three years ago, and there were still a lot of unknowns. It was a new category. We didn't have a digital showering product, and he is very good at—he is the most experienced project manager in Moen, and he has delivered a lot of good products, including several that have won awards in the industry. So I chose him because he's the most knowledgeable and also had huge success before in introducing a lot of innovative products in Moen. He's very good at working in this gray area.

So, any previous work in new business development, either within the company or in other companies, and an appreciation for how the current company operates, are important experiences for people in this role. At John Deere, the marketing A-1 on the JD Water business was hired from outside of the company. He had worked in Europe, in a smaller business, and then joined Deere. He had been through some different roles in business development, strategic marketing, and in consumer products, across different parts of the company. He was described as a guy who could understand the company culture and "think like a Deere person," but he had also had exposure to other approaches to marketing, other business models, and other product categories, thus giving him a larger set of scripts to draw from in developing the marketing strategy for the JD Water business.

In sum, A-1s need to draw on their skills, experiences, and personal characteristics to put together workable high-quality systems to as quickly as possible capture a market while recognizing there will be room for increasing efficiency down the line. They need a different type of logic than those in incubation and need to think creatively and broadly about sourcing, inputs, and processes. In short, they need to know how to scale a business, and be sensitive to the organizational changes that the new business will exact upon the company.

A-2: GENERAL MANAGER, NEW BUSINESS

Whereas A-1s are the functional experts, A-2s are general managers of an emerging business platform. People who occupy this role are neither fish nor fowl. They cannot claim their business is in experimentation mode, as an incubation program manager can. They must deliver, just like any business unit manager. At the same time, the A-2's mode of delivering may well run afoul of the company's tried-and-true operating model, so they are not part of the mainstream either. As one A-2 described his role:

So . . . you're in the valley of death. You're out of the phase of being able to say, "This might not work (because we're experimenting in incubation)," and you're getting to the point where it's actually an existing business . . . that's what you're trying to get done. A lot of people throw rocks at you, so you have to have a very thick skin. You have to be very determined. You have to be able to sort through a lot of conflicting information about what's really important, because stuff is going to fly at you all the time. You have to be able to set up processes that are new and different. Create your own processes, not just run existing processes. What I mean by processes is, I mean assets, operational things, sales and marketing, routes to market because you're making something out of nothing.

But of course it's not all pain! The acceleration leader on Corning® Gorilla® Glass described how motivating it is to be in this "neither fish nor fowl" role. He'd worked in discovery and also in ongoing businesses but prefers the acceleration space:

My love is working in the new, but not the real exploratory stuff. I like to work with customers and turn it into products, and head it towards manufacturing. For example, with Corning® Gorilla® Glass, the exploratory marketing team is out finding applications and does a first engagement. Once the customer is ready to start talking about cost, they'll transition it to us and we'll help sort it out and see if there's a path to follow. If yes, we'll start taking it to the next stages, e.g., ten or fifty pieces to do a qualification. We make the parts in house but also are setting up external suppliers so we can feed this application development. Following that, the customer may say he wants changes or doesn't want it, or "let's go." If the latter, we need to set up a supply chain, get them more details, and take that next step.

Responsibilities

By the time an I-2 New Business Platform Leader gets through with the emerging business' experiments, there are multitudes of opportunities and applications, some of which may appear more promising in the near term and other "killer apps" that show great promise but may require more time and investment. All of them seem exciting, and the company has declared a willingness to back this business with sizable investments. But each is fraught with pitfalls. The A-2 must guide the growth strategy and manage its execution. To do this, the A-2 shoulders three or four key responsibilities.

First is to down-select from among the many promising opportunities the incubation team has developed and focus on staking a claim in the first market application. General Managers must understand which of the many leads to focus on now and which to save for later. The organization has made investments in cultivating many possible applications but the A-2 needs to prioritize by examining how quickly each can scale, how much market share they can win, and which priorities best align with the organization's overall strategic vision. The early part of acceleration is a critical time to focus and scale rather than to experiment with lots of options. This decision may not make the A-2 popular. As one described it:

It's about getting a multitude of insights, combining them, and then making a choice and focus. When I started as the head of this business platform we had a portfolio of opportunities. We had a front end pipeline which was almost 50 percent of our total budget—and a development pipeline which was also 50 percent, and we were trying to do that all with a budget of about nine million dollars. And I said, "Nobody is going to like this, but if we truly want to be successful, then we need to avoid smearing ourselves too thinly. Let's make a choice and then put 90 percent of the budget on that choice." So I killed one part of the business which, in my view, was not very promising, and I decided to move all the resources in one area and said, "We need to make this work, because if it doesn't work, then we're out . . . we need to show success." You cannot muddle along for years, trying to make it work. Make a choice. Be daring enough to make a choice and see if it works.

At the same time, A-2s must be preparing for the future, evaluating options for expanding beyond the first market entry point and first product formulation to developing a whole family of products and a complete business enterprise. A key criterion for evaluating new opportunities is strategic relevancy to the company and the path toward fulfillment of the robust opportunity landscape that was originally envisioned in discovery. Otherwise, these opportunities will fail in the corporate environment. "We try to look for links to what we have and what we know," one A-2 told us.

Some of those links are more aspirational than real, since much of the point of incubation is to develop new competencies that the general manager now begins to leverage into multiple markets as a platform of business, to fulfill the strategic intent that was articulated at the outset. Moen's MotionSense™ faucet that we described earlier was just the first product from a platform that the company is leveraging to bring smart sensing into household plumbing fixtures. DSM's Advanced Surfaces Emerging Business Area created new solutions that originated from technology developed for optical fiber coatings. There are many, many ways to grow those business platforms. The A-2 is responsible for protecting the company from falling into the "breakthrough opportunity, incrementally executed" trap as it gains visibility and comes under pressure to grow rapidly and begin producing profits.

A third responsibility A-2s carry is to help their companies develop a culture of openness and perfectionism in seeking the proper talent. Acceleration leaders described the need for culture change in their companies, where pride had always been taken in doing all of the development work for their innovations themselves. But for strategic innovation, as we saw in incubation, accessing competencies from outside is critical. In acceleration, leaders must ensure that those competencies are brought in to the company, sometimes at great expense. When IBM's Silicon Germanium project was growing rapidly, the company opened an office in Cambridge, Massachusetts, primarily for the purpose of gaining first access to the specific and relatively rare types of physicists and engineers graduating from MIT that were needed for this new growth area. Corning added biologists when their life sciences business was clearly taking off. DSM added solar materials expertise for their advanced surfaces business. Moen added electrical and computer systems engineering to their primarily mechanical engineering stable of technical expertise. Marketing and sales expertise will also be added as new business applications come online. "We cannot limit ourselves to ourselves," is the mantra we heard from acceleration managers. While incubating businesses contract out the experimental work, acceleration requires commitment of funding, not only for physical facilities but also for the right expertise.

Finally, A-2s are responsible for working with the A-3-level growth council to prepare the mainstream organization, and the new business itself, for the new business's assimilation into its ultimate organizational home. This is no small feat, as we have seen in some of the stories in this chapter. The A-2 who earlier described having rocks thrown at him was referring to his previous experiences in having grown several new businesses within one of the largest business units in his company. Legitimizing new processes that work for the emerging business but that don't necessarily fit the current core processes requires intensive attention, education, negotiation, and oversight. Otherwise, all of the investment a company makes in incubating and building a business model is lost. The A-2's responsibility is to make the new business repeatable, predictable, and operationally clear enough that it can be considered part of the company's core business over time, even if its operating routines vary from those of its host business unit.

Tasks and Activities

To accomplish all these responsibilities, the general manager of an accelerating breakthrough business divides his time between (a) working with his team to maintain the momentum of growth in the face of many forces of resistance; (b) working in the market to create the relationships necessary to scale market demand and the company's ability to supply it; and (c) working with the company's leadership to prepare the mainstream organization to assimilate this new platform into a current line of business, or create a new one.

Regarding the first, we heard from many general managers of emerging businesses, as well as the A-1s working with them, how the daily grind of organizational resistance or technical challenges would get them down. Every little bump in the road meets with an organizational "I told you so" or "You can't do that because . . ." coupled with the fact that there seem to be so many "easier" opportunities that provide short term wins. One acceleration team member described it this way:

We get very excited at the beginning of a breakthrough opportunity and rush it through to launch, and we quickly move on to something else and lose that excitement about the innovation. When we start having issues with the commercial path, we give up on those innovations. Supply-chain issues, or any hiccup on operations, we give up on it. When there are hiccups with new breakthrough businesses, it's easy for the operating units to say, "It's not working; let's keeping making our bread-and-butter stuff." That's because there's more volume on other projects, and this is such a small volume, so nobody is excited about the breakthrough product anymore. They think that the market doesn't care about that product, so why should we spend more time making it, versus moving on to something else that makes more revenue.

This same acceleration team member later elaborated on this point and spoke specifically about a current new business:

One of my concerns with the [current new business we're working on] today is exactly this. We're all excited about this product and we're doing a great job trying to make it right, but any one hiccup in the supply chain (and there's a huge supply chain on this product), could kill this product, and that's what I'm worrying about. We have done that before. We have done that so many times. We have so many great innovations and we—have called it quits and moved on to something else, because it's no longer exciting anymore.

Another new business manager in a different company told us:

You have to always search for the truth, and push but not give up too early, because there are always barriers in the way. You can think of ten reasons to kill any of these.

So the general manager is the one who sets the vision, reminds her team of the bigger picture, and of the value they are bringing to the company's future, and helps them persevere. It's rewarding and draining at the same time.

Besides working with their business teams, A-2s spend significant time in the market. They initiate new partnerships and sunset others that may have worked well for incubation but cannot be leveraged for scaling the business. The selection process of external partners and hires is more unforgiving than in incubation. Since incubation is about testing and experimenting, everyone knows there's no obligation to move forward. But in acceleration, commitments are made regarding market applications, technological solutions, and the competencies that the company must incorporate for competitive advantage. Even though one partner may have developed an interesting manufacturing process technique in incubation, for example, they may be too small of an organization to carry it forward to scale. Or the company may determine that the process is crucial to maintain in house and so decide to invest in adopting those processes and acquiring that type of equipment themselves. The acceleration manager works with company leaders to determine which of these strategic investments are needed, finding those partners or sources of talent and hiring them as individuals or, if needed, acquiring relevant companies to complement the breakthroughs that the business has developed and nurtured.

Finally, A-2 general managers invest a substantial portion of their time interacting with the leaders of the Innovation Growth Council about decisions on capital investments, hiring, strategic direction as new opportunities arise, and integrating the accelerating business platform into one of the lines of business, or as its own business unit, as seamlessly as possible.[2] As soon as the ultimate organizational home is identified, the A-2 works with members of that BU to align objectives, add members from that unit to his team, and determine a workable transition plan.

One might wonder if A-2s seek one another out to share their experiences, learn from one another, and check one another's progress as a way of support. We do not find evidence that they are willing to invest their time that way. The job of growing a business is all consuming, and they don't find enough value added to trade attention to their business for time spent with one another. One told us he and his peers considered themselves like a fraternity or band of brothers, since they were all "getting shot at all the time," but others admitted they tended to avoid any group meetings or formal structures for interaction because they sensed a competitive edge, and in fact perceived one another as rivals. Interesting but not surprising since acceleration requires resources and these general managers are fighting for their share from the same growth fund.

Performance Metrics

The A-2 is measured on three important dimensions: delivering on the value proposition to the customer, growing sales, and demonstrating a path to profitability, in that order. Delivering on the value proposition comes first because it drives market acceptance, and with that comes profits.

One of the projects we studied delivered more than $25 million in incremental revenue within two years, which was a huge win for that company. But revenue targets were not the primary metric, quality was. As the A-2 for the new business platform described it,

"Everybody, including the CEO was telling us 'what's important is quality.' Making sure that when we deliver innovation, it's executing correctly—delivering a quality product was far more important than getting the cost right. Quality was also more important than timing, so when we communicated to our sales group, we did not commit that we're going to ship it on a certain date. There were still too many unknowns, and quality came first."

Another strategic innovation general manager mentioned the importance of demonstrated excitement via customer engagement as a critical metric. "We didn't make the measure of success the generation of immediate revenue. We made the measure of success the act of cocreation with customers, rapid prototyping, innovating together." Any of these demonstrations of market enthusiasm, including new codevelopment partners, referrals, or repeat customers all signal that value is perceived in the market, and they foreshadow growth. All of these signals help the mainstream organization recognize the value of assimilating this new business entity into the core when it's ready.

Before a new business can move from an accelerating business to a mainstream one, though, it must demonstrate cost economies and a path to profitability. Prior to that time it is a resource drain, and, since operating units are measured on their profit margins, they cannot be expected to make the required investments unless it's over a very short timeframe. While an accelerating business does not need to be in a profit position, senior leaders will be looking to see that it will ultimately turn the corner.

Selection Criteria: Choosing General Managers for Strategic
Innovation–Based Businesses
It'll be obvious who the general managers of emerging businesses should be. They're broadly experienced, ambitious, and have demonstrated that they can take on a strategic initiative of some sort previously. Some may be surprised when they're tapped to run an emerging business that is still so immature, since they've often managed much bigger budgets and more personnel than an early accelerating business requires. Others will view this as a natural next step, having taken on risky projects over the course of their careers, as with each of the other innovation roles, we'll describe what we can about their personal characteristics, skills and expertise, and the critical experiences that we observe lead to a successful A-2 performer.

Personal Characteristics
A-2s are mature, strategic thinkers blessed with a strong dose of confidence and plenty of ambition. They're driven by very clear objectives. One told us, "What is important for me is that I see the ultimate goal where we want to go. So if the flag is over there and that's where I need to go then that is fine. But if you haven't discussed the flag, then that is something I don't like." Clearly A-2s differ in this regard from incubation platform leaders, who are trying multiple approaches to achieve the best-value proposition, whatever that may be, and thrive on working in an uncertain environment. A-2s, in contrast, want a clearly defined goal and they'll figure out how to get there.

Reflecting on earlier experiences he'd had as an Incubation platform leader (I-2), one of our A-2s described his preference for the acceleration role, given its more practical, applied context:

I have fifty people, and we're working on three market applications. We're making lots of progress in all three. The good thing about this one is that, unlike some of the previous projects I have had in NBD, this one actually has a product, it's made in high volume, and so we're taking that product and not trying to change it too much, although we've found some ways and we're feeding that in. But I have a product and we have some customers and it can be applied.

A-2s are motivated by the idea that they could become general managers of one of the company's businesses of the future, and this is where we found problems since their role, which we previously described as "neither fish nor fowl," doesn't call for the type of person needed of a general manager in an ongoing business. If they were fish, by the time our study was over they'd moved on to another new business development project or another company. If they were fowl, they'd left the innovation function and had moved into a role in one of the operating units. None had evolved their business platforms to the point of transition to an operating unit and remained at the helm.

Skills and Expertise

As we noted earlier, the ambiguity in acceleration is more about how the business operates, scales, and fits into the company's ongoing operation, and less about finding new markets or technological solutions. So the skills needed of an A-2 are the ability to solve issues associated with scaling and conceptualizing the new business's operating model, in a manner that works with the larger company's objectives. Once the leadership team decides which markets to prioritize, the rest follows.

The A-2's expertise, then, is in managing the transition from a model of working with first-of-a-kind customers to a high-growth businesses. He is skilled at operational execution, but in a new space, where the business is developing and institutionalizing processes and people is the main concern. The A-2 is able to design his organization and leadership team, conceive of the natural market segments in the application fields the business is cultivating first, drive that marketing strategy, and motivate the team to dramatically improve yields, production schedules, and supply-chain management in order to reduce costs.

General managers of emerging businesses can manage expectations regarding pacing and strategic direction in the face of many diverse customer requests, and can modify operating plans as the business environment responds. A-2s are broadly skilled in operations, marketing, finance, and strategy. This broad base helps them understand complex systems so they can design an operating model that will fit the emerging business's needs rather than "copy-pasting" from the past. They do not operate like Six Sigma black belts, in that they're not so heavily focused on weeding out deviations as they are on developing new processes that are moving the business in the right direction. We heard several use metaphors like, "We're laying the tracks while we're driving the train," to describe their skills. Others can perfect those processes once they're in place.

Finally, A-2s have the patience to build an operation step-by-step, rather than prioritizing speed of the growth. So while there is an urgency to generate sales and growth, focus on growth at the expense of solid infrastructural development could result in failure. The ability to balance this tension is required since the A-2 has to manage a wide variety of internal stakeholders to ensure that the business model that is evolving will be accepted within the organizational unit that is ultimately adopting the business. The twin abilities to stay focused on delivering the value proposition to the market and evolving the company's enthusiasm to incorporate this new business is their sweet spot. One of the A-2s we encountered summed up the skills and experiences needed for the job this way:

So typically, it's people that have had experience in commercial businesses, but aren't so locked in their thinking that they think that that's the only way we do things, which in our company is a very difficult thing to find. They have to have a lot of business savvy because there's a lot of stuff going on at once. There's a lot of ways to get lost on the way between a really good idea and making money. They have to have a very strong business acumen. And they have to have very strong people leadership skills because inevitably, it's unbelievably stressful in the valley of death. You have to be able to keep people calm and focused and believing in what you're trying to do.

Background and Critical Experiences

As with any general manager, the A-2 should have had a broad array of experiences, and it helps if he's had several of those outside of the current company so that he can offer creative solutions that he may have seen elsewhere. A substantial portion of those broad experiences should have been associated with growth opportunities or having brought something to fruition before. The A-2 should have scaled something before taking on this "big bet" responsibility, since acceleration involves a large commitment of resources. Some of the A-2s we encountered were program managers within an operating unit and had taken a new initiative there and grown it. Others had actually started their own companies. Cross-pollinating those two experiences is especially valuable: building a business from scratch forces the leader to develop new processes, but growing an initiative from within the company provides experience in managing all of the stakeholder relationships necessary and ensures the internal networks are functional. The A-2s we encountered had been in some form of new business development and project management roles for growth initiatives, either on the technical or the business side, for decades.

The biggest problem with A-2s occurs when they have been selected too early in their career or are too narrowly experienced within a single functional role. They may be bright, well educated, full of energy, and be considered high-potential leaders, but that is not enough for this role. To be successful, A-2s require a number of trips around the block to manage the complexities and challenges, both in the market and in the company, of commercializing a strategic innovation business platform. An executive in one of our study companies reflected this opinion:

Where we've had less success has been with people in the five- to ten-year career window, that started at our company, had only ever worked at our company, and where it got ingrained into them that the company way is the only way. We send some of our high potential's off to get their MBAs, and some of them come in and think they're going to run the company in five years, and this is the only way to do things, but they don't quite have the wisdom yet to realize there might be multiple ways to do things.

A prototypical career path to successful acceleration general manager is the person who led the commercialization of Corning® Gorilla® Glass. He holds an MS in electrical engineering and started his career working for the consulting firm Booz Allen, as a technical staff member in the communications systems practice. After five years he joined Corning as an applications engineer in the fiber optics group. There, he began to work with customers and, over time, was promoted to product manager and then worldwide marketing manager for one of Corning's highest-volume and fastest-growing businesses. He held various product line management roles over that time period and began working in new business development on newer, more uncertain initiatives in 2002 when Corning was growing its emerging optical networking business. He served as program manager for several projects including one of Corning's big bets that ultimately failed because of technical challenges. He describes himself as having always migrated toward newer products and initiatives, and had held business related roles for more than fifteen years. So he migrated away from a technical career track early in his career and held a variety of roles in multiple divisions so he was well networked.

We might assume that once the incubation platform leader and his team has worked enough promising pathways for the emerging business, scaling it would be smooth and straightforward. Through the stories of the people described here we see that the A-2 role is by no means a lightweight job. It is still a risky, uncertain venture, although with different dimensions of the uncertainty matrix as the focus compared with incubation. In addition, the A-2 lives with greater scrutiny from the organization's leaders because they're investing significant resources in acceleration. To be successful, A-2s need the help of an executive team who is engaged and willing to back them up as they create new, and different, platforms of business for the company. We turn now to that final role in our matrix, the Innovation Council.

A-3: INNOVATION COUNCIL

At the A-3 level we break with our system and identify a governance committee rather than an individual to fill this role. Acceleration, as we've seen, is the expensive part of strategic innovation. It requires enormous investment to build plants, hire people, sometimes acquire companies, and scale up the business. So the A-3-level responsibilities are shared across a senior executive team, guided by the CNO.

The Innovation Council is of course aware of the incubating businesses in the strategic innovation portfolio as they percolate along. Ideally, council members are highly engaged in the development and reconsideration of the domains of strategic intent that guides innovation investments. Only in this way are they prepared to back an emerging business as it hits acceleration. The reality is, though, that many senior leader councils are not very engaged in the company's strategic innovation agenda. More often, one or two senior leaders sponsor and protect projects along the way, but when those executives move on, commitment to the new business evaporates. One R&D director described his company's pattern of failing to invest to scale new businesses this way:

We start these things. We dump in hundreds of millions of dollars, we get to about year five, year six, and then typically we see movement at the top, and that's where you lose sponsorship. Then everybody gets nervous, and if you're not close to commercializing or things don't look good, people starting asking, "Why are we doing do this?" and the naysayers come out real, real quick. Everybody likes to say, "See I told you so. That would never work."

By instituting a truly functional Innovation Council, the responsibility for sticking with decisions to invest in an emerging strategic innovation business is likely to be borne more broadly across the top of the organization. That doesn't mean decisions won't change, but if they do, it's more likely because of unexpected changes in the emerging business itself rather than corporate courage and commitment. In this section we clarify the responsibilities and metrics to help companies institute productive, valuable A-3 councils.

Responsibilities
The Innovation Council's responsibility is to oversee the incubation and acceleration portfolio in light of the company's chosen domains of strategic intent, to make the investment decisions regarding which of the incubating platforms should be accelerated, and to monitor progress of those

new business platforms prior to their transition into an existing operating unit or a newly formed unit.

There are few businesses operating at any point in time in a company's acceleration portfolio because acceleration is the point in an emerging business's development cycle that requires the heaviest investment. Therefore the council attends intensively to the one, two, or perhaps three high-growth businesses at any given time. For each of those, much of the uncertainty has been reduced, a path to market has been charted, and the key concern is scaling the business to a point where it can stand on its own relative to other established businesses with which it may compete for resources once it transitions into a division of the company.

The Innovation Council must provide adequate resources at this point, so the emerging business isn't starved. Several of our participating companies noted that ensuring a critical mass of people to execute acceleration of a strategic innovation business was a perennial challenge. At a time when follow-up and focus on execution are critical, underresourcing the potential new business is a surefire road to failure. Process and product development engineering, field support personnel, and customer service personnel are all necessary. Manufacturing oversight is critical as well, since, as one person told us, "The manufacturing process is likely new and must be 'bird-dogged.'" Frequently there is acquisition activity to fill resource and skill gaps. Last, time and attention must be allocated to the strategic planning needed to plot the future course of the business, given that opportunities may be flooding the gates, or not.

At the same time, flooding an accelerating business with resources won't necessarily make it succeed any faster, since acceleration general managers are advised to build their businesses patiently. Innovation Councils have to balance their desire for quick successes with the recognition that truly strategic innovations can require significant behavioral and structural changes in the market, and that takes time. A-3 councils monitor the strategic innovation portfolio's composition and pacing of emerging business in a way that matches the company's capacity to invest, its ability to absorb them and in a manner that responds to a continuously changing business climate. Finally, the Innovation Council helps manage the transitions of emerging business areas into designated business units, or arranges for a new unit to be organized to house them. These final transitions are politically difficult for everyone involved and require an active senior leadership council to ensure there is a healthy reception for these businesses of the future.

Tasks and Activities

The trick for Innovation Councils is to find the right balance between involvement in projects and involvement in the portfolio. By this we mean that councils can become overly involved in directing emerging business platforms, rather than letting the new business' leadership team educate the council members. IBM's Emerging Business Opportunity (EBO) initiative in the early 2000s time frame provides an excellent example of strategic coaching.[3] The A-3 council was composed of the senior vice president of corporate strategy, the senior vice president of research, and the corporate controller, and was staffed by the vice president of strategic planning. Together they met with each accelerating EBO team monthly. There was no preset agenda and no template for a review. The agenda was set by the A-2 general manager of each EBO, who brought problems and barriers, and questions he was facing, to the meeting, along with whatever A-1 team members he needed to have in the room. The A-3 team viewed its job as helping the EBO leader and his leadership team resolve organizational barrier problems and maintain the link to strategic intent as each new decision point and opportunity arose. That's a lot of very senior man-hours devoted to nurturing strategic innovations, but IBM's CEOs Lou Gerstner and later, Sam Palmisano viewed the time investment as crucial to the company's future.

When the A-3 team wasn't working directly with or on behalf of the EBO's, they were discussing the portfolio, its pacing, and investments needed over time. They watched to see that the allocated funds were, in fact, being spent rather than siphoned off onto near-term initiatives. The portfolio-level diagnostics were developed and presented by the two strategy executives, who played the role of chief innovation officer and orchestrator, whom we discuss further in Chapter 8. But they could not have made decisions or taken action without their A-3 team counterparts.

Metrics: How Should an Innovation Council Be Assessed?
Ultimately, this body's success is determined by two metrics. First is the extent to which they manage to fulfill the company's strategic intent through bringing new businesses that address emergent opportunity landscapes to market at a desirable pace. Second is the extent to which those new business platforms are successfully assimilated into the mainstream organization and maintain their growth trajectories, or, if not, the organization learns from their experience with them and enriches its understanding of those opportunity spaces.

Several Innovation Councils we've encountered express these goals operationally by targeting specific incremental revenue objectives. We want to caution companies about potential unintended consequences of these goals. First, many times companies find themselves in need of replacing rapidly declining revenue streams, so revenue borne of emerging new businesses from the strategic innovation portfolio may be replacing those evaporating businesses rather than providing top line growth. Secondly, revenue is a derivative. It is a consequence of other things. Measure the primary drivers, not the derivative. Otherwise, Innovation Councils who feel pressure to deliver to stockholders will find ways of accomplishing the revenue goal in ways that may shortchange the strategic innovation agenda. There are many ways to drive revenue, and organic growth through game-changing innovation is only one.

Selecting the Innovation Council Team
For all the other roles, we addressed selection criteria. The issue at the A-3 level is really one of composition: Who should be a part of the Innovation Council? How big should it be? What about the backgrounds and characteristics of its members is important?

We know that an Innovation Council should be composed primarily of corporate-level executives, since they are responsible for the health of the company, and, theoretically at least, are not looking out for the prospects of one business unit over another. New businesses rooted in truly strategic innovation may cannibalize current parts of the mainstream organization. At the very least they'll create the need for dramatic changes in business models (such as in Kodak's case), reporting structures, revenue flows, and skill set needs. For these reasons a longer-term, broader view of organizational strategy is needed from the A-3 council. As in the case of IBM, the council should include at least the senior executives of strategy, R&D, and finance. Including the COO and CEO is also warranted since acceleration investments are not only large but will impact the strategic direction and competitive advantage of the company. Some companies include senior representatives from each business unit, and others use one or two spots on the council for BU representation. They will then rotate the various BU leaders through those seats on the council so that, over time, each BU is represented, but no single BU has undue influence over the council's investment decisions. It is important to have BU senior leader exposure to the council and its workings, since BU leaders are inherently invested in the company's future. This exposure provides leadership development opportunities at the most senior levels of the company. The council's size could hover between eight and twelve. Too small and there will not be enough inclusion to be credible. Too large and decisions won't get made.

A number of the companies we studied have not created an Innovation Council until later in their journey of building an innovation capability. One recently developed an Innovation Steering Committee after ten years of working at discovery and incubation. There were many misses in their early days. Great ideas were generated and incubated at least partially, but none made it out into the market. The first successfully accelerated project required so much engagement on the part of senior leadership and throughout the business units that the CNO and CEO recognized the need for an A-3 type of governance structure.

Personal Characteristics and Critical Experiences
Members of the A-3 Innovation Council are motivated to ensure their company is healthy beyond the next quarter. They are willing to accept and motivate change within their companies.

To make those kinds of strategic investments, the Innovation Council must understand how strategic and breakthrough innovations in high uncertainty spaces tend to unfold. Killer apps don't happen overnight. Experiments that don't work out are not failed projects. They're learning opportunities that support a growth platform in which the company is building a capability and asserting itself. Organizational mind-sets are oftentimes too myopic. External partners are a must. These are just a few of the defining characteristics that we've seen over and over. Council members should be familiar with these and others. Many have read, attended conferences, and otherwise educated themselves on the phenomenon. Others would be wise to do so.

A-3 members have typically been promoted to executive positions through the operational excellence engine of the company . . . because that is where careers are made. So it takes a special set of skills and talent to understand when and how to make the steady investments in emerging businesses for which the outcomes are still fairly ambiguous, when the company needs to scale them. Some are able to make decisions under uncertain conditions, but others are paralyzed. When an A-3 team is paralyzed, all of the discovery and incubation in the world won't get the breakthroughs out the door. The most important thing is that, if they know this is a trait of theirs, they recognize it and partner with someone who can help them through the process. That's why the chief innovation officer has to be a well-respected leader of the A-3 team, and must be able to facilitate the team's work.

ACCELERATION IS MORE DIFFICULT THAN IT APPEARS

Acceleration is where the big investments are made. It's also where the risk is highest, although that risk is dramatically mitigated by an effective incubation function. It requires courage, focus, and strategic execution. The most challenging management practice we find is the temptation, and, indeed, the practical reality in many companies, to accelerate an emerging business within a current operating unit or division. When that happens, the A-1 functional experts, the A-2 general manager, and the business itself must be managed as exceptions. If acceleration was treated as part of the innovation function rather than as an exception in an operating unit, then the actions, responsibilities, and metrics associated with these critically important players will align with the needs of the new business platform, and companies will have a more successful hit rate.

For each accelerating business, A-1 functional experts create and hone the business model. At the same time the new business's general manager steers the course of the business, ensuring it remains connected to the company's declared strategic intent as opportunities for expansion arise, or as competitive forces drive the business in different directions than expected. In conjunction with the Innovation Council, the accelerating business must seek a home within the company's current divisional structure, become its own business unit or, worst case, be spun out of the company. The Innovation Council must constantly remind the organization of strategic innovation's emerging businesses' crucial role in creating the company's future, and ensure that the revenue and operating models that are emerging in the accelerating businesses are not crushed by the organization's current norms and routines. It sounds simple, obvious, and rational, but we all know it is a tall order.

At this point we have covered nine roles associated with strategic innovation that together provide the resources and expertise for the discovery, incubation, and acceleration capabilities required for a successful innovation management system. They're quite different from one another. Strategic innovation doesn't succeed in any sort of systematic way if a company doesn't assign responsibility for each of these roles. There may be many multiples of people holding the first level roles in discovery, incubation, and acceleration. Most are midcareer people, with a good working knowledge of the company, solid networks, and the energy, enthusiasm, and skill for innovation. The second-level personnel are typically of an executive level, or certainly aspire to it. The top level of our innovation matrix are senior executive leaders, responsible for the company's future welfare.

Now we turn to the glue that binds it all together—the chief innovation officer and his or her support team. You'll recognize many of these roles. They've been around in most companies for a long time, but perhaps have not been considered as part of an Innovation function . . . until now.

8 THE CHIEF INNOVATION OFFICER AND INNOVATION SUPPORT ROLES

In this chapter we address the "glue" that holds the innovation function together. These are internal organizational consultants, innovation process facilitators, and other staff members and leaders who enable discovery, incubation, and acceleration activities to work well. Most do their work in the background, assessing the innovation management system and finding ways to improve on it. These professionals monitor the innovation portfolio's health, forge relationships with parts of the mainstream organization necessary for getting work done on behalf of the innovation function, and facilitate and support the work to set the company's innovation strategy. They can be cheerleaders for those experiencing the roller-coaster ride of strategic innovation. They sometimes find themselves nurturing and comforting those in distress or experiencing too much frustration.

The people who occupy these support roles maintain expertise in all kinds of innovation practices but they are not connected with a project, a platform, or a revenue-generating business. They are typically viewed as costs to the company, and may not be recognized as valuable . . . a common criticism of any staff person in an organization. However, they are an important presence in the innovation function. We find that those in innovation support roles tend to love their jobs because of the exposure they get to so many aspects of innovation and their role in helping others make it happen. They told us the following:

If you like innovation, this job is like being a kid in a candy store.

This environment is very inspiring. I work closely with top management. We are allowed to do things that nobody else can do.

You can see all the different business groups within the company. You can work with a broad group of people. You can leverage the differences that you see. You can create synergies between people, which is great.

But they also noted that they work in the background, indicating that people who like to stand in the spotlight are ill suited for a role in innovation support. The following analogy to a movie production director that one of them described exemplifies their crucial role but their distinct difference from discovery, incubation, or acceleration personnel:

We set the stage. We ask the actors. We write the script . . . We even hire the audience. But when the curtains come down, and the title of the film [goes up], we're not there.

We find in many instances that innovation support personnel do not report to the chief innovation officer, but they should. Typically they report up through the R&D organization. Yet the chief innovation officer maintains a broader perspective, beyond discovery, and these process effectiveness and portfolio monitoring roles encompass that entire innovation mandate.

There can be many different ways to organize and label staff roles that support strategic innovation, including process facilitators for idea generation sessions or strategic intent development sessions, and partners in the finance, business development procurement, legal and human resources functions who understand the special needs of the SI group and provide meaningful support.

Here we focus on two critically important categories: innovation facilitators, and what we call the orchestrator. We return to the CNO at the end of this chapter and complete the picture of the innovation function by describing that crucial role as leader of the function and integrator of innovation with the rest of the company's ongoing activities.

INNOVATION FACILITATORS

People in an innovation facilitator role shoulder a wide variety of responsibilities and engage in many different activities to support the innovation function. These activities can be grouped into three basic categories.

First, they train company members on the use of tools and frameworks that provide structure for innovation projects. They address innovation projects across the spectrum, from incremental to breakthrough and everything in between. In this way they work to improve the company's innovation effectiveness, help evangelize the proper language for different types of innovation, and ensure that company members are using the tools and frameworks most relevant to the degree of innovativeness and concomitant level of uncertainty they are grappling with. Many innovation facilitators train product development teams on Stage-Gate® processes and teach innovation black belt courses for those seeking to improve their new product acumen. But to be effective, they must also understand the innovation function's role in the company and how breakthrough innovation is managed differently from new product development. They must have learning-based project management tools in their arsenal that serve strategic innovation projects.[1] In that regard, innovation facilitators constantly scan the environment, attend conferences, work with external consultants, and benchmark others to ensure they're as up to date as possible on the most effective techniques for managing innovation. Our experience is that these people walk a fine line between internal pressures to standardize all processes and promoting the notion that different types of innovation require different tools and processes.

A second responsibility is to facilitate important events and meetings that are specific to the strategic innovation agenda. Two of those are idea-generation events and senior-level meetings to develop and review the company's currently articulated strategic intent and progress toward it.

With regard to idea generation, we mentioned in our discussion of the discovery capability (Chapter 5) that many companies initiate the search for breakthroughs or their next domains of strategic intent through a bottom-up approach, by hosting idea jams, idea fairs, and other "creative" events. Part of the innovation facilitators' responsibilities are those associated with designing, organizing, and managing these events if companies decide to stage them. They may also be involved in managing the resulting onslaught of ideas, and helping organize the ideas as input into the discovery function where they can be shaped into compelling business opportunities with game-changing potential.

In addition, innovation facilitators may participate in strategic intent review meetings that are held at the senior levels of the company. While at times external consultants are used for guiding these meetings, the innovation facilitator staff's participation is important since they monitor the portfolio of innovation projects and platforms. In this role they can reinforce the concept of strategic intent as they work with the rest of the members of the innovation function on projects, platforms, and the balancing of the portfolio of innovation investments. They need to be aware of the domains that have been decided on, those under consideration, and the senior leaders' perception of those being worked, so they can provide additional support as needed.

Third, innovation facilitators provide strategic coaching and encouragement to discovery and incubation teams. Table 8.1 shows the distinctions between this type of coaching and the substantive coaching that the level-two Opportunity Domain Leaders and New Business Platform Leaders provide in discovery and incubation.

In short, substantive coaching is more specific to the business platform of concern. In contrast, strategic coaching helps teams recognize what they have learned versus what they're assuming, helps them prioritize which assumptions to test, and works with the team to identify efficient ways to do so. Strategic coaches help innovation teams clarify the strategy of their emerging business opportunities, given the high-uncertainty context in which the team is operating. They help teams see the forest when they're blinded by the trees, and let teams know that the ambiguity they're experiencing is normal given the nature of the innovation they're cultivating. Many team members are new to the world of high-uncertainty innovation, and appreciate knowing that the context they're operating in is to be expected.

The principle underlying strategic coaching is that the team knows more than the coaches do about the details of the emerging business. Strategic coaches do not dispense advice, but instead ask leading questions that help ferret out uncertainties. By listening to the team members talk and

TABLE 8.1   Two Types of Coaches

	Substantive Coaches *Opportunity Domain Leaders (D-2) and New Business Platform Leaders (I-2)*	Strategic Coaches *Innovation Facilitators*
Source of Expertise	Firsthand experience on related projects.	Study of innovation management practices and coaching of many teams.
Critical Experiences	Have executed strategic innovation projects before. Learned by doing/failure.	Exposure to numerous strategic innovation projects over time.
Nature of Expertise	Experience or educational background in the substantive domain.	Innovation process experts. Distinguish breakthrough from incremental innovation and apply relevant processes and tools.
Nature of Broker/ Network Help for Teams	Leverage their networks on the team's behalf.	Encourage and teach teams how to expand and exercise networks.
Nature of Their Value to SI Project/Business Teams	Dispense advice/wisdom. Make decisions together with the team.	Help team members arrive at their own conclusions for next steps.
Success Metrics	Success depends in part on the project's outcome.	Success depends on value project and platform personnel place on their services.

reflecting it back to them, they help the team identify the priorities to be tested, areas of potential risk, and choice points. They can facilitate the team's decisions about which of their many hypotheses or assumptions are most critical to the project's progress and should be tested next. In other words, the strategic coaching process elicits from the team members the next steps they need to take. Coaching sessions help the team move closer to strategic clarity about the nature of the new business that is emerging. One experienced coach described the way he worked with a specific team that was involved in incubating a new business:

I helped them to reflect on, OK, if you find this, what do you do then? If you have to make a choice, what do you do then? So I simply took a mirror and I continuously fed them with, what should you think of? Who do you need to help you? What could you do? What are the options? So select the right people, empower them as much as you can, and sit on top of them to help them and coach them and help them to make decisions. That's the best way to do incubation.

Oftentimes we see that teams neglect organizational uncertainties in favor of advancing the project on technical and market fronts. Yet if the organizational and resource issues are not addressed, then the project may end up without the commitments needed for accessing the right external partners or internal business unit support as needed. The strategic coach helps the team move toward decisions about how those hypotheses will be tested and records the decisions for the team. He keeps them honest and doesn't allow them to focus on the parts of the project that are easiest for the team to tackle.

Our company representatives who described the need for coaching told us:

One thing that we talk about is how we get them to nonintuitive clarity sometimes . . . they're like, oh, my God, I hadn't thought about that or yeah, you're right. And it could be about their people. It could be about their market. It could be about their product.

They require a lot of hand-holding to get them through this.

They seem lost in the market because the market isn't even there, they don't know the processes.

These people need assurance that they're OK because a lot of their work is failure.

I have frequent contact with them. Because team leaders, just like probably everyone else, like to feel the connection with the organization, like to feel that they're making a difference, and they also like feedback, constructive and otherwise. And so I probably see five or six of them a day, whether it's, you know, casually, or a call.

Strategic coaches are good listeners: empathic and nonjudgmental. They are able to solicit comments and opinions, and set an inclusive culture. They have reflective listening skills in that they can summarize key points they hear coming from various team members and articulate them back to the team. They can see patterns in the discussion and draw them out. They're credible, smart, and quick to pick up on undercurrents in the team's discussion in order to surface latent issues.

They ask open-ended rather than leading questions to facilitate teams' learning and identification of next steps in their business's evolution. At the same time, they can be quite directive, in that they keep people on point and don't let conversations wander too far. They know when to guide teams to diverge or converge in their thinking by recognizing patterns in the business's growth through their accumulated experience with many similar teams. Good strategic coaches tend to have a long history with the company and know its strategy and the boundaries of strategic intent, so they can help teams recognize when they need to test organizational sensitivities.

Sometimes people who have been through a strategic innovation assignment cycle off and coach others for a while. They want to help develop others and their recent experiences make them credible. We find that they enjoy working with project teams while not being held responsible for the project's progress, since working on an emerging business can be so intense. Three years after they initiated their Emerging Business Opportunities (EBO) program, IBM began using people who were part of their EBO teams that had "graduated" into mainstream businesses as coaches for new EBOs. They had developed expertise that was transferrable to new EBO leaders. We met people in DSM, Sealed Air, and other companies who did the same.

Conversely, people who've spent time coaching sometimes aspire to move into a project role. While the skills are not the same, the interest is there and they've had the opportunity to learn through working with many teams. This turns out to be a promising and fluid career pattern for those with innovation ambitions. One process facilitator turned incubation project leader told us, "I would have been much less ready for this role [heading a project] without having the experience of being in the consultancy role."

Assessing an innovation process facilitator's performance is not as difficult as it may seem. When you have encountered skilled process facilitators, you know it. They challenge the team's collective thinking and may offer unconventional interpretations of the data. They're demanding of the teams and groups they work with and hold people in working sessions accountable for producing actionable, meaningful outcomes as a result of the session. Innovation team members admit that they would not have arrived at the same conclusion were they to have forged ahead on their own. Teams leave coaching sessions feeling energized and more confident about the next steps they need to undertake.

While facilitators and coaches provide support at the project and platform level, and in facilitating the senior-level meetings that help the company stake its claim on the future through choosing it arenas of strategic intent, the innovation function needs other staff and leadership activity. The orchestrator plays a key role in monitoring, diagnosing, and plugging gaps in the innovation management system and its portfolio of opportunities.

THE ORCHESTRATOR[2]

One of the most important aspects of an innovation function, just like all other organizational functions, is its permanency. Rather than starting and stopping as many new ventures' groups have in the past (on average a four-year life span), an innovation function remains in place. Indeed, our purpose throughout this book has been to describe innovation roles as a way to further institutionalize innovation as a permanent function.

But there is only so much strategic innovation an organization can handle at any point in time. Sometimes the company's capacity for absorbing new businesses is constrained, by external or internal forces. At other times, the organization is crying for more and wants breakthroughs immediately. Still other times, the company cannot absorb any more new business platforms but wants to leverage what it has into new "adjacent" areas, as these opportunities are still replete with plenty of uncertainty and not likely to succeed via a Stage-Gate-like process. The reality is that organizations experience an ever changing capacity for strategic innovation. The orchestrator plays an important role in helping to match the innovation function's activities and portfolio with the company's appetite for more breakthroughs.

The orchestrator bears the twin responsibilities of (a) ensuring the innovation function is working properly and (b) ensuring that it is aligned with the company's capacity for innovation. He shares these priorities with the CNO, and serves as the CNO's associate—sort of an innovation operations executive—in pursuit of these objectives. However, their priorities are flipped. Whereas the CNO's primary concern is the latter, making sure the relationship of the innovation function aligns with the company's capacity to absorb innovation; the orchestrator is primarily concerned with the former, ensuring the effectiveness of the internal workings of the innovation function itself. Specifically, he attends to the innovation portfolio's health, raises concerns as needed, ensures that the discovery, incubation, and acceleration competencies are seamlessly linked, and implements continuous improvement changes within the innovation function once he and the CNO agree.

Regarding the innovation function's effective operation, the orchestrator must ensure that the discovery, incubation, and acceleration capabilities are working well, that projects and platforms are moving along at a reasonable pace from discovery to incubation and from incubation to acceleration, and that the pipeline into discovery is able to refresh the innovation system as needed.

He must also consider that the project, platform and portfolio levels of the function are well integrated, since that is how the innovation function is designed to handle risk. For example, the orchestrator evaluates whether the opportunity domains and business platforms at level two in our matrix are actually robust enough, with multiple options to explore and develop, rather than glorified projects that are focused on a new product line or market. In this way, a setback in any single level-one opportunity or project provides learning for the platform level but is not necessarily a showstopper. On the other hand, level-two domains and platforms that are hitting bumps in the road at every turn should be sunsetted, and the portfolio refreshed. Someone needs to call attention to those withering opportunities if the teams are not doing so themselves. At the same time, the array of level-two opportunity domains and emerging business platforms should represent a diverse field of initiatives, so that the failure of any one still leaves plenty of new growth businesses on the table. DSM moved from four to two emerging business areas over five years, and then added one new one. GE similarly fast-tracked one of its Advanced Technology Programs to a business unit as it became clear that the innovation was just a bit more than incremental. Over the four years of our study they stopped several others and initiated one or two new ones. These things happen, but, just as venture capitalists rely on one or a few of the investments to win big and carry the rest of the portfolio, so too does the innovation function. That can only happen if the new businesses are cleverly diversified across technology bases, markets, time horizons, and the degree of alignment with the company's current businesses. All of these risk management techniques are designed into the innovation portfolio's structure, and it is the orchestrator who watches carefully to make sure those design elements are holding steady.

Beyond its diversity, the orchestrator monitors other aspects of the strategic innovation portfolio's health. He ensures that there is an agreed upon set of objectives for the portfolio's characteristics,[3] and monitors those as key performance indicators (KPI's) of the innovation function. Some of these metrics include the portfolio's churn rate, its size, its composition within discovery and incubation, its alignment with the company's articulated domains of strategic intent, the pacing of programs across discovery, incubation, and acceleration, cross-portfolio synergies, and commercial returns.

In monitoring these aspects of the portfolio, the orchestrator is driven to diagnose the innovation management system and find ways to improve it to meet those KPI's. One orchestrator described to us a point at which he realized the incubation portfolio was bloated, and that emerging business platforms that had been growing in revenues for some time and were seemingly ready were not being transitioned to acceleration. After a bit of investigation and reflection he concluded that the innovation function leadership enjoyed the kudos they were receiving for the revenue growth, even though incubation metrics were not supposed to include revenue growth, and that the emerging business platform leaders didn't want to come under the scrutiny of acceleration metrics. These were the wrong reasons to keep the new businesses in the incubation portfolio, and so he voiced the concern and the businesses were transitioned to acceleration. He had succeeded in a very important exercise . . . making sure that each part of the innovation function was fulfilling its role, not that of another, and that each was being held accountable for the relevant metrics rather than the metrics that they could easily meet.

Another orchestrator we encountered described a benchmarking study he led the company in every two years. Conducted by a large global consulting firm, the study involved eliciting responses to a survey about the company's innovation system. He collected 750 responses from across the organization. Those were compared with the company's own responses from the past years to note points of improvement and setbacks, and with results from other participating companies in the same industry. The orchestrator used those responses as input into his ongoing assessment of the company's innovation function's health. Other orchestrators described periodic times of reflection, diagnosing for themselves and with others what was working well, what was not working well, and what was missing in their company's innovation system. *Innovation diagnostics* is a term they used regularly. Once diagnosed, orchestrators address the identified weaknesses with a continuous improvement mind-set.

Ensuring that the DIA system is working well at the project, platform, and portfolio levels is the orchestrator's primary responsibility. At the same time he must also connect the innovation function with the rest of the organization, in order to gain access to needed expertise resident in the company to help with specific issues that the emerging businesses are facing. The orchestrator also supports the chief innovation officer in ensuring that senior leaders remain committed to the company's stated strategic intent as it starts coming to life through the emerging businesses that are incubating. In this capacity, he works with innovation steering committees, reports on portfolio metrics, and maintains relationships with other support functions such as purchasing, legal, public relations, and HR. To effectively manage those relationships, orchestrators typically identify one or two key stakeholders in each of these support functions who are comfortable with novelty and ambiguity, and who enjoy innovation. He advocates for their support of the innovation function to their supervisors if necessary, since the work they need to do on behalf of innovation may depart from the normal procedures of their department. Legal agreements for joint development partnerships in incubation, for example, may not be able to specify the outcome of the work a priori, but instead focus on describing the objectives on an experiment or trial to be conducted. Negotiations with new suppliers may require that the purchasing department support a different business model than the company has used in the past. And the HR/OD function needs to understand enough about strategic innovation that they can clearly describe and identify potential candidates' skills, competencies, and backgrounds that would fit any of the roles described in this book.

Effective orchestrators are reflective systems thinkers. Their credibility comes from a long history of solving company issues, typically in a variety of roles. Many we've seen are late stage in their careers, but midcareer works as well. The most important point is that an orchestrator has an eye for continuous improvement and critically assesses whether creeping changes in the innovation function's mandate are healthy or are taking the wrong turn. They behave like auditors and cheerleaders at the same time. While they monitor the innovation function's effectiveness and implement improvements, they are simultaneously making sure that the rest of the company is aware of the innovation function, its role in the organization and any and all success stories for which it can claim credit.

THE CHIEF INNOVATION OFFICER (CNO)

We first described the CNO in Chapter 6, in the capacity of incubation director. There we noted his responsibilities associated with managing the portfolio of new business platforms that the company is currently incubating.

The CNO also holds an executive leadership role in the company as head of the strategic innovation function. In that capacity he carries two major responsibilities, which parallel those of the orchestrator, but are reversed in priority as discussed above. The CNO's top priority is to ensure the company incorporates strategic innovation into its DNA. To that end he focuses on the health of the firm's innovation culture so that strategic innovation can flourish, and he defines, cultivates and maintains the proper linkage between the strategic innovation function and the mainstream organization. Second is to maintain the health of the innovation management system itself so that it produces.

LINKING STRATEGIC INNOVATION WITH THE MAINSTREAM ORGANIZATION

As part of managing the link between the strategic innovation function and the rest of the company, the CNO must watch that innovation remains on the organizational agenda and, in fact, is viewed as imperative. She works to make sure the innovation function is embedded in the company's financial, planning, and budgeting systems in a way that confers it organizational legitimacy and reduces threat of on-again, off-again commitments. In other words, she protects it from being viewed as an appendage, an afterthought, or a once-in-a-while, ad hoc activity. She is responsible for delivering new business platforms that will become the company's growth engines of tomorrow, along with other forms of organizational impact including cross-portfolio synergies, uplift, and spillover effects that come with innovation investments that are leveraged in a healthy way.

To that end, she consistently educates other senior leaders about the realities of how markets for evolutionary and breakthrough innovations actually unfold so that their expectations are aligned with the realities of what the strategic innovation portfolio can deliver. "Our leadership is committed to strategic innovation intellectually, but not in their gut" is a phrase we've heard several times from innovation personnel. So excellent CNOs cultivate their relationship with senior leadership to become a trusted confidant and overcome this resistance. We know of CEOs who have their CNOs on speed dial because they (the CEOs) know that their own instinct is to decide in favor of operational excellence and short termism rather than in favor of an innovation mandate when faced with the many daily decisions required of them. They know they need to check in with their CNO. That's progress, and a sign of the respect afforded to innovation in a growing number of companies.

The CNO must recognize changes in the organization's capacity to support and absorb new businesses born of strategic innovation. As part of this he must determine whether to cooperate with or challenge his peers in their perceptions of whether it's time to slow down the investment in innovation or stay the course. A CNO can reduce or expand the innovation portfolio, stall its progress or speed it, or even alter the innovation function's mandate to incorporate adjacencies and other forms of strategic innovation in recognition of these realities. But no matter what these modifications are, he carries the responsibility to advocate for some level of continued investment rather than a complete shutdown on innovation commitments when the environment changes. Just as marketing budgets increase and shrink given economic realities, but are never stamped out completely, so too should the innovation function be managed. It is the CNO's job to ensure this happens.

To accomplish such ambitious goals, the CNO must be able to gain and maintain the commitment and participation of other organizational leaders, who have more immediate responsibilities. He leads the conversation among the senior leadership that determines and periodically revisits the company's chosen domains of strategic intent. He makes sure that the innovation portfolio is linked to that strategic intent and, in fact, informs it. He situates the strategic innovation function and portfolio amongst the incremental innovation and other new product development activities in the firm, and rationalizes the company's collective incremental, evolutionary and breakthrough innovation management systems. He chairs the innovation council, which evaluates progress of the emerging business opportunities and makes investment decisions. He recommends which of the emerging incubating businesses are promising enough and mature enough for transition to the acceleration portfolio and monitors that they are receiving adequate resources, given the competition for resources with the immediate needs the organization is facing. Finally, he works with company leaders to ensure smooth, effective transitions out of the innovation function and into a receiving operating unit, or a new unit if one is to be created, for emerging businesses that have reached a sufficient level of maturity to stand on their own.

Managing the interface between his function and the rest of the company is more difficult for the CNO than for other organizational leaders (CMO, CFO, or other senior vice presidents) because the innovation function is focused primarily on the firm's future. Therefore, he must link innovation actions and investments to the firm's present situation and encourage others to consider issues beyond the current. It is precisely this challenge that organizations struggle with, and the identification of a permanent role with that focus provides the opportunity and agenda for the firm to take care of its future through growth and innovation initiatives.

INNOVATION FUNCTION EFFECTIVENESS

Besides her work to maintain the innovation function's legitimacy and interfaces with the rest of the company, the CNO is concerned with the effectiveness of the function itself. If it cannot deliver results, it will become increasingly difficult for the company to support a strategic innovation function and may revert to a championing model. That is why developing the expertise associated with discovery, incubation, and acceleration and their system-level interactions is so crucial. In this regard, the CNO's concerns differ from those of the orchestrator, who manages the progress of opportunities and emerging businesses within the portfolio. The CNO uses the portfolio's progress as a signal, but just one signal, of the Innovation Function Management Systems' health and productivity. She monitors all of its elements, shown in Figure 8.1 and reprised from Chapter 2.[4]

On this score, the CNO's concerns include the innovation function's budget (and its consistency over time), the adequacy of its talent pool, and the consistency and uniqueness of its mandate, ensuring that it is not creeping too much toward incremental innovation given the constant pressures to produce immediate results. He makes sure the innovation committees that make portfolio decisions are properly composed. As we mentioned earlier, complete representation of all the business unit leadership, for example, is not necessarily the best practice. The innovation function is agnostic to the company's current situation and business unit structure and is more

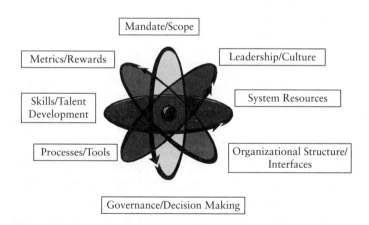

FIGURE 8.1   Management System Elements
Source: Reprinted with permission from John Wiley & Sons, from Gina Colarelli O'Connor, Richard Leifer, Albert S. Paulson, and Lois S. Peters, *Grabbing Lightning: Building a Capability for Breakthrough Innovation* (San Francisco: Jossey-Bass, 2008). Copyright © 2008 by John Wiley & Sons, Inc.

concerned with ensuring that new businesses requiring significant structural changes in the company are afforded the considerations they need.

The CNO ensures that the roles required to manage the portfolio are established and filled by people with the right skills and experiences, and that they are rewarded appropriately given their work is of much more uncertain outcome than most other roles in the organization. He is concerned that the processes used for project management are the right ones rather than just those the organization is comfortable with, and that a culture of creation and experimentation, combined with urgency and disciplined execution is maintained and reinforced.

He is concerned with the innovation function's ever evolving structure. Besides the discovery, incubation, and acceleration activities, many chief innovation officers incorporate other mechanisms to ensure a steady stream of inbound innovation opportunities and options for exit. Some of these include a corporate venture capital fund, a spinout model for emerging businesses that have potential but don't yet fit the company's capability set, and a technology licensing office. The degree of centralization of the innovation function is also part of the CNO's concern as he evolves its structure. Several advocate that strategic innovation should be taking place in the business units themselves, and assume the responsibility for overseeing that the innovation function is extended into those business units and is fully supported there. All these activities, and other types of experiments as well, serve the interest of the company's ability to renew itself through innovation, and the CNO designs them into the innovation function as needed.

Finally, the last element of the management system is metrics. The CNO identifies, gains commitment for, and delivers on metrics that are relevant and meaningful for strategic innovation. Ultimately, of course, the innovation function is responsible for producing new businesses that are based on game-changing innovation in the industry and the company, but there are many interim indicators of this longer-term prize. The CNO clarifies those, reminds the organization of their importance, and makes sure they're reported regularly in order to gain the recognition of the innovation function's contribution to the company's well-being and long-term health.

In actuality, the CNO role is still relatively rare. While the recent movement to appoint chief innovation officers in large companies is appealing, in many cases we find this title is but a recasting of the chief technology officer or vice president of R&D's job title, with little change to her responsibilities. This leaves little formal recognition of the new business creation responsibilities at the project, platform, and portfolio levels that, in many companies, are severely understaffed and lack proper role models or definitions. In a show of progress, several companies that participated in our research program are on their second or third CNO, and have modified the background and critical experience set they're looking for, from those with technical training and a bit of experience in the business units as a technical expert, to a much more rigorous combination of technical education, business education, and experience in both.

Beyond those critical experiences, we know the following about the characteristics of CNOs that help them succeed: They're systems thinkers, highly strategic, and are driven by the opportunity to harness the organization's knowledge and resources to solve big, complex world problems. They're visionary and inspirational, but also decisive. "He can describe a dream for the company through 2025," representatives in one company told us. Others echoed the same sentiment about their own CNOs. But that wasn't the case for all.

Several companies set up a great infrastructure for strategic innovation but had a weak CNO, who, among other missteps, did not develop and gain buy-in for strategic intent among the company's leaders. Those working in the discovery and incubation parts of the innovation function described their frustration with the lack of boundaries for vetting project ideas that were coming forward, and the resulting short-term perspective used to evaluate each singular opportunity:

We look at megatrends . . . where the world is headed, but if I had to say what the strategic direction is, it is to "move into the new/new space of new technologies and new markets." It was more of an objective or metric than a strategy. We have started to build our portfolio with "anything goes." Then I heard someone from another company describe their portfolio strategy for new business creation at a conference, and I told my boss that we should really work to put something like this together. We tried to do that ourselves but quite frankly—and my boss has been a great mentor to me and a good, good friend of mine and we get along wonderfully, but his boss (the CNO) never really blessed it . . . so it is still out there. You can make any subject area that you pick fit that model that we put together, so it doesn't help. We haven't gotten there yet. So I think part of the problem is, we really do have good strategies for our three business units, but we don't have much strategy for new business creation.

The ability to manage a high-powered innovation council, create a culture for innovation, and execute the portfolio's development with a real options mentality are crucial skills for a CNO. To develop these skills, most have had experience across discovery, incubation, and acceleration, and also in the business unit settings. They've done the project work but also the strategic foresight development work. Their breadth of experience allows them to understand each of those environments and maintain credibility with many different constituents. After all, this person is the one leading the company toward its future. Without organizational credibility, she cannot have influence.

We are aware that this description sounds like a one-in-a-million person. This is likely because companies have not yet had the focus, clarity, or opportunity to groom the CNO of the future. They've also not had the opportunity since the role is so new. What we've observed so far has been the starting point that helps develop a proper profile for this role, so that companies can begin to identify talent early on and institute development and succession planning, as they do for other executive leaders. We have, in fact, met several very effective CNOs in the course of our research. We highlight one here.

THE CHIEF INNOVATION OFFICER AT DSM

Rob van Leen has held the role of CNO at DSM for more than ten years.[5] He was the company's first CNO, having been appointed in 2006 by CEO Peter Elverding. In 2000, Elverding had set out a significant vision statement for DSM, called "Vision 2005—Focus and Value." The document conveyed the need to continue DSM's transformation from commodity chemicals into more value-added products, thus enabling its entry into higher growth and leading-edge markets. DSM had begun by establishing competencies in life sciences and performance materials. The vision included doubling sales to €10 billion by 2005, with more than 50 percent of sales to come from newly acquired companies and 80 percent from specialty products.

In 2007 Elverding moved on from DSM and Feike Sijbesma took over as chairman of the management board and CEO. He was just as committed as his predecessor to accelerating DSM's innovation efforts. Elverding and Sijbesma had both offered van Leen their trusting confidence that he could do the job as CNO. Elverding is reported to have declared to van Leen upon offering him the job: "Nobody else is better equipped to do it, so you have to!"

Van Leen had come to DSM in 1999, via the acquisition of Gist-Brocades NV, a Dutch yeast company that had branched into enzymes and become a leader in penicillin and food ingredients. There van Leen had been R&D director of Food Specialties. He held various roles in DSM, and by 2006 he was the business group director of DSM food specialties, developing its nutrition competency area. He held a PhD in molecular biology and an MBA, and had led breakthrough, evolutionary, and incremental innovation projects. By 2006 he had developed a strong reputation and high levels of credibility within DSM.

Interestingly, he and Sijbesma had worked together previously at Gist-Brocades, and knew they complemented one another's strengths well. Their ability to work so closely together has been described by others in the company as a contributing factor to DSM's success in innovation to date.

That said, there was no clear assignment when the new post was announced in 2006. So, van Leen's first task was to define the job himself. One of his first undertakings was to establish a new organizational setup that built on DSM's recent restructuring of R&D. In that arrangement the traditional central research lab was replaced by a "hybrid model" where competence-oriented groups were created to serve the entire company, but were located in specific business groups. Centers of Excellence in Biotechnology, Nutrition, Organic Chemistry, and Materials Science were established, each in a different business unit and geographic location. A corporate-level research group was maintained, to keep the technology base for those competence-oriented groups at a state of the art level. Directed by the CTO, it consumed about 10 percent of the total research budget.

The R&D restructuring was in place in the early 2000s. Additionally, divestitures and acquisitions had accompanied the new competency development initiatives such that, by 2005, approximately 80 percent of DSM's sales were of specialty products. In 2005 DSM instituted "Vision 2010—Building on Strengths," a strategy focused on reaping the benefits of the portfolio transformation undertaken during the preceding years.

It was in this context that van Leen recognized that even such a fundamental portfolio transformation would not automatically translate into strong and sustained innovative prowess. He believed that DSM needed an integrated approach to take innovations to market, and established the DSM Innovation Center for that purpose in 2006. The center was purposely designed as a business-oriented group rather than a staff support function. It incorporated its own HR, controller, and budgeting and planning functions. In addition to those business support groups, the DSM Innovation Center is composed of an innovation process excellence team, technology licensing, DSM venturing, the corporate technology officer (yes, corporate R&D reports to the CNO!), the Business Incubator (DSM's term for identifying and elaborating opportunities), and then a set of incubating and accelerating opportunities, called Emerging Business Areas (EBAs). The Business Incubator focuses on DSM's stated areas of strategic focus for innovation, including climate change and energy, health and wellness, functionality and performance, emerging economies, and the intersection of life sciences and materials sciences. The most promising businesses from the Business Incubator were expected to be pursued as EBAs, and the others, either too small or less strategically linked, were to be transferred directly to a business group or sold off. The move to these stated innovation focus areas occurred in 2008, two years after the DSM Innovation Center was formed, as van Leen and his team realized the importance of working beyond individual projects toward a portfolio of strategically chosen platforms. The director of the Business Incubator at the time stated:

DSM should anchor into areas and not focus on products. Focusing on different projects within an area makes us less vulnerable and more flexible. Management should first fence the boundaries where the business should be, then let the Incubator and the Business Groups work within these fields.[6]

By designing and implementing this structure, Rob legitimized strategic innovation within the company, ensured it is embedded in the company's financial and planning systems, clarified the mandate of the Innovation Center vis-à-vis other parts of the innovation function in the company, and maintained a healthy portfolio of EBA platforms.

There has been turnover in DSM's portfolio of EBAs. The Innovation Center began with four in 2006, in the domains of industrial biotechnology, biomedical materials, personalized nutrition, and specialty packaging. By 2010 they recognized that not all the EBA activities were evolving in a direction that would add sustained value to DSM, so they reduced their focus on the two domains of personalized nutrition and specialty packaging and partnered with other companies to commercialize those. They've since ramped up their investment in the remaining two by beginning to acquire small companies with complementary resources, and have added one new EBA on advanced surfaces, which moves them into the solar energy domain.[7] Combined with the original two, now called DSM Biomedical, and DSM Bio-Based Products and Services—company leadership is targeting a combined sales level of €1 billion by 2020 from these three new EBAs, all the while remaining one of the leaders on the Dow Jones sustainability index, in keeping with their corporate commitment to a healthy natural environment.

Rob led the design and development of the Innovation Center, hired his own leadership team to build it, and got the portfolio started. Those who work for him, directly and indirectly, describe his leadership style as insightful, inclusive, and enabling. What follows is part of an interview in which we asked others about him:

Question: What are the qualities that make him the right fit for the job of CNO?

Answer: First of all he is extremely smart. He has a very broad view of the role. He has been an R&D director but he also has been a business group director. He has seen both the R&D part and the business part. That is a very nice combination because he can engage in the content of the discussion on the technology, market and business sides. He can follow and he can guide, and he has credibility.

Question: Is he a challenger? Or sort of an encouraging and nurturing person?

Answer: I would say that our CEO is more of the challenger—he challenges you all the time. Rob is not so much a challenger. He is more of a person who would ask critical questions. He gathers people around him within the innovation center that are quite independent, and can do their own job. You only have to steer them a little bit. He is not the constant challenger. He is more of a person who gives people space to do their things and to work on their projects.

Question: What motivates him?

Answer: He is not a person who jumps into everything. He is more balanced. But this is an example, to show what motivates him. Once we had a discussion where he said . . . "You know, it would really be great if we could make meat of all kinds of leftovers or waste. Because it is possible . . . just proteins and . . . it comes from the content of meat so it really is very simple. How you get the taste right may be a challenge, but the content is not that difficult. It would be great if we could do something in terms of sustainability and what we want to do at DSM for the world . . . to make meat out of waste."

Question: So he is a bit of an idealist?

Answer: Yeah but very realistically.

Question: A realistic idealist??

Answer: He has a realistic view on things. He says that it will be great and then he can tell you why it is or is not possible and what time it would take, but most probably in twenty years' time that is possible.

Question: So he can kind of set out what a vision could be and then people can rally around that. Is that the idea?

Answer: Yeah, but he gathers those people around him who have ideas on their own. He gives a lot of room and some people can handle it very well and for others that is more difficult. If you ask him for a complete roadmap, he would not give you that.

From this discussion we see that Rob's leadership style seems to be based on inspiring and motivating smart, like-minded people with his grand visions, coupled with the expertise to discuss the details of how such a vision might be accomplished at the technical level. He's inspiring and intellectually stimulating as a leader.

When asked to describe his responsibilities, Rob responds with equally grand description: to bring innovation to a higher level of performance throughout the company. His performance is measured on four criteria: innovation sales, pipeline quality and value, building the right team, and health and quality of the innovation infrastructure. The first of these means that he has concern for innovation that is happening in the business units as well as in the innovation center. In fact, DSM has been aggressive in setting sales objectives from innovation, expecting that over a five-year period they'd double their sales resulting from new products, services, and processes. As Rob described it:

It was clear that everybody looked at me to make sure that happened, but most of those sales came from the running businesses. So we were expecting much of this to come from the existing business groups and only very little from the innovation center. There is a big lead time for the emerging businesses which means starting an innovation and investment in a certain field, but the point where it yields substantial sales, in our case that can be ten to fifteen years down the road.

So if we wanted to really make an impact we also had to look at speeding up existing projects and platforms that are developing in the existing business groups—and we started to develop new fields in the innovation center outside the scope of the existing business groups at the same time. The only hope would be that in probably five to ten years we will see reasonable sales from the innovation center. We stuck our neck out for 2020, so fifteen years down the road we want to create €1 billion of additional business from what we have started in the innovation center. It's really a stretch target, but we can achieve it partly by acquiring young business start-ups and accelerating their growth.

To guide the innovation center's portfolio strategy, Rob participates in the company's Corporate Strategy Dialogue (CSD), an event that takes place every five years. Senior leadership conducts an "overhaul" of their strategy and determines their emphases for the next five years at the portfolio level. Rob described the importance of that plan in guiding decisions he makes within the innovation center:

We follow that plan very diligently. So you could say between 2000 and 2005, we decided to get out of petrochemicals. After 2005, we decided to focus only on life science and material science and we divested additional basic chemicals and our more cyclical businesses. We also said that we need to be more externally oriented and market driven instead of operational excellence oriented and now we have said we have more or less shaped the company. Now what we want are two strong pillars in life science and material science, we got it all through organic growth now or local innovation and acquisitions in the fields that I have just mentioned. We also have set some clear targets, and for the next five years, that is the route.

While the corporate strategy dialogue is a very useful exercise and helps the innovation center, Rob also notes that a five-year planning horizon presents challenges when incubation may take fifteen years for some of his emerging business areas:

Our mismatched planning horizons present an interesting dilemma. I constantly need to remind people of that phenomenon, so even though people know this and have the history—we have several of those projects where we can clearly show how long it takes and how long the returns are negative, you have this, say, relative impatience which usually starts to kick in about after about three years. But when they start saying, "Wow you have spent so much money and we haven't seen anything back from it and that is after five years," well, most of them are in complaining mode. I have to explain this to the analysts and so on but it is a matter of, I would say, keeping your back straight and going on. This is increasingly difficult of course, so the early successes help you to get continued support. In that respect in biomedical after about two and a half years we bought a small company that was growing very rapidly, very comfortably and that has definitely helped the image and the confidence of the senior management and the stories we could tell externally. And we hope to do that in the other EBAs as well. That helps you strengthen the story, you increase the speed and of course then people see that it will really be there, and recognize that this was not only a story on paper but it is tangible.

These insights into Rob's decisions and actions show the expertise a CNO must have to successfully advocate for innovation and maintain its legitimacy in the company in the face of the natural tensions that arise between the innovation mandate and the mandate for short term financial performance. He also balances the organic growth and acquisitions, since neither on its own allows an established company to create new business platforms that bring real value to the marketplace in a timely fashion.

In order to be successful at convincing others, Rob has to ensure the innovation function is working well. Together with the orchestrator, chief innovation officers make decisions to implement changes in the structure and processes for developing and nurturing their portfolio. Rob instituted changes early on to conduct more elaborate discovery and incubation activities prior to labeling an opportunity as an EBA. He described these early days in the Innovation Center as follows:

Today, the EBAs are very different from what happens in the incubator within the Innovation Center. But at the beginning, they weren't so differentiated. Our current structure and process of course did not exist when we started all this. Today, an EBA will emerge from this assessment of trends in the world and technology and feasibility and so on. But when we started in 2006, we came up with this concept of EBAs without having an incubation period except for the fact that for instance in biomedical we had some scattered projects running already in R&D for two, three years, but there was no strategy and no goal. We just thought that it might be interesting to do something with biomedical materials.

In that Corporate Strategy Dialogue of 2005, we conducted a more strategic analysis and we confirmed that biomedical will be an interesting area. It will grow. People will get older. They need replacement of body parts and so on. We have a lot of understanding of people's bodies, of drugs, of materials so this is an opportunity space with DSM and we should go for it and then we founded the EBA immediately. Now that is a bit dangerous because you basically don't take time to figure out whether that idea was good, you just sort of jump in immediately and the same was true for something we call then white biotechnology. Now we call it Bio-Based Products and Services, and you could say those were lucky shots or they were close enough to what we already have to be a success. The other two EBAs, Specialty Packaging and Personalized Nutrition, were conceptually extremely interesting but we have far less history, far less fit. So the trends were right I think they were also confirmed on the last five years but the fit to DSM, turned out to be less than we anticipated and that is the reason why after . . . the next evaluation we decided to abandon them again.

Rob strengthened discovery and instituted incubation as he realized that they were not taking enough time to scope and explore the opportunity platforms and their potential fit with DSM. Every idea sounded good at the beginning (as is the case with most of the companies in our research), but as the opportunity unfolds in incubation, the business model may require a number of adjustments in order to align with the company's vision of its operating model for the future. Just jumping into late incubation and acceleration didn't work. However the issue was diagnosed, it was up to Rob to add those capabilities and make those changes . . . and he has.

Of all the skills and characteristics a CNO requires, a will to protect the company's future through strategic innovation and the ability to execute on behalf of that agenda is by far the most crucial. One might argue that all members of the company's executive leadership should demonstrate these characteristics. But while others may be more focused on risk management and defensive protection, the CNO's job is most directly related to the company's growth and renewal agenda. In that capacity, her responsibility for managing the relationship between the innovation function and the rest of the company is her key priority.

Rob has experienced the struggles associated with matching the Innovation Center's ability to produce interesting growth opportunities for the company beyond what it is able to absorb at any single point in time—a good problem to have. That matching function is a constant refrain we hear from CNOs, but Rob is looking for creative solutions to leverage those opportunities in different ways, as are many of his counterparts in other companies. They are revisiting ways to spin out such opportunities and maintain an equity share, with rights to buy them back at a point in time. Others are structuring joint ventures with companies who can help leverage the potential breakthrough into markets or applications that the company does not currently have an interest in developing directly.

In the case of DSM, Rob is working with the senior leadership to embed the innovation function more deeply across the entire company, so that strategic innovation becomes a more broadly accepted activity, with greater participation from other parts of the organization. He is attempting to institutionalize innovation as a permanent business function just like any other. He's extending his reach, his influence as a corporate executive, and his impact, owing to some of the successes that the Innovation Center has generated. Rob is also forging a better understanding of the competencies necessary to successfully develop EBAs. In the passage below, he reflects on the challenges associated with the innovation function's success and the vision he has for extending its reach:

Well one of the problems, you know, is the success rate that we have. We basically have a huge budgetary problem now because we have too many initiatives that look very promising and they all need more resources. We are at a stage where you really need to kill stuff that potentially is very significant. We are bringing that discussion to the corporate level innovation council which is the collection of innovation directors of all the business groups that I am chairing. We are trying to manage the radical innovation over the total company, so not only looking at the radical innovation in the innovation center, but also what are we doing in the business groups. Can we develop and use a similar system to characterize them and then come up with a proposal to develop them in the most optimal way within DSM? Maybe we'll stop some things, or bring things together, start other things but spend the money currently being invested in radical innovation across the company more wisely.

Obviously this is a sensitive topic. Until now, I have been encouraging people [in the business units], helping them and so on. Now we are sitting together and discussing the quality of the innovation portfolio of each and every group. We are going through cycles of discussion of each business group's radical innovation portfolio and in the fourth quarter, we will see when we have consolidated that and whether we want to make changes.

We are looking at two things. The first is to see if the balance between incremental and radical per business group is optimally aligned with strategy, and you could say we are providing advice on that. The business group leaders can do what they want within their business group. But secondly, we are going to consolidate the radical innovations at the DSM corporate level, and say maybe "Business Group A" should do a little bit less and we are going to take away money over there and we are going to put that in "Business Group C" because they have better opportunities when we take a DSM corporate look. That will be rather unusual in DSM because the business groups really have the primary say in how they run their business, and do not want interference. This will be the first time that we are going to do that and that is why we need to be very careful how we go about it. Basically I am working towards the process where they are already part of the discussion so that we arrive at a jointly agreed conclusion.

As CNO, Rob is adjusting the innovation portfolio so that each part is operating under the management system that best fits it mandate. He clarified that he did not think removing all of the evolutionary and breakthrough innovation from the businesses was the right thing to do, but that it was his job to keep track of what was happening where.

I think the business groups should be involved in radical innovation because you are not only there for today, but also for the future. Your successor should also have a pipeline of opportunities to manage . . . not only a dying business. So of course you can debate about the degree of radicality that belongs there and I think, in the Innovation Center we should take on more radical projects than what they are doing. We have an interesting grid on which we plot all the initiatives to keep track of these things.

And it also means that we need to manage that part of the grid together to do the best things for the company. I think the only way this will work is when everybody is fully in the process, it's completely transparent and we go through an evolution together. I am certain that in a couple of years from now, we will be able to do this much, much better.

At the end of the day, Rob's concern is that everyone on the innovation council and beyond, essentially the leadership of the company, is in agreement with the way responsibility, accountability and the management system for strategic innovation is set up, and that DSM's future health is their collective objective. Stockholders couldn't ask for much more.

INSTITUTING A STRATEGIC INNOVATION FUNCTION THROUGH PEOPLE

At this point it should be apparent that there are many roles to be filled if a company wants a strong, sustained ability to leverage strategic innovation for competitive advantage. We all know that R&D is critically important, but it is just the beginning. Discovery, incubation, and acceleration have to be instituted as capabilities, and that means people need to know how to execute them, and those groups have to be managed. Projects collect up into business platforms, and those comprise a company's portfolio of new business options for the future. Those platforms are not the result of a creative idea somewhere, but rather of discussions about the company's desired position in the future, based on its current competencies and perspective on emerging new areas that it should create and dominate. All of this requires leadership, in the person of the CNO, who is supported by a second in command that orchestrates the innovation portfolio, along with a bench of strategic coaches, facilitators, and educators.

It all sounds so rational. It's probably not too difficult to spot people who perform these roles in your company today, if you really get a good look. The problem is the lack of formal recognition of these roles, the resultant turnover in these jobs, and companies' inability to retain and properly leverage that talent. And this is specifically why we need to institutionalize the innovation function! In Chapter 9 we examine practices that companies are trying in order to achieve a true capability for strategic innovation. They're attempting to move beyond "one-off" innovation jobs and projects to developing true career paths for innovators. We're at the very beginning of this journey, as you'll see, but the uptick in attention to innovation roles and careers is indeed occurring, and it is exciting to see.

9   DEVELOPING AND RETAINING TALENT
Career Paths for Innovation Personnel

It's said that to develop expertise one must invest significant time in deliberate practice,[1] in some cases up to ten thousand hours. That's five human years of work focused on attaining expertise under the tutelage of a mentor or instructor. To be sure, an avid debate exists on the relative contributions of inborn talent and practice in the achievement of expertise.[2] However, every contributor to the debate signals that both are important. Several note that companies don't pay much attention to the concept of deliberate practice. Certainly we find that to be the case with innovation.

The fact that companies don't leverage this rather well-known principle of expertise development should not be a surprise. People are ambitious. Staying in one job for too long sends a bad signal . . . that you are not interested in moving up the career ladder. But at the end of the day, companies need expertise. It should not all reside in one or a few individuals, it has to be more broadly present in the company. That means we need people who have years of experience in an area, and who are willing to train and mentor others who wish to develop a similar expertise. We need organizational memory and organizational expertise for strategic innovation.

Everyone we have spoken with declares that they have improved their ability to commercialize strategic innovations the longer they've been at it, and, specifically, the more projects they've been involved with. Sticking with one project forever doesn't help. Cycling across multiple opportunities does.

Although most of the people we studied only stayed in their roles for eighteen months to a couple of years, many expressed a desire to make their career in innovation. Some managed to find a way, but for most career advancement wasn't an option if they chose to stay. Throughout the last several chapters, we described innovation roles and the selection criteria managers can use to fill them with people who will be more likely to succeed. To be sure, some are more capable than others at new business creation, just owing to their innate characteristics and abilities to handle the unfamiliar and unexpected.[3] So finding and selecting the right people for clearly defined roles to begin with is important. But that is just step one.

Our interest is to address the development of talent management policies that will help companies (a) build an expertise for strategic innovation and (b) make strategic innovation an enduring organizational capability. To accomplish these twin objectives, companies need to address two additional concerns associated with talent management: developing people through some version of deliberate practice and retaining them.

Many companies interested in competing on the basis of strategic and breakthrough innovation have provided people with stimulating innovation-based assignments and jobs, or allowed intrapreneurs the freedom to break rules. But our research shows that most organizations are not providing realistic opportunities for innovation careers. This disconnect is important: it is the firmament of an innovation career path, not an inconsistent string of assignments, that can help build expertise and drive the company's organic growth and renewal agenda. Simply stated most companies may be creating innovation jobs, but not innovation careers!

We start this chapter by illustrating the career development advice that innovation experts are receiving now. We offer our thoughts for a better way, and then describe some emerging talent management approaches that are in the works and build on these to offer suggestions that we believe can bear fruit.

CAREER PATH OPTIONS FOR INNOVATION EXPERTS: CURRENT PRACTICE

Chapter 3 described a number of career-related challenges that innovation experts face. Now that we have developed a framework of innovation roles, it is important to take a look at the types of advice those who aspire to become innovation experts are typically given to succeed in their organizations. In a nutshell, they are given two options if they want to stay in innovation: Cycle in and out of it periodically, or make sure your project succeeds.

Option 1: Cycle In and Out of Innovation

The theory behind the "cycle in and out" advice is that innovation projects are viewed as "on the fringe" of the organization. To be effective, one needs influence, and to have influence, one needs to maintain and at times rebuild his credibility in the organization (after an innovation "fringe" assignment). The only way to do that, according to this view, is to alternate fringe projects with high profile core initiatives that are backed by senior leaders. Each assignment may be a two or three year stint. This concept is shown in Figure 9.1.

Peter, a vice president in one of our participating companies, described his career in terms of these cycles. He joined the company to help build a service-related innovation that could have complemented the heavy equipment part of the company's mainstream business. After several years of incubation, this opportunity was beginning to show real promise. But just then, Peter was coached that he'd been "on the fringe too long," and needed to get "back on track." He was moved to a mergers and acquisi-

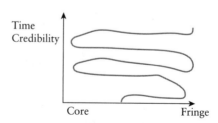

FIGURE 9.1   Cycling In and Out of Innovation

tions role within the core part of the company, where he worked on several very high profile projects. He told us the following:

> I realized that all the experience I had prior, which was almost four years on the innovation project, was regarded as not relevant at all. Actually some people told me, "You need to forget about it." And I said, "I don't want to forget about it. This was a very interesting experience. We learned a lot." For me, it was a tremendous experience, which has always been discounted by the enterprise.

He announced that he was leaving the company, and was convinced by several senior business unit leaders to stay. They claimed that the business unit needed "change agents" like him, and asked him to lead a major reorganization within the business unit . . . again, a high-profile but mainstream role. After several years in that position he was finally deployed on another "fringe" but potentially breakthrough project, where we encountered him at the time. Peter reflected that his credibility and influence in the company were not established until he had filled a mainstream role, since the innovation projects were "in a remote location, and because you're working on things that are atypical—and are very easily discounted by folks in the division."

As companies begin to take the development and articulation of a strategic intent seriously, and use it as a reference for their innovation initiatives, working on a breakthrough innovation project should no longer be considered a "fringe" activity. However, even if the work is considered critical to the company's future, most operating unit leaders will still consider it as fringe. It it's not urgent, it's not important to many company managers, and the innovator's reputation is affected by that perception.

Another reason for advising aspiring innovation experts to cycle between innovation projects and core projects is because the activities and resources needed for creating new businesses conflict with the typical metrics required to reward and promote people inside large companies. The Hay Method©, the prototypical performance evaluation system used in many large industrial companies, is implemented in such a way that a person's promotions, salary, and job classification are highly related to the number of people reporting to him and size of the budget he oversees. But we've seen that discovery, incubation, and even acceleration don't work that way. Instead, the innovation expert relies on a small core team and a nimble budget for quick investigations and learning experiments. There is no heavy investment until acceleration. An incubation platform director explained:

The idea that a person working in innovation could move up to a Band 7 with so few people reporting to him is viewed as a reward in and of itself. He's over-compensated based on the typical system of having larger numbers of people and bigger budgets . . . a Band 7 in a business unit might have supervisory responsibility for 180 people. People in the innovation group had few reports at that level . . . but were at that level because of the difficult nature of the work itself and its value to the company. That said, there is nowhere to go beyond director level. I had hit a ceiling.

This conflict baffles innovators' bosses. They don't want to stir up trouble by operating outside the traditional assessment system. In one case, a senior executive knew he needed to promote his incubation portfolio leader, Sue. The next promotion, however, was beyond what her budget and authority level would have suggested if the Hay Method was followed. He ended up promoting her but did not allow it to be announced in the company newsletter, for fear of stirring up a reaction within the company ranks. A decision like this is good for Sue in some ways but not others. In fact it undermines her authority since she will not be able to leverage the position power that comes with her new title. Interestingly, other career ladders exist that contradict the Hay Method, and companies have come to accept them. The most obvious is the R&D technical track, in which job titles and promotions exist that parallel managerial roles but are granted based on the researchers' recognized scientific expertise. So, if it can happen in R&D, why not in innovation?

Finally, recall the story of Mitch, who we introduced in Chapter 3. Mitch was the person who joined his company along with a set of peers from a prestigious MBA program. Unlike them, he opted to lead an innovation project which was composed of a small team with a right-size budget and breakthrough possibilities. The venture failed, due to no fault of his own, and Mitch found himself behind his peers on the promotion schedule because he hadn't managed "big enough" projects. Recall also that the option he was offered at that point was to cycle out to a business unit in a role that was more appropriate for people who were three to five years behind him so that he could "catch up."

Mitch took the offer and moved to Europe to assume a customer-facing role in an operating unit. Not surprisingly, he found that he was a "rough fit" there, claiming that the assignment would have suited him five or six years earlier in his career. It was understimulating at best, but he stuck it out for a while as he continued to look for a way to get back into innovation. When he expressed that desire to his boss, however, the response was: "You're good at innovation management, but you've already done that." As if it were a checkmark on a promotion path, rather than an actual career opportunity in and of itself. "I took the job in the customer-facing side of operations, and couldn't find a good way to cross back over into innovation," he told us.

Eventually Mitch was offered a plum role as staff to the Innovation Portfolio council. "Finally I got released," he told us. He wanted to grow another business, or indeed a portfolio of businesses, and thought this job might provide access to the set of potentially breakthrough opportunities the company was investing in, so that he could pick his next gig. But he quickly found that the opportunities were too early and underdeveloped for his skill set and patience level at that time.

Mitch felt like he was neither fish nor fowl. "I was waddling back and forth between two career tracks," he told us. He enjoyed taking opportunities that "looked like they have legs" and finding a way to scale them. He was not happy in operations forever, and he was not happy with the very early stage, undeveloped business concepts that were coming from the discovery part of the portfolio. "You have to know what it takes to scale a business," he claimed. "You get that experience in an operating division. You have to know what it takes to make a sale." Based on our framework, Mitch was indicating that he was best suited for a role in acceleration. But the company didn't have clearly defined innovation roles, or the understanding that some people could make their careers there.

The consequence was that the company lost Mitch. He left to consult in new business creation for other companies. Peter has also left. Sue, the woman who was promoted outside the Hay Method, remained in her role for another five years before leaving the company. What do we make of these outcomes? It's not the case that everyone wants to stay in innovation . . . but those who do have a tough time. And companies need to keep these people if they want to build an expertise in breakthrough innovation that they can use for their competitive advantage. They may not need ten thousand hours of practice, but they need more than they're getting now.

Option 2: Make Sure Your Breakthrough Succeeds!

Many company leaders and innovation pundits today promote the "passion model" for innovation. It's startling how many times we heard about the "brass ring" that Mitch mentioned as the promised career path. No guarantees, of course. Start with an idea, nurture it through incubation, scale it, and, lo and behold, you will become the general manager of a business!

Figure 9.2 represents this "ideal" career path. "They held out this beacon: go and develop this business and then you can run it," Mitch (and many others) told us. But in the back of his mind, he admitted hearing a small voice that said, "I bet that doesn't happen often." He's absolutely right. It's the seemingly obvious career path, but on closer inspection it sure doesn't make sense generally and happens only rarely if at all. Why?

First, as we've described in previous chapters, the skills necessary for discovery, incubation, and acceleration all differ. Inventors, starters, and opportunity scopers (discovery personnel), for example, typically are not interested in growing a business the way that acceleration personnel would be. Similarly, those with ambition to be a general manager may be equipped

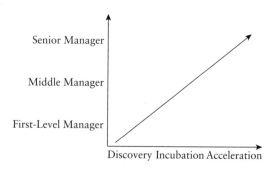

FIGURE 9.2   The Seemingly Obvious Career Path

to scale an opportunity, but find the pivoting and experimentation necessary in incubation too amorphous for their liking. The same thing happens in the start-up world. Venture capitalists add "professional managers" to their venture companies when they achieve a certain size. There are exceptions (Bill Gates at Microsoft, Mark Zuckerberg at Facebook, Steve Jobs at Apple, Fred Smith at FedEx) to be sure, but they are rare.

Second, some innovators don't find the supposed brass ring an attractive option. One of our company representatives described his firm's evolution in career path planning for innovation personnel that shows an increased understanding of this phenomenon, but reflects a foggy perspective and lack of confidence of what the right approach should be:

We have, unfortunately, a fairly long legacy, in many of our new businesses that were cultivated inside the corporation. The original inventor of the technology or the idea somehow was force-fed into the role of the general manager of the business . . . Talk about a duck out of water, and they were frustrated and upset and we put them in a position to fail. The way we handle it now, people can evolve according to their skills, whether they're a program leader or an inventor, maybe become the CTO of the business versus the CEO. We're still evolving there, but we're . . . I think we've got it reasonably right.

A third problem with the promotion path described in Figure 9.2 is that, in many industries, the time frame of one project outpaces an individual's capacity to wait for a promotion without appearing to have stalled. Businesses based on innovations in advanced materials, pharmaceuticals, optics, or many other fundamental sciences may take longer to incubate and accelerate than one's career life span can tolerate. One incubation platform leader responded to a question about any frustrations he faces in his role, and he led with this:

First of all, the career path is unclear. No, I shouldn't say it's unclear; there's really only one good option, and that is the intent of most of these new business opportunities is to grow them into something large enough where it becomes a division, and then whoever was leading that, like myself, basically, it was pitched to me that, hey, if you can make this successful, you'll be a general manager running this new division. Well, you know, one thing about innovation is, you don't hit every pitch out of the park, and these innovations take time. They don't hap-pen overnight, so, candidly, I'm a bit frustrated that it's been almost four years now, and are we making progress, yes, but the stuff takes longer than you had expected. You asked me the question why am I still doing it, and it's because I believe in this project. But the day I stop believing in it, is the day I'm either going to ask for another job, or find another company, to be candid. I'm not doing it for the pay. I should say I'm doing it for the potential reward because, at least in companies like ours, you know, we only get a big hit about once every ten years. If you are able to foster a big hit, you are rewarded quite well. However, if you get singles, instead of home runs, you're really not rewarded very well, and I think that's one of the challenges the company has to think about. Starting new businesses is extremely difficult, and how do you insure that you have the right people doing it, and reward them so they don't get frustrated to the point where they say, "Screw it, I'm going to go do something else."

Besides the long wait time to adequately cover incubation, the business's growth plan may not be accepted by the designated receiving operating unit. If the new business finds a home in an established division, it cedes control over personnel decisions and strategic direction to the division's leadership. As one company representative told us:

I used to believe that a person could come in, lead a venture, and then move to the business with the venture. However, this is often viewed as an "acquisition" by the business unit. So there is some loss of control of destiny.

Finally, project leaders or champions can become biased, and their commitment to the venture may overpower the true evidence that dem-onstrates its value. Since they and their teams are betting their careers on one business's success, signals of trouble in the new business platform can lead to undesirable behavior on the part of the team who depends on its success. If the risks of admitting that a project is failing are too high, the team may drag the project on beyond its useful life . . . at least until they find employment elsewhere.

Clearly we need to think a different way. Given what we know about the requirements for managing an emerging business opportunity, what are some logical ways to think about innovation careers?

AN ALTERNATIVE: RECOGNIZE DISTINCT COMPETENCY SETS

Once we realize that hierarchy is needed to manage not just projects but platforms and portfolios of strategic innovations, it opens up opportunity for careers within discovery, within incubation, and within acceleration. So an alternative and natural model for career advancement is to develop promotion paths within each of those functions, as shown in Figure 9.3. In this model, a person is recognized for level-one expertise and is promoted to level two, and potentially level three, within his or her competency area. If an individual elects to move from discovery to incubation, or from incubation to acceleration, the move would be lateral, until the person demonstrates the skills necessary to achieve the next level within the new competency area.

One incubation leader who had previously overseen discovery illustrated the reason for lateral moves between discovery and incubation based on his experience in mentoring those who were trying to make the move:

In my previous job in the company, discovery was reporting to me. And what I saw in these people is that they had really good ambitions and intelligence. They all want to step out—they see it as a step up to go to incubation, OK? In discov-

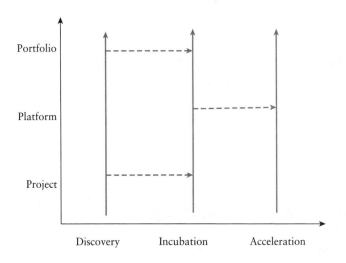

FIGURE 9.3 Proposed Innovation Career Paths

ery, they are used to looking outside the company, and they find things, and then they want to take the next step. But then some of them become frustrated that they find this challenging opportunity, and cannot do anything with it. And then I encourage them, "Just go ahead. Make something out of it. Just do it. If you need to go, just go after it." But they are reluctant. Something in them is holding them back. So my view is that you need a kind of information lovers for discovery. They have pretty good analytical skills and they're smart thinkers. They see cross connections. But then the step to really make something out of it, to start interviewing those companies and to see what you can do and to offer and to create momentum in your own company, to find supporters who also think it's a nice idea and to—that is quite a challenge for them.

One I-2 New Business Platform Leader reflected on his ambitions in response to our questions and realized, upon reflection, that he'd rather cycle within the incubation-acceleration transition for multiple emerging businesses than take one single business into maturity . . . but, understandably, he wanted to be recognized for that specific talent:

I can see going into acceleration. I want to push it into production, get sales going, create a viable business but do I want to be the guy that's helping run a factory or run a $200 million operation? I can't say that's in my DNA. I would want to stay with that business for several years to help build it up, but I don't know if I'd want to run the daily operation. I'd create new partnerships, and get it up to scale. There isn't much room to ascend vertically, so what you want is to get credit for your work, interesting jobs, and some progression financially and recognition. It's personal, what different people want, I want to grow, and to be seen as a guy who's developed some successes. If we're successful, I want to be recognized for that work, but maybe I will go do another one.

What is described here parallels the role and expertise seen in serial entrepreneurs: they incubate and grow their businesses but don't see themselves as running a company when it becomes a large operating concern. This path is rewarded, even lauded, for serial entrepreneurs, but performing similar functions within a corporation is currently unthinkable.

The same approach applies with acceleration. Functional specialists at level one may aspire to become general managers of a business over the course of their careers, but only within the development phase we have called acceleration.

Breaking with Traditional Promotion Criteria.   The career path model we are proposing makes sense from a skill set and experience perspective, but it breaks traditional rules for promotion, which require individuals to demonstrate responsibility for bigger budgets and an increasingly augmented span of control in order to get promoted. But, as we mentioned earlier, in the world of high uncertainty innovation, big budgets and lots of people are not always critical to developing a new business. The managerial skill set needed to drive the long-term success of the firm is not necessarily connected to expansive headcount and escalating budgets.

Innovation expertise is of immense value to the company and should be rewarded through promotion. Otherwise, those with expertise in incubation, for example, may continue to be recycled on project after project and never have interaction with senior management, even though they are responsible for cultivating opportunities that lead to new platforms for growth of the company. One of our company respondents has been incubating projects for seventeen years, yet has not had a promotion for the past eight. While year-end bonuses have been used to reward him, his frustration at the lack of opportunity for interaction with company leadership ultimately caused him to take an extended leave of absence, presumably to look for his next job.

DEVELOPING INNOVATION TALENT

We like to develop expertise in people. We develop people who are good at operations, people who are good at R&D, whatever it may be. But it doesn't appear that there's a good approach for developing people who are really good at new business creation.

So the people doing that step out work [on the technical side], they're actually progressing better than the people on the business side. Now, on the business side, I think that's where you get caught. I hear a lot of stories from different people that have gone out and tried to do a venture, and it doesn't work out, and they kind of plateau at a certain point.

As these statements from people at two different companies reflect, there's typically a wide disparity between companies' claimed desires for breakthrough new businesses and their investment in developing people to cultivate them. However, that's not the case everywhere.

A few leading-edge companies are experimenting with approaches to developing innovation talent. As we finished our most recent research study, two companies were instituting training programs for persons identified as innovation high-potential talent. The first company assessed their promising performers along three capability dimensions, shown in Figure 9.4, and those who met the qualifications would be identified as a "global talent leader" for one of three talent pools. The company's human resources / organizational development team was designing a series of critical experiences and master classes for each of the three types of talent to strengthen and develop the potential that these individuals showed in their initial assessments.

The three talent pools share the three competences listed at the intersection of the circles in Figure 9.4:

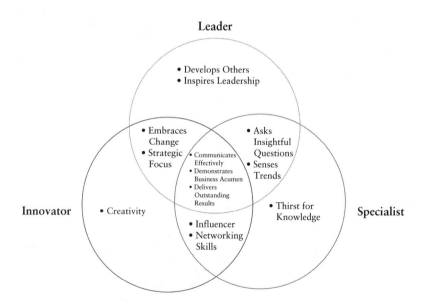

FIGURE 9.4 Three Talent Pools

Source: Reprinted with permission from Lars Enevoldsen, PhD, Group VP, Technology & Innovation, Grundfos.

- Communicating Effectively

- Business Acumen

- Delivering Outstanding Results

It is encouraging to see the thought leadership behind expanding the types of leadership needing these three competencies to include corporate innovators.

Behind each of the competencies, a set of descriptor statements exist that help assess an individual's fit with a specific category. The unique descriptors for the innovator evaluate creativity, shown in Table 9.1.

The company did not limit the innovator talent pool to new business creation, but sought these people from all areas of the company, and deployed them throughout as well. The director of talent management explained their thinking:

The way we have defined it is not limited to breakthrough innovation. It could be incremental innovations that we're looking for as well, so it's not specifically within the area of our new business creation entity. It could as well be within our sales or our production organization, or it could be within other parts of the organization where we say we really need this approach of innovating our business. So it's not, for example, about how will they improve a production line. It's how do we think about production in the future? If we have to turn around or think out of the box, and to be more creative, we will call on one of our global innovation experts. It's about the ability to embrace change.

TABLE 9.1   Creativity as a Skill unique to Innovation Leadership Talent as perceived at Grundfos

Creativity Generates original and innovative ideas; sees opportunities and combinations of ideas that others don't.
+ Spots brilliant concepts. + Suggests innovative ideas, not just relying on the most obvious solutions. + Spots ideas and pursues them. + Generates ideas quickly and takes the initiative. + Acts on creative ideas and drives them forward. + Encourages others to come up with new and innovative ideas.

Source: Reprinted with permission from Lars Enevoldsen, PhD, Group VP, Technology & Innovation, Grundfos.

This company also worked to design equivalencies into the job-grading system for the innovation roles, recognizing that span of control over a large number of direct and indirect reports was not necessarily relevant for assessing innovation expertise. Some of those comparisons are shown in Table 9.2. Rather than the Hay Method, this company used the Mercer job-level system, and so those codes are shown in Table 9.2. While we don't have the descriptions of all of the roles, even for Innovation, and while the Mercer job-level system is not straightforward or easily defined, the comparisons are interesting. Even more interesting and important is that this company has made the effort to draw them. The talent management director explained:

What would be the driver for people to take on a role in our breakthrough innovation area, if the only way that we honor people is linked to this very big span of control, when, in fact the uncertainties associated with working on breakthrough innovation is a much bigger determinant? The ability to collaborate with customers, and to conduct all of the analysis to find out whether there's a market for this or not, even in industries we don't know today are also important. It's a different type of work.

We find it interesting that discovery is ranked at a lower level than incubation. This ranking makes sense for companies that are more likely to seek younger people for the Opportunity Generator role, as many do. In that regard it is nice to see a more junior-level pathway into the innovation function.

The second company that instituted training used a more personalized approach. While many people experience a personalized career development approach in partnership with their superiors, we were impressed by how systematic this company was. Individuals were nominated as potential innovation talent rather than formally assessed. Once someone was nominated, the director of organizational development for the innovation function worked with the heads of discovery and incubation to map out a development plan for the person, similar to a plan for any high potential leader. However, this plan was centered primarily within the innovation function, where the person would spend a number of years rather than a short rotation on a predefined series of positions.

TABLE 9.2 Role Comparisons in the Organizational Hierarchy

Mercer Level	New Business Platforms	Marketing	Development and Engineering	Product Line Management
62		Global Marketing Director	D&E Director	Global Product Line Director
61	Innovation Director			
60				
59	Head of Projects			Global Program Manager
58	Chief Incubation Manager	Marketing Manager		
57			Chief Project Manager	
56	Innovation Manager			Senior Product Manager
55	Incubation Project Manager		Lead Project Manager	
54				Product Manager
53	Discovery Project Manager	Marketing Project Manager	Senior Project Manager	Senior Product Specialist
52				
51		Communication Specialist / Marketing Coordinator		Product Specialist

The director of organizational development and director of incubation described two aspects to a person's development, which mirror most executive development plans. The first was the set of knowledge, norms of behavior, and processes a person needs to understand in order to conduct new business creation activities. This list included things like the following:

- Stakeholder management: How to identify and convince relevant constituents in the organization to align with you on an issue or a project.

- Building, composing, and managing a team that is working on a high-uncertainty project that requires an entrepreneurial culture.

- The types of tasks and activities that need to be accomplished for the role.

To accomplish this training, the company was developing an innovation curriculum as part of the suite of professional development courses that it ran.

The second aspect of development they described is that of the person's attitude and mindset. Openness, lack of defensiveness about not having command over all of the facts given a context of high ambiguity, and a constant sensitivity to opportunities were some of the elements they mentioned. These, they admitted, were harder to develop or coach. They take a longer time to nurture in a person and come more naturally to some than to others. These are, in fact, some of the factors that differentiate people with innovation talent.

Once nominated, a "high-potential innovation" person is enrolled in a number of traditional management training workshops associated with attaining leadership roles in the company, but was also assigned to a project or series of projects to give them the right experiences, with heavy doses of feedback provided. The company also created events designed to give people opportunities for practice. For example, the company sponsors a business plan competition, which is viewed as an important development experience for innovation personnel. They practice articulating opportunities in a way that captures senior leadership's attention (since senior leaders are the judges), and, if they win, they practice managing a project / new business opportunity under the watch of seasoned experts and innovators. There are numerous other experiences in which innovators can participate that will earn them the "scar tissue" that company members told us was necessary in order to be a successful corporate innovator.

The vice president of HR and communications for the innovation function told us the following:

Right now, for example, we are nominating people in the biomedical organization, and we have a lot of debates about it. We are nominating a person who is not yet there, but we are really convinced she can make it. She needs some coaching, and we will put her in a management position that is a stretch for her. It's a different environment, but we are quite convinced that she will be able to take it up. We select people whom we can trust to make the next step. Creating the nominations has been helpful. Our management development system puts you in a position beyond your demonstrated capabilities, and lets you go, to see what happens.

In each of these two companies, it is notable that the HR/organizational development people are highly aware of the specific characteristics of strategic innovation itself. They understand the nature of developing and commercializing high uncertainty innovations, including the processes, systems, culture, and metrics required. Both were assigned to serve the innovation function specifically. These companies stood in stark contrast to most others we studied. In most cases, the HR/OD representative was either assigned to R&D (rather than to a new business creation function) or there was no assignment at all. Many company representatives we spoke with complained that much of the HR/OD function of the company had been outsourced or was run as a lean support service. There was no one for the orchestrator to educate or coopt to help with the HR/OD aspects of the innovation function's agenda, and no incentive for those on the internal skeleton crew to learn about the unique aspects of the innovation functions they are supposed to service.

PILLARS AND APPRENTICES
In most of the companies we studied, development occurs through apprenticeship and mentorship, but without any specific thought about the development opportunities within innovation or a well-designed career path. Most of the level-two leaders (Opportunity Domain Leaders in discovery, new business program leaders in incubation, and new business general managers in acceleration) selected their own team members . . . or had promising young "high potentials" foisted upon them in a rotational role on their way to a general manager position. Not much thought was given to truly outfitting the innovation function with people who could contribute in the most effective manner.

All the level-two people we spoke with decried the short rotational assignments given to the high-potential leaders in training. One director of discovery began requiring that anyone electing to come onto their discovery group commit to a minimum three-year stay. "It takes a year for them to get used to this job, a year to ramp up, and by the third year they are really contributing," she told us. Her decision automatically eliminated the discovery group from the set of required rotations on the high-potential leaders' development pathway. Even though the discovery leader recognized that she would lose access to these talented people as a result, she was too frustrated with spending so much time apprenticing people who took their leave before they could contribute anything of substance to change her mind.

A common format, though not formalized, is for one person to remain in the second- or third-level role (platform or portfolio level) for a lengthy period of time. Some people called them tentpoles and others referred to themselves as pillars, but those that we encountered were all in the position because they loved it and had elected to trade off career advancement. Many were in the last jobs prior to retirement. One described his passion and decision to stay this way:

So, you know, I finally landed in something that I'm really passionate about that I enjoy coming and doing every single day, and I really don't want to go anywhere anymore. I've done that whole career ladder shift thing, and I'm happy doing what I'm doing as it stands, so. And I think that they're happy that I'm still here.

The pillars have accumulated experience in innovation over many projects, and enjoy bringing others along. Sometimes, people just need to be shown through role-modeling behavior, as in this scenario that one incubation leader described:

On one project I'm running now, that opportunity was already recognized. It was already on the list, and discovery and business intelligence had been completed. It was kind of a joint venture with the business group, so the project manager to incubate it was assigned from the business, rather than from the Innovation group and guess what? Nothing happened.

My boss asked me to take a look at it. He said, "Please interfere and make something happen there." I waited awhile, and still nothing happened, so I decided to give it a kick myself. I went to a company and started discussing the concept, and all of a sudden the project manager and team were right behind me. Now the whole project team was energized, but everybody had just been waiting for somebody to take an action and reach outside of the company. Once the project manager saw what I did, he followed immediately. He was a very young guy but he recognized what should have been done. So when I decided to give it the kick myself, he advised me which company to talk with. He had talked with their technical manager, but he could not get a meeting with a higher level person. And I could make an appointment with the COO. So we had this meeting with the COO and—yeah, there was some common ground to work on and then the whole thing started.

So, he had to learn how to leverage my seniority level in the company. I know how things are decided, how things move, to get the project started—inside the company, too. He needed help with that.

Another incubation platform director described a more closely managed relationship with his I-1 apprentices. He has them watch, learn, and then analyze what happened:

Well, mostly what I do is I'll bring them in and work with them very, very closely on their project in the beginning. As an example, I'll go out with them to go talk to customers and negotiate joint development agreements—all of that kind of stuff. I'll sit down with them, and we'll work on the whiteboard together. It's like a one-on-one mentoring relationship. Like an independent study with a professor or whatever. And I can't do more than one at a time because there's not enough hours in the day, right? So that's generally what we've done.

There are two guys in my group right now that are both fabulous that started off as being really smart technical guys, and then for the first six months they were over here, they spent a lot of time with their uncle Mike, you know. They get better and better at different pieces, and then they're off and running.

The pillars and tentpoles of the innovation function that we encountered seem quite effective. They help others develop their innovation expertise through deliberate practice: identify a weakness, watch, practice, get feedback, and try again. But the lack of succession planning or formal development of the next generation of innovation experts worries them. One signaled her plans to retire in two years and worked on succession planning, but each of the people she identified as a potential successor was poached for other jobs. That does not send a strong signal about the relative importance of strategic innovation in a company.

RETENTION MECHANISMS

In Chapter 1 we described the turnover rate among people in the innovation function. Over a three-year period, 71 percent of the people we observed left the innovation function in their companies, and 20 percent left the company altogether. Even more concerning, however, is that, of those who left the company, 53 percent took innovation roles in other companies. Retaining innovation talent in the company and within the innovation function are important managerial concerns. Companies are leaking talent in an area in which they say they're seeking to cultivate it.

What can companies do to retain people in innovation so their expertise continues to mature, and the company benefits as a result?

We suggest three actions:

1. Legitimize innovation as a permanent function.

2. Assess people's performance and reward them based on those role descriptions.

3. Develop career paths within innovation for people who want to make a career of it, and develop meaningful roles within innovation for those who would like to experience it but realize it's not their endgame career goal.

These are not happening today.

Legitimize Innovation as a Function

Formalizing innovation as a function provides people with a permanency and safety net to undertake tasks that the company needs to realize its future. That means it is understood that the context in which they're operating calls for practices that recognize the high degree of uncertainty and lack of structured problems. One of our participating companies installed an incubator program in one of its largest business units. The director of that program described its effect on peoples' behavior in this way:

We have been able to put some safety nets in place for people. We talk with our teams to learn their reactions to this experience, and what almost always comes out from those discussions is that this whole idea of fast failure, from a prototyping standpoint, scared the pants off of them at the beginning. But they got more comfortable with it as time went on and they knew it wasn't going to be career ending if it didn't work out, since we now have this special pot of money and this incubation program. It allows us to use our creativity to start running around out there and start talking to customers in ways we don't usually talk with them . . . like, "What would you think if we . . ." and "Would you consider being a pilot company for this? Would you be the alpha site? Would you be the beta site?"

Given a specific program name that signals strategic innovation (such as an incubator), a budget, and a mandate, the people functioning within it will, over time, align their behavior to accomplish the objectives of innovation.

The director's comments are well taken, but he's dealing only with people who are just starting out. What about those people who have been in innovation for a while? Role clarity, a mandate, and a budget are a great beginning, but after a while, people want to be recognized for what they've done, even if their projects have not resulted in killer businesses. That leads us to our second point.

Reward Appropriately
Unfortunately, there is a gap in the reward system, in particular for those who undertake the business side of strategic innovation. When asked why he was having such trouble attracting entrepreneurial business talent to work on his more uncertain but potentially strategic projects, one R&D leader explained:

Well, we know that technology people get motivated by technical challenge, not by money or position. It's really about doing something that's breakthrough, it's exciting. So, naturally if you have something that has some level of sponsorship, we can usually attract some of the right technical people. The more difficult part is getting the marketing and the businesspeople excited. I would say most of those people tend to be more risk averse because those positions are not rewarded within the company. It's very difficult to get the marketing and business development types to be more entrepreneurial because they recognize the way they get promoted is to be in a more mature business. Especially if you're dealing with ambiguity, it's difficult getting the right kind of leaders to drive that. You know the entrepreneurial leaders who can manage by influence, who can work with a technical team or business team, it's hard to find those kinds of people.

When asked why it was so difficult to keep her business people, one level-three discovery director told us, "Well, there is a risk issue because you may work on things that don't count for anything." Clearly this situation must be remedied.

Activity-Based Rather Than Outcome-Based Metrics. When a project is fraught with high levels of uncertainty on multiple dimensions, there are many factors at play beyond a project team's control. The likelihood of a positive commercial outcome is impossible to know. Under those circumstances, it is more appropriate to assess project team members' performance on the basis of other factors . . . those that are under their control. We are suggesting that innovation personnel be rewarded on the basis of activity-based outcomes, rather than performance-based outcomes. By this we mean that they have engaged in the behaviors and activities that we know are aligned with success, even though the probability of success is lower than in the incremental innovation world. Have they gained new insights that we didn't already know? Created new partnerships? Identified possible applications for a business concept that the company hadn't previously considered? Designed clever experiments that tested critical uncertainties? Attacked the most critical uncertainties first, rather than the ones they're most comfortable handling? Are they disciplined in their approach to experimentation? Do they carry out the experiments and evaluate the results strategically? All these issues are under the innovators' control, and they should be rewarded for executing them well. If they do, the company will benefit from new opportunities, new relationships, and eventually from new, strategically driven, businesses. But also, importantly, the company will be much more likely to reward and retain innovation talent. Simply removing the threat of punishment, such as a stalled career or threat of a layoff, will greatly increase the number of talented people who come forward to work on strategic innovation projects. New business creation talent exists. It's plentiful, but it is latent, hiding within organizational designs and structures that squelch it. If we align incentives with the work to be done, they'll come forward.

Financial Incentives . . . the Good and the Bad. One company in our study instituted a performance incentive plan for new business program managers (I-2s in our innovation roles matrix), which requires them to set objectives that are appropriate for the time period and maturity level of the project. Bonuses are granted based on the degree to which they achieve the objectives: 50 percent of a standard bonus for some level of progress toward them, 100 percent for achievement of the objective, and 150 percent for surpassing expectations. As long as the objectives are developed specifically for the high-uncertainty context of BI, this approach encourages and rewards the right practices, and aligns the extrinsic reward system with the intrinsic rewards that attract people to innovation in the first place. As with everything, the devil is in the details, to make sure that the agreed-on objectives are realistic. However, we see this as a promising practice.

Other forms of financial incentive structures appear to work against the goals of an innovation function. These include phantom stock for the team and offers to spin the emerging business out of the company to let it develop on its own, with a promise to buy it back if the new business remains aligned with the company's strategic intent.

Phantom stock in the emerging business for the team can create an "us vs. them" mentality within the organization. Rather than unifying the identity of the emerging business with the identity of the mother company, this incentive system separates those identities.

Spinouts are great for the emerging business but may not work as well for the mother company. The emerging business tends to lose alignment with the company's strategic intent when choice points about business models, fields of use, and even IP strategy crop up. The whole point of having an innovation function is to help develop these opportunities in a manner that brings the company's intended future to fruition. If an emerging business opportunity clearly has no relationship to that intended future, spinning it off early makes sense. However, if it does show promise as a path toward executing on the intentions of the company, why spin it out, even temporarily? It's better for the company to build a well-designed innovation function that helps rather than hinders the evolution of those emerging businesses.

Our objective is to develop a corporate level expertise in strategic innovation by instituting innovation as a function. That means it is treated like other functions in the company. Its reward system should be aligned with the mandate of the function. That mandate is to provide options to the company for whole new platforms of business or game-changing renewal of existing businesses. Using similar financial incentives that other executives enjoy, but that are aligned with the context of strategic innovation rather than that of ongoing operations, is a promising practice and one that will help strengthen a company's innovation function.

Design Innovation Career Paths

Over time, as aspiring innovation experts gain experience within discovery, incubation or acceleration, or broaden their exposure across D, I, and A, they can become true innovation subject-matter experts. As their expertise grows, they need career path options. Most report that they are paid fairly well and are valued by their immediate bosses. What they lack is a path for meaningful promotion within innovation. The words of this innovation "pillar" convey the frustration she experienced in finding ways to reward and retain her people:

There is no doubt in people's mind that our people are excellent, and our people receive pretty good bonuses and stock options and other sorts of things like that. That is not the issue. The issue is the career ladder that we are on.

One of our biggest challenges is that we have some people who like doing and are very good at doing what we have asked them to do in this opportunity identification and early incubation activity and yet we don't have a good way to reward them and keep them. We have some subject matter experts who are really great at particular things like value analysis, but we don't have a career path for that. So the people that you want to keep, how do you reward them appropriately and give them the career path that they need?

The answer is to reward outside the Hay Method and add career paths for innovation experts. Chief innovation officers can work with their organizational development and HR communities to design promotion paths for people interested in staying in innovation. These paths can also be designed to include those interested in spending an adequate amount of time in the innovation function before moving on to a general management role. These folks can then be better general managers as active collaborators and receivers of accelerating new businesses because they truly understand the nature of strategic innovation.

Within discovery and incubation, specifically, two paths upward would be available, similar to the parallel career tracks that the R&D community has institutionalized.

The Specialist Career Track: Innovation Fellows. Just as some R&D scientists thrive on conducting bench-level science and bring increasing levels of value to the firm over time owing to their accumulated knowledge and experience, so, too, do serial innovators, who identify and nurture business after business in companies.[4] And just as some R&D scientists resist promotion into a managerial role, so, too, do some serial innovators. Companies have responded to R&D scientists who prefer to remain on the technical track, and who have contributed in an impact way through their technical talent, by instituting a technical career ladder. A parallel innovation specialist career path for serial Opportunity Generators, serial incubation specialists, and serial accelerator specialists is in order to recognize their increasing value to the firm over time and to permit them to continue to engage in the activities at which they excel.

In one of our companies, the head of discovery wanted to institute an Innovation Fellows designation.[5] Similar to the Research Fellows that are recognized in the company's Hall of Fame and with such a special title, Innovation Fellows would be recognized and rewarded for contributions made on the basis of their specialized new business creation expertise. They are expected to continue to contribute in that manner, and to be a source of mentorship for others.

This particular director wished to nominate a person who was expert at value analysis as an Innovation Fellow. She defined value analysis as scoping large breakthrough opportunities and the potential value they could bring to the market. Building on this idea, one can imagine an Innovation Fellow label that would recognize Incubation expertise and one recognizing acceleration expertise alongside these discovery talents that she mentioned. This kind of a recognition system allows new business creation experts to be rewarded for applying their expertise over and over to a diverse array of opportunities, similar to the R&D Fellow status granted by many of the companies we have studied.

In another approach, the director of a discovery and incubation group within a very large business unit instituted a series of titles that aligned with the traditional functions' levels. As he describes below, they were granted on the basis of innovation expertise rather than the size of a person's budget and number of direct reports. He noted that the function is very narrow, so there is little room for assuming managerial responsibilities, and wanted to provide a way for people to move up in the traditional organizational hierarchy. This is exactly what we recommend as the specialist career ladder:

I'm a bit of a pillar myself, because I've been doing this job now for seven years in total. So I'm sort of the memory, and I pass that on to the others as they come through. But you do need people who are going to stick around.

We've talked about this with our HR support, and asked them how we can find ways to give people that recognition, so that they don't need to move to get the career development piece. How can we do that when we've got experts that we want to keep doing what they're doing, and when that's what they're best placed to do?

So we've put in levels for promotion here, within our group. They typically come in at an associate director level. They can move to director and then to senior director level. So we create that internal level of title that allows them to develop in that way, and then we can set goals for them, so that, if they have a good year, they can be considered for promotion. That means a different title and different pay structure.

As far as different responsibilities associated with these titles, it's hard within a narrow group. They take on mentoring responsibilities for new people coming in.

Within a few companies we see the beginnings of career path designs for innovation specialists. These are weak signals, but they're important because they indicate emerging trends. Although we do not find widespread use of an innovation specialist track, we believe it offers great promise for companies wishing to develop their capability for strategic innovation in a way that can fit the organization's ever-changing environment.

To make the innovation specialist track work, several companies are experimenting with some rather specific practices that make a lot of sense. These include an innovation talent pool to offer a way for people to cycle off one project and on to the next, coupled with a pool of ready opportunities or projects, and a matching function.

Maintain an Innovation Talent Pool

An innovation talent pool is composed of people who wish to recycle themselves onto strategic innovation projects, much like consulting firms deploy their associates on one project after another across different clients. The innovation talent pool would include both discovery and incubation specialists, most of them level one but some level two. Individuals in acceleration businesses that do not succeed could come back into the pool as well. However, we believe that most accelerating businesses will grow and the functional specialists that occupy those roles will stick with them for a lengthy period of time. As their businesses move into an operational excellence mode, they, too, would be welcome back into the innovation talent pool.

Innovation experts can be deployed across a variety of different technology and science domains as they accumulate new business creation experience. Those who are designing and managing innovation functions can assign them to projects in different fields to help them broaden their experience across technology and market spaces. The skills and acumen that discovery and incubation personnel have, as described in the preceding chapters, are not characterized as much by their depth of expertise in any single technology or market area as by their ability to learn about new ones quickly, to understand the significance of the performance attributes these technologies can provide, and to ferret out the implications for creating value. Experienced people can come up to speed fairly quickly on how to work with scientists and inventors to translate the technology into business opportunity. It's part of their skill set.

After being deployed across a number of projects within discovery or within incubation, people on the innovation specialist career track could be promoted to a discovery or incubation specialist 2, respectively. Those labels would be affiliated with a director or senior director level in the company's hierarchy, or whatever level the company decided was appropriate. Each company needs to calibrate these roles in relation to other more traditional roles in their existing hierarchy. We noted in Table 9.2 that discovery level one and incubation level one are located at different levels in the company's organizational hierarchy. Ultimately a person in the specialist pool could be granted innovation fellow status, assuming it was merited.

Differentiate the Innovation Talent Pool from the Employee Redeployment Pool

The talent pool is a useful approach for ensuring innovation specialists can stay within the innovation function. The companies who were considering instituting it, however, voiced concern about reputation. They anticipated that an innovation talent pool would be viewed as a redeployment pool for people whose departments are downsized or reorganized, or whose project had failed, presumably owing to their mismanagement. Such a pool is the parking spot for people who must wait it out while looking for their next role in the company. If the person cannot find his next job soon, he's out. We don't see the concept of a talent pool of innovation project managers in this negative light, but instead as a more progressive concept. As the director of organizational development for one innovation function described:

You need really some people who are capable of being active in different kinds of projects. And that's not easy because the project's background could be different than the specific expertise of that person. So now I think we are almost there, but it has to be perceived as a positive . . . that we have people, they are on the payroll of the pool and that it allows us to assign them to different projects in different stages. So it's not the kind of negative, oh, my project failed

. . . I have to go to the pool. We have to turn that around. Otherwise, it's so negative. It's not right—I have to get the leaders' commitment to this before we take it up.

A talent pool provides a ready supply of increasingly sophisticated expertise to the strategic innovation mandate. In addition, a waiting inventory of opportunities to develop, or incubation projects to work, is critical. The supplies of innovation talent and innovation options to be worked on needs to be matched . . . not perfectly, but close, in order for this to work.

Maintain an Inventory of Breakthrough Innovation Options
While some companies think of their innovation projects in a "pipeline" framework, it's better to think of them as portfolios within domains. That way, every time one is killed, for whatever reason, another is there to take its place. The purpose of discovery is to help generate that interesting pool of projects, driven by the declared domains of strategic intent. Quotas of business concepts for discovery personnel and opportunity generation cycles are two of the mechanisms we described in Chapter 5 as interesting approaches for ensuring that there is always an inventory of opportunities available for incubation. The simple fact that those quotas and cyclic processes are in place ensures that incubation personnel are matched with opportunities to develop on a regular basis. As they cycle off of one investigation they can take a break and enter the innovation talent pool for a bit, or immediately cycle on to the next opportunity cluster. So a ready "bench" of opportunities or projects to take up is one key to reducing the risk to innovation personnel of having a project defunded. Whereas in many companies that event could mean the person is left without a job, or needs to find something outside the innovation group, companies with a true innovation function recognize the need to build in a steady supply of opportunities in order to maintain a healthy portfolio as well as to retain their talent pool.

There are both positive and negative consequences to this approach. The positive is that teams are less likely to hold on to a project that is suffering a long torturous death in order to save their jobs. They are more likely to be honest about the project's increasingly narrowing opportunity landscape as they explore or experiment in different fields of use as long as they know they will find another opportunity to work on. The negative potential consequence is that innovation personnel may see more attractive options in the project pool and recommend shelving the one they're working on just as they begin to dig in to the challenges, in favor of picking up a fresh new opportunity. One of the orchestrators we spoke with expressed this concern:

To match the talent pool, we need a waiting list of potential projects that have not yet been started. And so that lets the teams know that, "OK, if this project fails, we can start the next one." So a project pool is an important part of the equation—but it is also the difficulty because, for all projects you have to go through the difficult time . . . where you need people to be really sticking their neck out for the project or venture they're working on. If—at the first headwind they say, "Well, this won't work . . . let's go pick up another project"—that's a problem. Everything looks great at the beginning, and then you start to dig in to it and find the challenges.

Teams may present too optimistic a picture, or too pessimistic a picture. The coaching sessions are important for helping them resist these temptations. So, too, is the composition of the talent pool. It requires discovery, incubation, and acceleration personnel. To enrich the pipeline we need discovery personnel, but to work those opportunities, incubation personnel who find them absolutely captivating are important. Fortunately, a vibrant talent pool will allow innovation leaders to deploy the right people on the job at the right time.

Sabbaticals

One last point about rewards and retention for innovation specialists: if people are deployed on one project after another, they need a rest in between. This is intense work, and people can become overly committed to a project. Allowing for short sabbaticals in between helps them let go of one, decompress, and move on to the next. If a project moves forward and they are expected to disengage, they need a time away before they can get their mind focused on the next one. If a project fails and they were particularly committed to it, they need a chance to regroup before they can be motivated to pursue the next one. One person we spoke with had just returned from a leave that he was granted because of his extreme disappointment with the company's decision not to continue its commitment to the project he had just worked on:

You need to be able to cope with [failure] in order to do this well. And I think that's underestimated by a lot of people in multinationals that this is a particular profession that you need to master, and you simply cannot just put people on it and then expect that it works out. No way.

Another reflected the intensity of time that sometimes occurs as these projects ramp up, and indicated appreciation for her boss's show of concern:

My boss believes in working hard, but she believes in recovery time. When I finished a project with long hours, she said, "I don't want to see you for two weeks, I don't want you online or on e-mail. I don't want to hear from you."

Given that projects are subject to dramatic pivots or to being shelved completely, we need to separate the project's end from the person's career outlook. The expert pool concept allows for that. It parallels the consultant company model in many ways. As projects come to a close or moves to the next phase, the consulting firm redeploys its people onto the next engagement. If there is downtime between engagements, the consultant takes care of administrative work, professional development work, or even involvement in client development or marketing collateral design. One can imagine a similar model for an innovation talent pool. When innovation experts are "between engagements," so to speak, they may use it for a sabbatical rest, for attending conferences or other events to broaden their exposure to new emerging scientific, social or regulatory trends of interest, or to help with some infrastructural initiatives that the innovation function is undertaking such as, for example, marketing communications to internal stakeholders. There's always plenty to do associated with the innovation agenda in a company.

THE INNOVATION MANAGEMENT CAREER TRACK
A second career path option is an innovation management track. These are the roles we described in Chapters 5, 6 and 7 as the second and third

levels of discovery, incubation, and acceleration, respectively. The move upward within discovery, within incubation or within acceleration would be from a project or functional specialist to a platform or more general manager level of a business domain, and then onto a portfolio role at level three. In each case, the complexity or the role increases, but the type of expertise gained in one level can enhance the wisdom of the decisions made at the next.

Table 9.3 lists certain critical experiences and demonstrated skills that one would need to move from one of the innovation roles to another, and from an innovation support role as coach or process facilitator to a line innovation role. As companies develop experience in institutionalizing their own innovation function, some of these patterns will emerge more clearly.

For the incubator level-one New Business Creation Specialist who prefers to move into a managerial role, the need for both higher-level strategic thinking as well as for coaching and advising is very high. By *higher-level strategic thinking*, we refer to the need to move from a consideration of individual applications of a platform to the development of an overall business strategy as the diverse range of application markets, the family of products, and the options for business models that the platform can generate is revealed through the experiments that New Business Creation Specialists conduct.

Thus a level-two incubation employee who moves up from level-one incubation assumes a managerial role and moves from a project-level work scope at level one to a platform-level scope, in which he is engaged with a suite of application probes and other projects that are each related to the new business platform.

Generally speaking, moves up the hierarchy require a broadening of skills and critical experiences, which will help the person apply them across multiple technology and market domains. Moves up also require greater focus on internal politics and on aligning domains and platform with the company's strategic intent, or stretching it to incorporate the emergent opportunities.

Moves from level two to level three in any of the competency areas require having had experience or deep understanding of all three

TABLE 9.3 Career Moves and Critical Experiences

Career Move	Critical Experiences Needed	Demonstrated Skills Needed
D-1 to D-2	• Has explored multiple applications within an opportunity domain, and developed multiple business concepts. • Exposed to multiple technical domains. • Exposed to multiple market domains.	• Articulate multiple opportunities from one platform. • Discern connection between platform and company's strategic intent. • Manage multiple small teams.
I-1 to I-2	• Executed multiple learning experiments and drawn conclusions. • Tested multiple applications of an opportunity and recommended first market entry strategy. • Contacted relevant external stakeholders to test out opportunity concept. • Convinced the market to try the opportunity. • Cross-functional project management.	• Strategic thinker. • Develop new business platform strategy. • Political savvy. • Coach and advise. • Broker relationships. • Manage teams of new business creators.
A-1 to A-2	• Has managed one function (marketing, development, manufacturing, service operations, finance) of at least one emerging business. • Program Management experience. • Operating unit experience. • Experience beyond single function: general manager experience.	• Solve urgent problems. • Financial management. • Real options mentality. • Incorporate scaling into design and execution of work.
D-1 to I-1	• Learn via experimentation. • Demonstrated interest in learning how to learn about markets or technology, whichever is the weaker skill.	• Thinks entrepreneurially. • Designs and executes experiments.
I-1 to A-1	• Experience in the functional role that will be assumed in acceleration. • Operating unit experience.	• Functional expertise. • Compartmentalize experimentation experience and focus on growth. • Work in a high-risk/high-pressure setting.
D-2 to D-3	• Managed teams of people who are "lovers of information." • Has developed a variety of opportunities within one strategic domain, several times. • Has had several domain landscapes accepted for incubation. • Experience with commercial policy (strategy, rules, operating procedures) and challenges.	• Visualize and articulate domains of strategic intent. • Guide domain leaders as they pursue opportunity landscapes. • Operate at a platform level. • Understands need to operate within an evolving organizational capacity.

(continued)

TABLE 9.3 (Continued)

Career Move	Critical Experiences Needed	Demonstrated Skills Needed
I-2 to I-3	• Has incubated more than one emerging business. • Developed and leveraged internal and external networks and communities for a specific emerging business. • Navigated internal political tensions associated with the emerging business. • Strategy setting. • Appreciation of commercial policy (strategy, rules, operating procedures) and associated challenges.	• Portfolio management. • Coach and advise. • Broker relationships. • Articulate and influence at a strategic level. • Devise strategy as well as execute.
A-2 to A-3	• General manager of at least one emerging business. • Operating unit experience. • Program management.	• Understands all aspects of running a business platform. • Manage under risky/high-pressure situations. • Well-balanced commitment to short-term and longer-term objectives.
D-2 to I-2	• Developed the domain landscape with multiple applications, several times. • Managed a team. • Design and execution of learning experiments and drawn conclusions. • Experience with all functions of a business, including operations, finance and marketing.	• Strategic thinker. • Develop new business platform strategies. • Cross-functional execution skills. • Political savvy. • Coach and advise. • Broker relationships. • Manage a team of new business creators.
I-2 to A-2	• Has led the development of an emerging business. • Operating unit experience. • Experience beyond single function: general manager experience.	• Cross-functional execution skills. • Political savvy. • Manage in a high-risk/high-pressure setting.
Facilitator to D-1	• Led idea generation processes and events. • Market learning. • Worked with inventors/R&D. • Presented new business opportunity ideas.	• Relate productively to external stakeholder community. • Market learning skills. • Articulate business concepts clearly. • Creative problem solving.

Role	Competencies
Facilitator to I-1	• Coached the design and execution of experiments under high uncertainty environments. • Conducted in-market fieldwork. • Relate productively to external stakeholder community.
Facilitator to A-1	• Functional experience in an operating unit. Has coached accelerating businesses. • Work in a high-risk/high-pressure setting. • Creative problem solving. • Functional expertise.
D-3 to CNO	• Has directed the discovery group. • Incubation experience. • Acceleration experience. • Operating unit experience. • Portfolio management. • Strategy development. • Works well with business unit leaders. • Understands business unit pressures. • Portfolio management under high uncertainty. • Long-term view with stepping-stone execution abilities. • Respect of senior corporate leaders.
I-3 to CNO	• Has managed the incubation portfolio. • Has worked with New Business Platform Leaders. • Has worked with R&D. • Acceleration experience. • Operating unit experience. • Portfolio management. • Strategy development. • Works well with business unit leaders. • Understands business unit pressures. • Portfolio management under high uncertainty. • Long-term view with stepping-stone execution abilities. • Respect of senior corporate leaders.
A-3 member to CNO	• Has made strategic innovation investment portfolio decisions. • New business creation, especially incubation. • Worked with R&D. • Portfolio management. • Strategy development. • Works well with business unit leaders. • Understands business unit pressures. • Understands the new business creation pressures. • Tolerates ambiguity. • Portfolio management under high uncertainty. • Long-term view with stepping-stone execution abilities. • Respect of senior corporate leaders.

competency areas. Incubation and acceleration directors also need previous experience within an operating unit so they understanding the opportunity and constraints that will eventually confront the emerging business.

Moving across the columns: People who desire to move from D to I, or I to A, or even D to A, can certainly do so, but in a lateral move. They need to learn that next job, since the skills required will be quite different.

Innovation support personnel, who coach and facilitate innovation teams, sometimes desire to move into the project portfolio activities as well. Their best entry point will depend on the kind of services and support they provided, combined with their experience prior to joining the innovation support team. Those who worked in idea management will be obvious fits for discovery, and those who coached teams through learning plans can jump into incubation. We have even encountered innovation support people who come from marketing backgrounds who may wish to leverage their functional experience on an accelerating business. All of these moves would be to level-one positions if they have not had previous program leadership experience.

ARE THERE ENOUGH INNOVATION JOBS TO GO AROUND?
While it is true that the narrowness of a corporate level innovation function implies a scarcity of openings at levels two and three in the company, we have seen small innovation groups that mirror our framework within many business units in large companies. We find, in fact, that there are quite a few level-two innovation managers peppered throughout these companies, and they are supervising teams. In most cases they are not linked to the chief innovation officer, if one exists, but in fact, most of the companies who have had a CNO position in place for any length of time are extending the reach of that role to link with these groups. They all need to be tied together, since their objectives and practices are similar. Just as all aspects of the marketing function ultimately report to the chief marketing officer, so, too, will every pocket of strategic innovation report to the CNO. When we look at it this way, there are more instances of innovation roles in large companies than one might imagine.

CUSTOMIZED CAREER PATHS

Once the innovation function becomes well established and its role in the company is understood, we observe selective movement in and out of it from people in business units. At DSM, for example, more people apply to work in the Innovation Center than there are available positions. The clearer the selection criteria for each role, the easier it is to find the right person. DSM appointed two EBA leaders who were both business group directors, who fit the profile of what was needed for each emerging business at the time. The VP of human resources management for the innovation function in one of our companies explained that the business units have a clearer understanding and greater appreciation of the innovation function's purpose now that it has existed for a number of years. The result is that those people who are ready to rotate off of an innovation project they may have been incubating for several years, but do not wish to cycle onto another one, are finding very attractive positions elsewhere in the company. The Innovation Center has struck a nice balance of talent flowing in and out of it:

Now there is a recognition of what we are doing in the Innovation Center. We have had some good results and we are just another part of the company. I think a couple of years ago, it was more difficult because then . . . especially in the operating businesses, they didn't know exactly what people here are doing.

Now we have a good balance of people wanting to come in and people wanting to move out, and I think it's OK. Sometimes, you have to change your team because you reach the next phase in a project, and you have to see if you have the right team composition. Maybe you need some other qualities and competences.

In fact, we would not prescribe any specific path, but more the design of a set of available paths for innovation experts. There needs to be a recognition of the critical experiences necessary for undertaking any one of the roles in the innovation function. The vice president for global talent management in that company explained:

The way that we are developing careers is not prescriptive. We do not want to be that restrictive, but more descriptive in the way that we think of the path the people can go—not the path you should go. We are painting different possibilities without making a formal innovation career path.

Every person's career path is individually crafted. Who among us is holding a job today that was part of our plan when we first decided what we wanted to do with our professional lives? Opportunities arise or close, and our unique talents reveal themselves through experiences and mentorship over time. What we are suggesting in this chapter, however, is that, just like every other function in a company, there should be an available set of career moves within innovation, and they should be based on a reasonable assessment of the individual and a way to allow him to leverage his earlier experiences into the next role. All options should be seemingly available, depending on his aspirations and talents, and match with the company's needs. Those options include the following:

- Stay within innovation function, but move on to new projects, new domains.

- Stay within the innovation function and move upward within a specific competency area.

- Stay within the innovation function and transfer with the project from discovery to incubation, or incubation to acceleration.

- Transfer out to a BU role after a period of several years.

Career development plans can detail the set of critical experiences one needs to move from her current role to an aspired one. Our point is simply that a transfer with the project—the "seemingly obvious path"—should not be the implicit assumption. Other options make much more sense.

A NECESSARY AND MANAGEABLE CHALLENGE

Developing and retaining innovation talent is a challenge in companies today, but it is clearly manageable. Every one of the prescriptions offered here has been used in other organizational functions. They're not new—just reconfigured to work for the strategic, future-focused work of innovation. Consultancies, R&D organizations, and established innovation functions employ the practices we are suggesting. Leaders of large, established companies are beginning to recognize innovation as a function. Formalizing development and reward systems, and career paths in particular, is a crucial step in making that happen.

With companies beginning to institute an innovation function, what else is needed to move innovation expertise from a role someone holds in his job to a profession? Chapter 10 turns to this topic.

10 INNOVATION AS A
PROFESSION

In February 2016 the CEO of BlackRock Inc., the world's largest investment management company, sent a provocative letter to the chief executive officers of the S&P 500 and large European corporations. In that
letter he urged them to figure out how to endow their companies' future
through investing in long-term, value-creating innovation, and to be transparent about it. Investors and, indeed, economies, need something more
than short-term stock price bumps, he claimed, in order to build a strong
foundation for society. And, he claimed, if given the compelling vision of
companies' strategic intent, short-term financial deviations will be better
tolerated by the investor markets. We quote the letter extensively here,
since it reflects a stunning change in the perception of one of the greatest
barriers to company investments in strategic innovation.

Over the past several years, I have written to the CEOs of leading companies
urging resistance to the powerful forces of short-termism afflicting corporate
behavior. Reducing these pressures and working instead to invest in long-term
growth remains an issue of paramount importance for BlackRock's clients, most
of whom are saving for retirement and other long-term goals, as well as for the
entire global economy.

While we've heard strong support from corporate leaders for taking such a long-term view, many companies continue to engage in practices that may undermine their ability to invest for the future. Dividends paid out by S&P 500 companies in 2015 amounted to the highest proportion of their earnings since 2009. As of the end of the third quarter of 2015, buybacks were up 27% over 12 months.

We certainly support returning excess cash to shareholders, but not at the expense of value-creating investment. We are asking that every CEO lay out for shareholders each year a strategic framework for long-term value creation.

Annual shareholder letters and other communications to shareholders are too often backwards-looking and don't do enough to articulate management's vision and plans for the future. This perspective on the future, however, is what investors and all stakeholders truly need, including, for example, how the company is navigating the competitive landscape, how it is innovating, how it is adapting to technological disruption or geopolitical events, where it is investing and how it is developing its talent. As part of this effort, companies should work to develop financial metrics, suitable for each company and industry that support a framework for long-term growth. Components of long-term compensation should be linked to these metrics.

We recognize that companies operate in fluid environments and face a challenging mix of external dynamics. Given the right context, long-term shareholders will understand, and even expect, that you will need to pivot in response to the changing environments you are navigating. But one reason for investors' short-term horizons is that companies have not sufficiently educated them about the ecosystems they are operating in, what their competitive threats are and how technology and other innovations are impacting their businesses.

Without clearly articulated plans, companies risk losing the faith of long-term investors. Companies also expose themselves to the pressures of investors focused on maximizing near-term profit at the expense of long-term value. . . .

We believe that companies are usually better served when ideas for value creation are part of an overall framework developed and driven by the company, rather than forced upon them in a proxy fight. With a better understanding of your long-term strategy, the process by which it is determined, and the external factors affecting your business, shareholders can put your annual financial results in the proper context.

Over time, as companies do a better job laying out their long-term growth frameworks, the need diminishes for quarterly EPS guidance, and we would urge companies to move away from providing it. Today's culture of quarterly earnings hysteria is totally contrary to the long-term approach we need.

To be clear, we do believe companies should still report quarterly results—"long-termism" should not be a substitute for transparency—but CEOs should be more focused in these reports on demonstrating progress against their strategic plans than a one-penny deviation from their EPS targets or analyst consensus estimates.[1]

The letter continues on to address other issues, but this excerpt is our focus. The letter has generated many cynical comments and much debate, but to us it represents a clarion call. Somewhat surprisingly it comes from a leader in the finance community—a community that has often been considered the bane of innovation's existence. Now it's up to companies to respond, and to do so they must develop a capability for strategic innovation. It must become part of the fabric of large, established companies.

In this book we have described a way to do that. Develop a well-articulated strategic intent, and a process for updating it every five years or so. Build an innovation function and make it a permanent department alongside accounting, finance, marketing, manufacturing, R&D, and all the rest! Create the right governance system and a somewhat consistent and persistent resource plan. Develop discovery, incubation, and acceleration competencies. Adopt the Learning Plan© and Discovery Driven Planning© as tools for new business creation projects. Operate at the project, platform, and portfolio levels simultaneously. Design a complete, well-integrated management system for it that aligns with the objectives of strategic innovation. Don't cherry-pick which elements of the management system (repeated again in Figure 10.1) to focus on or set to the side. Make it cohesive.

And, at the root of it all, select and develop the right talent. There will be no sustainable system without recognizing and instituting the innovation roles required for a strategic innovation portfolio. Company leaders must institute clearly defined innovation roles, and develop the selection and evaluation criteria to help individuals become innovation experts. They cannot expect expertise to develop if people are constantly rotated

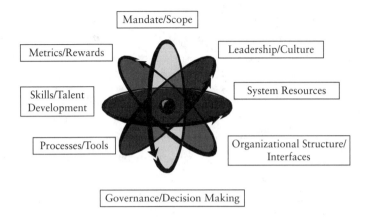

Mandate/Scope

Metrics/Rewards

Leadership/Culture

Skills/Talent
Development

System Resources

Processes/Tools

Organizational Structure/
Interfaces

Governance/Decision Making

FIGURE 10.1   A Comprehensive Management System for Strategic Innovation
Source: Reprinted with permission from John Wiley & Sons, from Gina Colarelli
O'Connor, Richard Leifer, Albert S. Paulson, and Lois S. Peters, *Grabbing Lightning:
Building a Capability for Breakthrough Innovation* (San Francisco: Jossey-Bass, 2008).
Copyright © 2008 by John Wiley & Sons, Inc.

in and out of strategic innovation projects, or expected to work on their
breakthroughs in the morning and their other projects in the afternoon.
It just does not work. The skills, attitudes, mind-sets, and time frames
differ too much. There needs to be clear recognition of the array of talent required and distinct activities to develop it. To continually seed and
grow a company's next platforms of business it needs to develop true innovation professionals, not part-time players.

Similarly, companies cannot depend on intrapreneurs or mavericks—
who operate on the margins of the system and are vulnerable to changes
in sponsorship on a moment's notice—to be the engines of the company's
future growth. And while the 15 percent free time rule sends a nice message about an organization's cultural support for innovation, it's an "at
your own risk" approach. Bootlegging resources and championing behavior are great examples of enthusiasm, but wouldn't it be better if we could
use the strengths of an organization to work with these folks, rather than
surround them like antibodies trying to attack a virus?

That means that companies must design roles and responsibilities for
innovation personnel, beyond those in R&D. Roles that are viewed as

legitimate across the company. Let them take the fruits of R&D and create wholly new business platforms. Provide them with stimulating career growth opportunities that leverage their innovation talent and interests.

The four appendixes at the end of this book summarize the suggestions offered in these chapters to help distinguish the unique innovation roles; compare them across the project, platform, and portfolio levels; and point to selection criteria for each of them. The first section of Appendix A details the responsibilities, tasks/activities, and performance metrics for discovery personnel, while the second section of the appendix outlines the selection criteria for these roles. Appendixes B and C do the same for incubation and acceleration, and Appendix D outlines the responsibilities and selection criteria for innovation leadership and support infrastructure roles.

These appendices provide leaders with templates to begin thinking about how to organize their people to institutionalize innovation within their company. Built from our research and interactions with dozens of innovation professionals, they can be viewed as a way of learning from the experience of others, and can be used as a starting point for your particular situation. They are in a summary form but will provide the foundation you need to develop the innovation roles that are right for your organization. We've spent two decades interacting with and interviewing innovators and executives of well-recognized companies across a broad spectrum of organizational levels, industries, and cultures. We've seen their approaches to managing strategic innovation projects, how they create innovation management systems, and—most recently—how they are attempting to develop innovation personnel. This has put us at the nexus of numerous forward-thinking companies that are constructing organizational designs for those wishing to pursue careers in corporate innovation and new business creation. We've been fortunate to be on the front lines to work with leaders as many of them take nascent steps toward institutionalizing innovation through the creation of innovation careers for their people.

Senior leaders wishing to chart a path to long-term organizational prosperity must remain persistent rather than allow for wild swings in commitment to strategic innovation. The presence of an innovation function must be as enduring as the presence of an engineering or marketing function. We may need to dial it up and dial it back, but we must not stamp it out. We need to break the cycle of four-year average life expectancies of innovation groups.

It's all possible. In fact, it's well within reach. Tremendous progress has been made since we began our research twenty years ago. But companies cannot do it alone. They'd be greatly helped if other institutions committed to developing innovation as a profession.

THE ROLE OF UNIVERSITIES

Universities can partner in this development, through their educational programs, research, and collaborations with companies. Business schools need to develop courses and programs in innovation management that recognize discovery, incubation, and acceleration as crucial and distinct domains. Pedagogical materials need to be developed, and students need to be recruited into the major. An ever-growing number of schools offer corporate entrepreneurship courses, but few offer a suite of courses needed to cover the entire set of management system requirements for breakthrough innovation in organizations. Courses designed to expose students to the processes and tools for commercializing advanced technologies under conditions of high ambiguity are important, as are courses in organizational change, stakeholder management, new network creation, and more.

Schools of engineering and science that are teaching students to articulate potential opportunities that arise from lab-based discoveries and inventions will help those students become valuable contributors to an innovation function. Partnerships between engineering and science schools and business schools for codesigned and cotaught courses associated with real innovation projects are even better. Combined degree programs, in which students major in one school and minor in the other are better yet.

Innovation functions in companies could be partnering with university programs such as these to provide course projects, internships, and entry-level apprentice roles as students who are aspiring innovators start their careers. Company innovation function leaders can participate on advisory councils for MBA programs, specialized master's programs in innovation management, or schools of engineering or science that focus on innovation systems.

Companies and academic scholars can continue to collaborate on research programs like ours to identify ongoing challenges to innovation success, or provide beta sites for testing new tools or techniques. Universities can provide outreach to company professionals, including workshops and training as new learning emerges about successful innovation management practices.

THE ROLE OF PROFESSIONAL SOCIETIES

The identity of a profession tends to gain recognition when professional associations and societies form to share best practices, network, and support their members engaged in those activities. Supply-chain management, for example, was viewed as a minor role in many ways until the Council of Supply Chain Management Professionals and Institute for Supply Chain Management were formed. Each holds conferences and has developed a body of knowledge, a set of educational and training offerings and a certification program. Others, like the Project Management Institute, the American Marketing Association, and the Product Development and Management Association, have done the same for their respective communities. Many welcome both academic and industry members and organize ways for them to interact with one another to further useful and insightful research.

There are several such societies emerging for innovation managers, including the European-based International Society for Professional Innovation Management, Product Development and Management Association, and the International Association of Innovation Professionals.[2] Both are just in the formative stages. Other organizations, such as the Innovation Roundtable and Front End of Innovation, organize conferences for those wishing to learn from colleagues in other companies or from recognized academics. The Industrial Research Institute, while focused primarily on R&D, has supported our own research and is keenly interested in supporting the development of an innovation management profession. Even the International Organization for Standardization, which creates the ISO business process standards, is recognizing the need to differentiate higher uncertainty innovation's tools and processes from those of incremental new product development.

These associations can further the development of an innovation profession as they find ways to offer value to companies and individuals. They provide an identity and vocabulary, and an opportunity to network with like-minded people and share experiences. Over time, if they succeed, they will help innovation become a recognized profession.

INNOVATION EXPERTISE: A NEW CAREER PATH

Innovation is, in our view, the next emerging business function. Breakthroughs need no longer be solely dependent on mavericks in the company who are willing to break rules, risk their careers, and sometimes, by sheer persistence coupled with serendipity, succeed. We can institute discovery, incubation, and acceleration roles, and support them with orchestrators, strategic coaches and innovation leadership. Organizational development leaders can work with chief innovation officers and orchestrators to recruit, select, and develop this talent. We know more about what it takes now than we ever have. CNOs are in an exciting position, and much hinges on their ability to quickly move along the learning curve so that they can build out their organizations with the right talent.

For companies to develop expertise in innovation, people need to develop expertise. For people to develop expertise in new business creation, they need to engage in it, stick with it, practice it. Some need to make careers of it. Others need a significant exposure to it so they can support those commitments of resources and support the outputs of the innovation portfolio. There's plenty of room to grow. We are excited to be part of this innovation journey that can shape the future of large, established companies and the game changers that are coming to market as a result.

Discovery Roles

	Opportunity Generator (Project Level)	Domain Leader (Platform Level)	Director of Discovery (Portfolio Level)
Role Characteristics			
• *Responsibilities*	Identify, develop, test, explore, and elaborate opportunities aligned with areas of declared strategic intent.	Build a pipeline of elaborated opportunities that fit company strategic intent. Coach Opportunity Generators.	Set climate and culture for development. Seed the company with possibilities for game-changing new businesses and influence strategic intent discussion. Motivate through planting of seeds and seeing they have the right climate to grow.
• *Tasks/Activities*	Scout, analyze trends, iterate with experts about imagined opportunities, produce white papers describing opportunities.	Articulate business concepts in ways that are relevant to the company and vet with key stakeholders. Facilitate discussions with business leaders to ensure alignment. Screen opportunities and connect them to create larger possibilities.	Communicate the company's strategic intent inward to platform leaders. Ensure company is engaged in ways to understand emerging technical advances. Align activities with the company's ability and willingness to deliver a new business or business restructuring.

	Opportunity Generator (Project Level)	Domain Leader (Platform Level)	Director of Discovery (Portfolio Level)
• Performance Metrics	Identification of nonobvious, robust opportunities.	Provide opportunity options whose value is recognized as worthy of incubation investments. Identify projects that will be developed further.	A motivated discovery team who is working to explore strategic new businesses of the future that the chief innovation officer and innovation portfolio board finds believable. A strong understanding throughout the company of the importance of scoping imaginative new business opportunities. Excellent partnerships with R&D and senior leaders.

Selection Criteria

	Opportunity Generator (Project Level)	Domain Leader (Platform Level)	Director of Discovery (Portfolio Level)
• Personal Characteristics	Motivated by learning and exposure to new things/information; challenger of status quo.	Creative, curious, inductive thinkers. Discerning, thorough, and well respected and well networked throughout the company.	Entrepreneurial. Highly strategic. Willing to chart new territory for the company and stretch beyond the company's business model comfort zone.
• Skills and Expertise	Holistic systems thinker who can integrate input from multiple sources and develop a clear statement of value for the market. Deep listeners.	Able to think across technology and business dimensions of a problem. Use and interpret evidence to validate an opportunity.	Understands the new business creation process from beginning to end. Can speak in business/ strategy language. Well recognized for functional background/ expertise. Able to delve into details as well as step out and look at the big picture.
• Critical Experiences	Experience with multiple learning styles, networker, connector.	Demonstrated expertise in the business or technology domain. Experiences in different functional areas. Experience in different domains of technology.	Some new business creation experience or exposure. Early career in the R&D area.

Incubation Roles

	New Business Creation Specialist (Project Level)	Director, New Business Programs (Platform Level)	Director of Incubation (Portfolio Level)
Role Characteristics			
• *Responsibilities*	Test, explore, and learn about identified opportunity spaces to build a case about its value as the foundation of a new business.	Lead the experimentation to determine potential of a specific potential new business area based on opportunity landscape developed in discovery.	Build a robust and viable portfolio of new business options. Responsible for decisions on resource investment.
• *Tasks/Activities*	Network to elaborate business models and the identified opportunity spaces. Observe and create scenarios to evaluate value of potential applications.	Help New Business Creation Specialists with experiments via strategic coaching. Network, broker relationships, bring people together. Shape the strategy of the emerging business.	Identify and develop emerging business area strategic innovation teams. Monitor the innovation capacity of the firm in order to resource opportunities appropriately. Remove internal barriers to emerging business progress. Facilitate business model development.

	New Business Creation Specialist (Project Level)	Director, New Business Programs (Platform Level)	Director of Incubation (Portfolio Level)
• *Performance Metrics*	Use of creative approaches to mitigating uncertainty around opportunities. Clarity of communication.	Successful guidance of an emerging business opportunity team to learn the actual value proposition across a variety of markets. Demonstrated successful transitions to other phases of strategic innovation. Successful internal stakeholder alignment.	Bring new business proposals forward to the company for which market enthusiasm has been demonstrated. Develop new business operating models that work and have some level of internal commitment behind it.

Selection Criteria

	New Business Creation Specialist (Project Level)	Director, New Business Programs (Platform Level)	Director of Incubation (Portfolio Level)
• *Personal Characteristics*	Appetite to explore. Motivated by charting new territories. Passionate about innovation but agnostic about particular projects.	Entrepreneurial mindset. Comfort dealing with ambiguity and uncertainty. Perseverance in the face of failure. Agile and adaptable.	Innovator driven by future health of the company. Allows for ambiguity among those who work for him and feels ok about that. Sets a culture of learning by experimenting.
• *Skills and Expertise*	Ability to design, carry out, and interpret creative experiments. Good at architectural and design thinking. Can create new networks.	Able to stimulate learning through insightful questioning. Debater, arbiter, emissary, matchmaker, negotiator, and mediator. Broker and strategic influencer.	Educates/evangelizes regarding need for strategic innovation. Brokers and negotiates on behalf of emerging businesses. Facilitates strategic intent by describing dreams for the future of the company.
• *Critical Experiences*	Demonstration of making something new happen in a large organization. Change agent.	Experience on multiple projects across multiple different units within multiple divisions or different companies. Change agent.	Helped design an innovation center to get a strategic innovation program started. Started and launched businesses. Broad professional experience with uncertainty, ambiguity, and and/or complexity inherent to strategic innovation.

APPENDIX C

Acceleration Roles

	Functional Leader (Project Level)	General Manager, Emerging Business (Platform Level)	Acceleration Innovation Council Member (Portfolio Level)
Role Characteristics			
• *Responsibilities*	Develop processes and practices relevant to the new business/opportunity.	Grow an incubated, emerging business to a point where it has predictable sales forecasts, yields, and a path to profitability.	Governance of strategic innovation activities at the enterprise level. Monitor progress and make investment decisions regarding the acceleration of platforms/or projects.
• *Tasks/Activities*	Conduct stakeholder analyses and develop stakeholder relationships. Solve problems within function of expertise associated with growth and scaling.	Design and structure functions, processes, for the new opportunity/business. Continuously improve to find path to profitability. Expand the business platform as opportunities unfold.	Help CEO and his/her peers understand how strategic innovation works. Evaluate options for investment and strategic potential given innovation capacity.

	Functional Leader (Project Level)	General Manager, Emerging Business (Platform Level)	Acceleration Innovation Council Member (Portfolio Level)
• Performance Metrics	Demonstration of workable processes and practices that will propel the new business.	Sales growth, new customers, partnerships, and instituted processes for reliability and repeatability of the new business's operation.	Achievement of company innovation aspirations. Successful launch of a new business or existing business revitalization. Successful assimilation of new business into mainstream corporation.

Selection Criteria

• Personal Characteristics	Growth and execution mind-set. Driven to build and facilitate business growth.	Mature, broad thinking, confident, strategic, and determined.	Long-term vision and willingness to accept and motivate change. Diverse group of corporate-level executives who have power, influence, and interest in growth through new business. Should include some who have an external focus.
• Skills and Expertise	Knowledge and understanding of how basic business functions play out in the company. Specific functional expertise. Able to solve problems quickly and through multiple approaches.	Able to translate business concepts into commercial operations. Develop processes and practices that are aligned or accepted by the mainstream company.	Demonstrated business acumen and judgment. An understanding of the importance of investing for long-term success.
• Critical Experiences	Demonstrated functional expertise, commercial sensitivity, and ability to execute a plan.	Experience in scaling and growing commercial operations. Skilled at partnering with multiple stakeholders to execute.	Promotion to executive level through demonstrated success in operational excellence. Demonstrated ability to make decisions under uncertainty or employ advice of those who are more comfortable in that domain.

Leadership and Infrastructural Support Roles

	Innovation Facilitators	Orchestrator	Chief Innovation Officer
Role Characteristics			
• *Responsibilities*	Breaks down barriers to strategic innovation acceptance. Maintains awareness of emerging tools and processes for managing strategic innovation projects. Communicates about and trains others in those tools and processes.	Ensures the innovation function is working properly and that it is aligned with the company's capacity for innovation. Communicates and advocates for the strategic innovation portfolio.	Responsible for delivering new business platforms that will become the company's growth engines of tomorrow. Develop governance criteria for strategic innovation. Ensures the incubation and acceleration portfolio align with the company's chosen domains of strategic intent. Defines, cultivates, and maintains the proper linkage between the strategic innovation function and the mainstream organization.

	Innovation Facilitators	Orchestrator	Chief Innovation Officer
• *Tasks/Activities*	Provide strategic innovation training and education. Facilitation of innovation events through designing, organizing, and managing these events.	Day-to-day management of strategic innovation portfolio. Ensure connections between the different competencies and their respective portfolios. Diagnose the innovation management system and find ways to improve it to meet identified KPIs. Strategic coaching. Manage strategic innovation budget. Work to prevent project relapse to incrementalism.	Gain and maintain the commitment and participation of other organizational leaders, who have more immediate responsibilities. Lead conversation about strategic innovation and corporate strategic intent. Chair the innovation council, which evaluates progress of the emerging business opportunities and makes investment decisions.
• *Performance Metrics*	Success in coaching and achieving meaningful outcomes of workshops. Impact of strategic innovation staging.	Healthy, robust strategic innovation portfolio with at least some projects recognized for their impact or on their way to making a recognized impact. Success in strategic coaching. Well-functioning innovation management system.	Ability to deliver new businesses and major strategic uplift in ongoing businesses. Recognition of importance of strategic innovation across all members of senior leadership team.

Selection Criteria

	Innovation Facilitators	Orchestrator	Chief Innovation Officer
• *Personal Characteristics*	Passion for facilitating the development and elaboration of innovation and new business opportunities. Good listener.	Reflective, systems thinkers. Passion for innovation. Strategic, portfolio oriented.	Driven by the opportunity to harness the organization's knowledge and resources to solve big, complex world problems. Visionary and inspirational, but also decisive. Idealist with a sense of practical realism. Will to protect the company's future through innovation and the ability to execute on behalf of that agenda.

NOTES

PREFACE

1. See https://www.iriweb.org/.

2. Richard Leifer, Christopher McDermott, Gina Colarelli O'Connor, Lois Peters, Mark P. Rice, and Robert W. Veryzer, *Radical Innovation: How Mature Companies Can Outsmart Upstarts* (Cambridge, MA: Harvard Business School Press, 2000).

3. Gina Colarelli O'Connor, Richard Leifer, Albert S. Paulson, and Lois Peters, *Grabbing Lightning: Building a Capability for Breakthrough Innovation* (San Francisco: Jossey-Bass, 2008).

4. Gina Colarelli O'Connor, Andrew Corbett, and Ron Pierantozzi, "Create Three Distinct Career Paths for Innovators," *Harvard Business Review* 14 (2009): 78–79.

5. As a result of the untimely death of one of the organization's cofounders and leaders, this organization has since folded (www.linkedin.com/company/954133?trk=tyah&trkInfo=clickedVertical%3Acompany%2Cidx%3A1-1-1%2CtarId%3A1435870426445%2Ctas%3AThought%20leadership%20institute).

CHAPTER 1

1. See http://www.kodak.com/ek/US/en/Our_Company/History_of_Kodak/Milestones_-_chronology/1878-1929.htm.

2. "Case Flash Forward: Kodak and the Digital Revolution (A)," Harvard Business School Case 6065-PDF-ENG, January 13, 2015.

3. See http://photosecrets.com/the-rise-and-fall-of-kodak.

4. Ibid.

5. Dana Mattioli, "Their Kodak Moments," *Wall Street Journal*, January 6, 2012, http://online.wsj.com/news/articles/SB10001424052970203513604577142701222383634. Mike Dickinson, "Kodak's Local Employment Falls to Nearly 3,500," *Rochester Business Journal*, http://rbj.net/2013/03/12/eastman-kodaks-local-employment-falls-to-near-3500/, March 12, 2013.

6. See https://en.wikipedia.org/wiki/Nortel.

7. Dorothy Leonard-Barton, "Core Capabilities and Core Rigidities: A Paradox in Managing New Product Development," *Strategic Management Journal* 13, no. S1 (1992): 111–125.

8. William Lazonick, "Profits Without Prosperity," *Harvard Business Review* 92, no. 9 (2014): 46–55.

9. See http://www.wsj.com/articles/hillary-gets-it-right-on-short-termism-1438124913.

10. Ibid.

11. Roger L. Martin, "The Rise (and Likely Fall) of the Talent Economy," *Harvard Business Review* 92, no. 10 (2014): 40–47.

12. See http://www.wsj.com/articles/mylans-leverage-to-resist-teva-deal-reveals-shift-in-rules-1438029585?cb=logged0.27827523419192196.

13. Lazonick, "Profits Without Prosperity"; Martin, "Rise (and Likely Fall)"; and private conversation with the chief innovation officer of a Europe-based company.

14. Norman D. Fast, "New Venture Departments: Organizing for Innovation," *Industrial Marketing Management* 7, no. 2 (1978): 77–88; Josh Lerner, "Corporate Venturing," *Harvard Business Review* 91, no. 10 (2013): 86.

15. Christopher M. McDermott and Gina Colarelli O'Connor, "Managing Radical Innovation: An Overview of Emergent Strategy Issues," *Journal of Product Innovation Management* 19, no. 6 (2002): 424–438.

16. See http://www.economist.com/node/15048819.

17. See, for example, Joseph L. Bower, *Managing the Resource Allocation Process: A Study of Corporate Planning and Investment* (Boston: Harvard Business School Press,1970); Robert A. Burgelman, "A Process Model of Internal Corporate Venturing in the Diversified Major Firm," *Administrative Science Quarterly* 28 (1983): 223–244; N. D. Fast, *The Rise and Fall of Corporate New Venture Departments* (Ann Arbor, MI: UMI Research Press, 1978); Gifford

Pinchot, *Intrapreneuring: Why You Don't Have to Leave the Organization to Become an Entrepreneur* (New York: Harper and Row, 1985).

18. Robert G. Cooper, *Winning at New Products: Accelerating the Process from Idea to Launch* (New York: Basic Books, 1985).

19. Robert G. Cooper, "Third-Generation New Product Processes," *Journal of Product Innovation Management* 11, no. 1 (1994): 3–14.

20. Rajesh Sethi and Zafar Iqbal, "Stage-Gate Controls, Learning Failure, and Adverse Effect on Novel New Products," *Journal of Marketing* 72, no. 1 (2008): 118–134.

21. Eric Reis, *The Lean Startup: How Today's Entrepreneurs Use Continuous Innovation to Create Radically Successful Businesses* (New York: Crown, 2013).

22. See http://www.forbes.com/innovative-companies/list/.

23. See https://hbr.org/1999/09/creating-breakthroughs-at-3m.

24. See http://multimedia.3m.com/mws/media/1084292O/3m-announcing-med-tech-external-press-release-pdf.pdf.

25. Louis V. Gerstner Jr., *Who Says Elephants Can't Dance? Leading a Great Enterprise Through Dramatic Change* (New York: HarperCollins, 2002).

26. Rosabeth Moss Kanter, *When Giants Learn to Dance* (New York: Simon and Schuster, 1990).

27. Interview with Joanne Hyland, previous vice president of Nortel Networks.

28. Alex Salkever, "Nokia's Security Connection," *BusinessWeek Online*, September 10, 2002, https://www.bloomberg.com/news/articles/2001-08-27/nokias-security-connection; Jonathan D. Day, Paul Y. Mang, Ansgar Richter, and John Roberts, "The Innovative Organization," *McKinsey Quarterly* 2 (2001): 21–31; Katherine Doornik and John Roberts, "Nokia Corporation: Innovation and Efficiency in a High-Growth Global Firm," Stanford University Case Number S-IB-23, February 2001, http://www.nokia.com/en_int.

29. See http://www.nytimes.com/2015/07/09/technology/microsoft-layoffs.html?_r=0.

30. Charles A. O'Reilly, J. Bruce Harreld, and Michael L. Tushman, "Organizational Ambidexterity: IBM and Emerging Business Opportunities," *California Management Review* 51, no. 4 (2009): 75–99.

31. Presentation by Mike Giersch, vice president, strategic planning, IBM Corporate Strategy Office (copresented with Gina O'Connor), at the IIR/PDMA Front End of Innovation conference, May 2007.

32. Mehrdad Baghai, Stephen Coley, and David White, *The Alchemy of Growth: Practical Insights for Building the Enduring Enterprise* (Boston: Da Capo Press, 2000).

33. Giersch presentation.

34. See https://www.bcgperspectives.com/content/articles/innovation
_growth_mergers_acquisitions_corporate_venture_capital/.

35. See http://www.globalcorporateventuring.com/; see also https://www
.bcgperspectives.com/content/articles/innovation_growth_mergers_acquisi
tions_corporate_venture_capital/?chapter=2.

36. We use the acronym CNO rather than CIO to reduce confusion with the
chief information officer role that exists in many companies.

37. See http://blogs.wsj.com/cio/2012/04/03/chief-innovation-officers-the
-growth-of-the-other-cio/.

38. Ibid.

CHAPTER 2

1. Much of the material in this chapter is reprised from Gina Colarelli O'Connor,
Richard Leifer, Albert S. Paulson, and Lois Peters, *Grabbing Lightning: Building
a Capability for Breakthrough Innovation* (San Francisco: John Wiley, 2008).

2. See http://www.theatlantic.com/technology/archive/2015/11/how-many
-photographs-of-you-are-out-there-in-the-world/413389/.

3. See http://www.nytimes.com/2015/07/23/arts/international/photos-photos
-everywhere.html?_r=0.

4. The details of this phase of our research are described in O'Connor et al.,
Grabbing Lightning. As noted in the preface and the first two chapters of this
volume, since describing and testing the management system theory and coming to
understand the necessary capabilities of discovery, incubation, and acceleration, we
have adopted the term *strategic innovation*, rather than *breakthrough innovation*,
to reflect the fact that companies benefit from an innovation management system
for any innovation initiatives with higher degrees of uncertainty than traditional
new product development processes can tolerate. The principles described in this
chapter apply to projects that are midrange on the spectrum of innovativeness, as
well as to those that are extremely innovative, that is, breakthroughs.

5. These four dimensions of uncertainty are those we've seen many times as
the ones that confront project teams focused on breakthrough innovation. All four
dimensions must be monitored and managed simultaneously. See Gina Colarelli
O'Connor and Mark P. Rice, "A Comprehensive Model of Uncertainty Associated with Radical Innovation," *Journal of Product Innovation Management* 30,
no. S1 (2013): 2–18. A learning plan framework is used to guide those projects.
For more about learning plans, see Mark P. Rice, Gina Colarelli O'Connor, and

Ronald Pierantozzi, "Implementing a Learning Plan to Counter Project Uncertainty," *MIT Sloan Management Review* 49, no. 2 (2008): 54–62.

CHAPTER 3

1. Robert B. Rosenfeld, *Making the Invisible Visible: The Human Principles for Sustaining Innovation* (Bloomington, IN: Xlibris, 2005). See also Gina Colarelli O'Connor and Chris McDermott, "The Human Side of Radical Innovation," *Journal of Engineering and Technology Management* 21 (2004): 11–30; A. Campbell, J. Birkinshaw, A. Morrison, and R. van Basten Batenburg, "The Future of Corporate Venturing: Companies Undertake Venturing for a Variety of Reasons. To Be Successful, They Must Be Clear About Their Objectives and Disciplined in Executing the One of Four Business Models Most Appropriate to Achieving Them," *MIT Sloan Management Review* 45, no. 1 (2003): 30–38; G. C. O'Connor and R. DeMartino, "Organizing for Radical Innovation: An Exploratory Study of the Structural Aspects of RI Management Systems in Large Established Firms," *Journal of Product Innovation Management* 23, no. 6 (2006): 475–497; A. C. Corbett and K. M. Hmieleski, "The Conflicting Cognitions of Corporate Entrepreneurs," *Entrepreneurship Theory and Practice* 31, no. 1 (2007): 103–121.

2. "Building a Better Innovation Model: What CEOs Can Do, and What They Should Not," CEO Forum sponsored by *CEO Magazine*, Mandarin Hotel, New York, October 4, 2007. See http://www.chiefexecutive.net. See also Jeffrey Kohn, Jon Katzenbach, and Gus Vlak, "Finding and Grooming Breakthrough Innovators," *Harvard Business Review* 86, no. 12 (2008): 63–69.

3. Alan Deutschman, "Building a Better Skunk Works," *Fast Company*, December 19, 2007.

CHAPTER 4

1. Gifford Pinchot, *Intrapreneuring: Why You Don't Have to Leave the Corporation to Become an Entrepreneur* (New York: Harper and Row, 1985).

2. See http://www.pinchot.com/2011/11/the-intrapreneurs-ten-commandments.html.

3. See http://www.fastcompany.com/3048522/hit-the-ground-running/3-ways-flat-management-structures-can-kill-your-business.

4. See http://www.holacracy.org/how-it-works/.

5. Ibid. See also http://www.forbes.com/sites/alisoncoleman/2015/07/16/holacracy-startups-can-learn-from-zappos-says-ceo-tony-hsieh/.

6. See http://www.forbes.com/sites/stevedenning/2015/05/23/is-holacracy-succeeding-at-zappos/.

7. Please see http://www.forbes.com/sites/jacobmorgan/2015/05/12/zappos-and-holacracy-is-it-worth-it/. Also of note is that holacracy is taking hold in software-based companies, where fixed specific assets are not a large consideration. By contrast, companies with heavy investments in assets that are not easily repurposed may hesitate to relinquish a more traditional hierarchical approach to decision making.

CHAPTER 5

1. See http://www.slideshare.net/rachelmercer/future-workforce-mshaped-is-the.

2. See https://www.fastcompany.com/55365/building-better-skunk-works.

CHAPTER 6

1. See http://fortune.com/2015/06/05/pepsico-ceo-indra-nooyi/.

2. Subsequent news releases indicate the platform is a four-ounce protein-dense drink to help women consume needed nutrients throughout the day (http://www.foodnavigator-usa.com/R-D/PepsiCo-seeks-to-patent-novel-high-protein-nutrition-beverages-in-4floz-hydration-units-as-protein-craze-gathers-pace). The product was envisioned to be the first launch of a new business initiative titled PLAY—for Protein, Liquid, Activity, You-time—which was focused on helping women fulfill their nutritional and health needs over the course of the day (http://www.foodnavigator-usa.com/Manufacturers/Have-you-had-your-P.L.A.Y.-today-PepsiCo-targets-women-with-new-protein-product-launch).

3. Mark P. Rice, Gina Colarelli O'Connor, and Ronald Pierantozzi, "Implementing a Learning Plan to Counter Project Uncertainty," *Sloan Management Review* 49, no. 2 (2008): 54–62.

CHAPTER 7

1. These technical requirements align with NASA's Technology Readiness Levels 8 and 9, which several of our interviewees mentioned as key milestones for acceleration. See "Technology Readiness Assessment (TRA) Guidance," United States Department of Defense, April 2011. See https://www.army.mil/e2/c/downloads/404585.pdf; https://en.wikipedia.org/wiki/Technology_readiness_level.

2. It may become clear at this point in the venture's development that the fit is not there and the A-3 team, together with the general manager must make the difficult decision to spin it out of the company. We expect that a clear articula-

tion of strategic intent, coupled with strong coaching throughout incubation would prevent a business from evolving to the point of acceleration before this decision is made, although in reality this may be the time that it becomes clearly the right decision.

3. IBM's EBO program is well documented in the academic and popular press literature. For additional details, see Charles A O'Reilly, J. Bruce Harreld, and Michael L. Tushman, "Organizational Ambidexterity: IBM and Emerging Business Opportunities," *California Management Review* 51, no. 4 (2009): 75–99; David A. Garvin and Lynne C. Levesque, "Meeting the Challenge of Corporate Entrepreneurship," *Harvard Business Review* 84, no. 10 (2006): 102–112; Robert C. Wolcott and Michael J. Lippitz, "The Four Models of Corporate Entrepreneurship," *MIT Sloan Management Review* 49, no. 1 (2007): 75; Gina Colarelli O'Connor, Richard Leifer, Al Paulson, and Lois Peters, *Grabbing Lightning: Building a Capability for Breakthrough Innovation* (San Francisco: Jossey Bass, division of John Wiley, 2008); and Gary Hamel and Bill Breen, *The Future of Management* (Cambridge, MA: Harvard Business Press, 2013).

CHAPTER 8

1. Several important tools of note are the following: the Learning Plan, described in Mark P. Rice, Gina Colarelli O'Connor, and Ronald Pierantozzi, "Implementing a Learning Plan to Counter Project Uncertainty," *Sloan Management Review* 49, no. 2 (2008): 54–62; the Transition Readiness Assessment Tool, found in G. C. O'Connor, R. Hendricks, and M. P. Rice, "Assessing Transition Readiness for Radical Innovation," *Research-Technology Management* 45, no. 6 (2002): 50–56; the Opportunity Recognition Framework, described in M. Rice, D. Kelley, L. Peters, and G. Colarelli O'Connor, "Radical Innovation: Triggering Initiation of Opportunity Recognition and Evaluation," *R&D Management* 31, no. 4 (2001): 409–420; the Discovery Driven Plan, found in R. G. McGrath and I. C. MacMillan, *Discovery-Driven Growth: A Breakthrough Process to Reduce Risk and Seize Opportunity* (Cambridge, MA: Harvard Business Press, 2009); and Critical Assumption Planning, presented in H. B. Sykes and D. Dunham, "Critical Assumption Planning: A Practical Tool for Managing Business Development Risk," *Journal of Business Venturing* 10, no. 6 (1995): 413–424.

2. The role of the orchestrator is described extensively in Gina Colarelli O'Connor, Richard Leifer, Albert S. Paulson, and Lois Peters, *Grabbing Lightning: Building a Capability for Breakthrough Innovation* (San Francisco: Jossey

Bass, 2008), chap. 7. Here we focus on the nature and characteristics of the person who fills the role.

3. An extensive discussion of metrics associated with the breakthrough innovation management system and its portfolio of emerging businesses is provided in ibid., and so it will not be repeated here.

4. Ibid.

5. This material draws from our interviews with van Leen and others who work with him, IMD Case #3-2111, "DSM: Mobilizing the Organization to Grow Through Innovation," authored by Jean-Philippe DesChamps and research assistant Daria Tolstoy, available through Harvard Business School Case series; and Rob van Leen, "Innovation Is in Our Genes: How DSM Transformed Itself Through Innovation," *Visions, Product Development and Management Association's Magazine*, December 2010, 14–17 (written at the time that DSM received the Outstanding Corporate Innovator award from the PDMA).

6. IMD case, "DSM," 8.

7. See https://www.dsm.com/content/dam/dsm/cworld/en_US/documents/dsm -integrated-annual-report-2014-review-of-business-in-2014-innovation-center.pdf.

CHAPTER 9

1. K. Anders Ericsson, "The Influence of Experience and Deliberate Practice on the Development of Superior Expert Performance," *Cambridge Handbook of Expertise and Expert Performance* 38 (2006): 685–705. Deliberate practice is defined as "activities designed, typically by a teacher, for the sole purpose of effectively improving specific aspects of an individual's performance." See https:// psy.fsu.edu/faculty/ericsson/ericsson.exp.perf.html.

2. See www.nytimes.com/2011/11/20/opinion/sunday/sorry-strivers-talent matters.html?_r=1&scp=1&sq=gladwell%2010,000%20hours&st=cse. See also Geoffrey Colvin, *Talent Is Overrated: What Really Separates World-Class Performers from Everybody Else* (New York: Penguin, 2008).

3. Charles E. Eesley and Edward B. Roberts, "Are You Experienced or Are You Talented?: When Does Innate Talent versus Experience Explain Entrepreneurial Performance?," *Strategic Management Journal* 6 (2012): 207–219.

4. Abbie Griffin, Raymond Price, and Bruce Vojak, *Serial Innovators: How Individuals Create and Deliver Breakthrough Innovations in Mature Firms* (Stanford, CA: Stanford University Press, 2012).

5. We are aware of the US government's Presidential Innovation Fellows program, which pairs technologists and inventors with governmental employees

to tackle complex problems. An internal corporate innovation fellow would not be the technical talent on the team, but rather the new business creation talent.

CHAPTER 10

1. See http://www.businessinsider.com/blackrock-ceo-larry-fink-letter-to
-sp-500-ceos-2016-2.

2. See http://ispim.org/ and http://www.iaoip.org/.

Page numbers followed by *f* or *t* indicate material in figures or tables.